D0462886

F R E S H

HEALTHY COOKING AND LIVING FROM LAKE AUSTIN SPA RESORT

Eat well and Be well!

3/2 04

FRESH
Healthy Cooking and Living from Lake Austin Spa Resort

Lake Austin Spa Resort
1705 South Quinlan Park Road
Austin, Texas 78732

Reservations and Information: 800-847-5637 or 512-372-7300
Email: info@lakeaustin.com
www.lakeaustin.com

Library of Congress Catalog Number: 2002112205
ISBN: 0-9619476-2-4

Art Director: Joe Warwick
Food Photography: Colleen Duffley
Food Stylist: William Smith
On-site Additional Photography: Colleen Duffley, Michael Hart, Andrew Yates
Editor: Darlene Fiske
Contributors: Terry Conlan, Robbie Hudson, Terry Shaw, Trisha Shirey, Hal Strickland, Lynne Vertrees, Tracy York
Acknowledgements: Jolyn Arehart, Mike Conner, Tracy Fitz, Suzanne Gonzalez, Amy Graham, Julie Purcell, Cindy Viator, Mel Wolf

All location photography was shot at Lake Austin Spa Resort.

Manufactured by Favorite Recipes Press® in the United States of America
First Printing: 2002

Dedication

With utmost respect and no small amount of affection, this book is dedicated to:

Pamela and the boys, Benjamin and Brendhan, who kept the faith, and who have not eaten poorly in the process.

Mike McAdams and Billy Rucks, our proprietors, whose singular vision for what Lake Austin Spa Resort might be has been matched only by their unswerving dedication to seeing it through.

Our completely remarkable staff, kitchen and otherwise, who honor this trust on a daily basis by bringing life and keeping it "fresh" with their combined and considerable gifts of body, mind and spirit.

And finally to you, our guests – our reason for being, who never cease to amaze, inspire and delight with your curiosity, strength, and appetite for life; and, who serve always as our constant reminder that the more we share, the more we have to share.

contents

preface

Not so very long ago, as occasionally happens, I had the opportunity to take part in a telephone interview with a journalist, this time from Los Angeles, who was gathering material for an article on spa food. Inevitably, as they all do, at some point in the proceedings, she popped "The Question."

"What exactly, in my opinion, was 'spa cuisine'?"

Now, I have been the executive chef at Lake Austin Spa Resort for eleven years, and this is a question I am asked all the time, but it is still one that I have a lot of trouble answering to my satisfaction (let alone theirs). Usually I just content myself and the interviewer by rattling off the same old "tired but true" litany about minimal fat, monounsaturates, increased soy, legumes and so forth, doling out the steady stream of spa "buzz" words that have become the common currency as regards the outside world and spa food.

This time, however, I surprised myself, and before I could think to stop, I blurted out the real truth. What I told her was, "To be honest, I am not exactly sure what spa cuisine is, but I'm pretty certain that whatever it is, we're not doing it here!"

Later, another journalist, another interview, and this "blasphemy" gets a second airing, this time abetted by a quote borrowed from the actor James Garner's response to a question about whether or not he had a theory about acting. I found it paralleled my own thoughts about spa cooking.

Journalist: "Do you have a particular theory or philosophy about spa food?"

Me: "I do. Never let anybody catch you at it!"

What I think I intended to convey in both of those instances was less heresy than a call for opening the gates (o.k., in my case the gates were already open. Like they say, it's easier to say you're sorry than to ask permission.) The problem with the concept of spa cuisine, at least as it is generally perceived, is that it's just too limiting to take us where we want to go, which is everywhere, and to let us eat what we want to eat, which is everything. What we need is a sort of 'unified theory' of spa food, a proclamation that the possibilities for healthy, genuinely satisfying eating are almost limitless. We need to be reminded that between the dim and distant outposts of gluttony and deprivation resides a very large space that celebrates eating, encourages diversity and respects the seasonal nature of things. The truth is, wonderful, wonderfully fresh food is all around us. Food that will sustain both our appetites and our imaginations. All we have to do to utilize it is to take a similarly fresh perspective, one that allows us to look both East and West, forward and backward, a 'food philosophy' that embraces all the good things in the present while still honoring the wisdom of the past. And the beauty of it all is that it's not that difficult to do because every significant, surviving food culture on the planet, however it may differ from the others, is grounded in an abiding interest in healthy, sustainable eating. We may have to shuffle a few ingredients or techniques about in response to the new century's sensibilities and we may want to employ some new versions of ingredients available to us, but essentially everything we need for this new (old) cuisine is already in place. As in 'every place'.

Even a modest perusal of our menus at the resort or the pages of this book will demonstrate this purposeful meandering. Side by side you will find a wide range of representative dishes from regional America, Mexico, the Caribbean, Europe, the Mediterranean, and all of Asia. There's Chocolate Pie to Phat Thai. Falafel to Flan. Pizza to Pork Pâté. There's even a Chili Cheeseburger, for goodness sakes! And more, lots more.

Every chapter is checkered with food from on high, and food from on low; food from the country, food from the town. Food from far away and food from your own backyard. You will find your grandmother's food; you will find food that your children will enjoy. Above all, you will find, I think, food that insists upon being eaten.

And for those for those of you who might think of this as new ground or of myself as a forward-leaning spa chef, I would say this: at the end of the day I'm just another cook doing what honest cooks everywhere have been doing for a long time - trying to put another good meal on the table. We can think of few callings higher.

Yours from the kitchen,

Terry Conlan

Introduc

Fresh ingredients. Fresh food. Fresh living.

A stroll into the Lake Austin Spa Resort lakeside dining room at the height of meal time is an experience abuzz with celebration and life. And, with three gourmet spa meals served each day as a part of any stay at Lake Austin Spa Resort, herein lies a glimmer of the heart and soul of the larger, more comprehensive experience provided every day of the year at our 19-acre spa escape, nestled against the water's edge in the Texas Hill Country.

We've called this book FRESH, foremost because the word clearly defines the commitment and philosophy Chef Terry Conlan and his staff bring to every meal prepared for our treasured guests, but also because it applies to every other aspect of the unique and highly personalized destination spa experience at Lake Austin Spa Resort. Fresh thinking, fresh movements, fresh relationships are all as integral to what can be expected from time spent at Lake Austin Spa Resort, as the food we serve each day. Abundant gardens, luscious accommodations, spectacularly creative spa treatments, an eclectic array of fitness classes & activities, and inspired Discovery programs... in all of these different aspects of life at Lake Austin Spa Resort, freshness abounds!

Aptly enough, the wonder experienced while dining with us begins in our gardens. Fresh vegetables, herbs, and aromatic flowers from our burgeoning organic gardens are harvested daily by the kitchen staff to add distinctive flavors and unmatched nutrition to many of the deliciously healthy meals served each day. You'll find many of these recipes listed in this book, and perhaps we'll inspire you to plant and grow some herbs, vegetables, and edible flowers in a garden of your own.

In addition to the many marvelous recipes for these dishes listed within, you will find an assortment of spa tips throughout this

tion

book which illuminate much about a healthy attitude and lifestyle reflective of the added benefits of a stay at Lake Austin Spa Resort. We'd also like you to know a bit more about us, who we are and what a visit to see us could mean to you.

Our greatest attribute is our size. We are large enough, with 40 fully renovated and aesthetically inviting rooms, to provide everything you need in a comprehensive spa experience and yet intimate enough to also insure everything you deserve from a highly personalized spa experience.

Our guest rooms feature sunlit bathrooms and Kohler steeping or soaking tubs, native Saltillo tile floors, woven rag rugs, all cotton fabrics, slip-covered down bedding and private patios divided by woven wood walls. Some of our rooms even have their own private gardens with hot tubs.

As a guest at Lake Austin Spa Resort you may choose from nearly 20 daily fitness classes and specialized activities, which may include Hill Country walks and hikes, kayak outings, sculling lessons, Hydro-bike™ cardio workouts, Nia, Pilates, Tai Chi, kickboxing, Spinning®, stretching, circuit training, step or water aerobics and Yoga among other inspiring activities such as cooking classes, garden tours and aromatherapy demonstrations.

In the tranquil surroundings of our Healing Waters Spa, you'll relax to the gentle touch of our expertly trained therapists. More than 50 skin and body treatments are designed to reduce stress, increase resilience and revitalize your mind and body.

We hope you'll find in your perusal of these pages as much a lifestyle guide as a recipe book, as inspiration for good living as much instruction for cooking, and thus a reflection of the experience we provide our guests each day at Lake Austin Spa Resort. And, whether you've visited us before, or are only coming to know us by way of this book, we also hope these pages may inspire you to come see us again or to come discover us anew.

appetizers

appetizers

appetizers

Shrimp Spring Rolls, Pg.28

appetizers

Artichoke and Green Olive Spread

No time to make your potluck contribution to the office party? Unexpected and hungry guests drop in? Or, just looking to up your daily thistle dosage (artichokes are members of the thistle family)? Stop right here. This is your baby. It requires no cooking; is made from ingredients you probably already have in your pantry; and goes together, beginning to end, in less than five minutes.

1 (15-ounce) can artichoke hearts, drained and rinsed
1 tablespoon extra virgin olive oil
2 tablespoons fat-free sour cream
2 garlic cloves, minced
2 green onions (green and white parts), chopped
1/2 teaspoon minced fresh rosemary leaves, or 1/4 teaspoon dry rosemary
1/8 teaspoon cayenne pepper
12 medium green olives, pitted and minced
2 tablespoons chopped fresh parsley

Place artichoke hearts, olive oil, sour cream, garlic, onions, rosemary and cayenne in a food processor; process until smooth. Transfer the mixture to a bowl and fold in the olives and parsley. Refrigerate until chilled. Serve with toasted baguette slices and/or raw vegetable sticks. *Yield: 32 (1-tablespoon) servings*

Nutrients Per Serving: Cal 13; Prot 1 g; Carbo 2 g; Fat 1 g; 41% Cal from Fat; Sod 45 mg

Warm Artichoke and Cheese Dunk

At Lake Austin Spa Resort, we set aside a place early each evening where guests can gather and socialize informally before getting down to the serious business of dinner in the dining room. There's always an hors d'oeuvre — usually a simple spread or dip with bread and raw vegetables. This warm, savory artichoke dunk may be the most popular of the bunch.

2 tablespoons olive oil
1 cup minced onion
2 cups fat-free mayonnaise
1/2 cup skim milk
2 tablespoons minced garlic
2 teaspoons Dijon mustard
1/8 teaspoon cayenne pepper
1/2 teaspoon salt
2 tablespoons chopped fresh parsley
2 tablespoons lemon juice
1 1/2 cups grated Parmesan cheese
2 (15-ounce) cans artichoke hearts

Place the olive oil in a sauté pan over medium heat. Add the onions and sauté until softened. Add the mayonnaise, milk and garlic; stir to combine and cook for 3 to 4 minutes. Remove the pan from the heat and add the Dijon mustard, cayenne pepper, salt, parsley, lemon juice, cheese and artichoke hearts; mix well. Spray an 8 x 8-inch baking pan with cooking spray. Spoon the mixture into the prepared pan and bake at 375 degrees for 15 to 20 minutes or until bubbly and slightly browned. Serve warm with baguette slices and/or raw vegetables for dunking. *Yield: 96 (1-tablespoon) servings*

Nutrients Per Serving: Cal 18; Prot 1 g; Carbo 2 g; Fat 1 g; 34% Cal from Fat; Sod 128 mg

Baba Ghanoush

There are arguments, good arguments, that civilization as we know it began in Mesopotamia, an area now generally referred to as the Middle East or the Eastern Mediterranean. One of the benchmarks for a civilized society certainly must have been the development of a "cuisine," a codified food culture wrought from common experience and applied over generations. Fruit, as it were, of first comprehending the cyclical nature of seasons and then, in a leap of faith, applying that knowledge to the agricultural practice of reap and sow, was a relatively stable food source. In time, that food source defined itself through what succeeded and what did not. What succeeded was prepared and shared. What was shared was prepared again, and so on until, eventually, the cultural fabric of a "cuisine" was woven as distinctive and real as any cloth. So, an old, enduring recipe such as Baba Ghanoush has antecedents still — a pre-recipe history, unwritten, but marked, when someone took an eggplant and threw it on the fire, discovering first that, lo, it was good and later that, lo, it was even better with garlic, sesame, and citrus.

1 large eggplant
3 garlic cloves, minced
1/4 cup tahini (sesame seed paste)
3 tablespoons lemon juice
1/2 teaspoon salt
1/8 teaspoon cayenne pepper

Pierce the eggplant all over 30 to 40 times with a toothpick or small skewer. Roast on a grill or under a broiler for 15-20 minutes until charred and softened. Then, turn once to char and soften the second side. Cool to room temperature.

Slice the eggplant into halves vertically. Scoop out the flesh and place in a food processor. Add a little of the charred skin, the garlic, tahini, lemon juice, salt and cayenne pepper. Purée until smooth. Serve with pita crisps (Page 29). *Yield: 48 (1-tablespoon) servings*

Nutrients Per Serving: Cal 12; Prot 1 g; Carbo 1 g; Fat 1 g; 48% Cal from Fat; Sod 25 mg

the essence of water

Fragrant waters are so easy to make that you can afford to be lavish. And you can use any herb you like. Particular favorites are lavender, rosemary, lemon balm, bergamot, hyssop, violet, thyme, lemon thyme, chamomile and elder. Men might prefer the scent of coriander, cinnamon or the spiciness of cloves. Pour 8 ounces of distilled boiling water over the herbs, let cool and then pour into a glass bottle. Keep a bottle of herb-scented waters in the bathroom or on the dressing table to use in your bath or as a refreshing after-bath tonic. In warm weather, dab your face with the scented water for a refreshing cool-down.

HOME SPA

Caponata

In quintessential Italian style, with quintessentially Italian ingredients, olive oil, wine, honey, tomatoes, capers, raisins, and olives are bound together with cubed eggplant to create a slightly sweet-and-sour, savory relish that you will find yourself eating until the bowl is empty and you are not.

1 medium eggplant
1/2 teaspoon salt
1 tablespoon olive oil
3/4 cup minced celery
3/4 cup minced red onion
3 tablespoons red wine vinegar
1/2 teaspoon honey
1 (8-ounce) can diced tomatoes, drained
1 tablespoon tomato purée
1 tablespoon capers
3 tablespoons raisins
16 pitted black kalamata olives, chopped
1/8 teaspoon black pepper
Chopped Italian parsley for garnish

Cut the eggplant into 3/4-inch slices. Sprinkle with salt and set aside for 30 minutes. Rinse the eggplant in cold water; dry with paper towels. Cut the eggplant slices into 3/4-inch cubes. Heat the olive oil in a sauté pan set over medium heat. Add the celery and onion and cook, stirring occasionally, until the vegetables are soft. Add the eggplant cubes and sauté for 2 minutes. Add the vinegar, honey, tomatoes, tomato purée, capers, raisins, olives and black pepper. Stir to combine and simmer for 15 minutes. Add a little water if the mixture becomes too dry. Remove from the heat and cool to room temperature. Refrigerate. Garnish with parsley and serve with bread rounds. *Yield: 128 (1-tablespoon) servings*

Nutrients Per Serving: Cal 6; Prot 1 g; Carbo 1 g; Fat 1 g; 42% Cal from Fat; Sod 24 mg

chefstip

Salt Of The Earth ✳ Sprinkled salt has a capillary effect on meats and vegetables. It draws moisture to the surface, which can be a virtue or a vice depending upon the circumstances. With certain vegetables, primarily eggplant and zucchini, pre-salting slices can draw out an inherent bitterness that is often present. The pieces can then be rinsed (to remove the salt) and patted dry before proceeding with the recipe (see Torta de Calabacitas recipe for an example). Conversely, salting meats, poultry, or fish too long before cooking creates an adverse situation with important moisture and juiciness being unnecessarily drawn out of the product. This surface moisture can also cause grilled foods to stick to the grill and sautéed foods to "stew" rather than sauté. For best results, salt lightly just prior to or during cooking.

Chick-pea Tapenade

The evolutionary history of a great cuisine, such as the one we generally refer to as "Mediterranean," is as necessarily complex and diverse as the multiethnic peoples who created it. Generally favorable agricultural conditions with long growing seasons and rich soil, coupled with a common sea to facilitate commerce and conquest, combined over centuries to create the seemingly endless, highly eclectic "buffet" we see today. And, although its strength is in its variety, certain commonalities — chief among them the reliance upon olives, olive oil, citrus, and legumes — emerge to lend definition to this cuisine. The use and re-use of these ingredients in all of the countries that make up this "melting pot" is the skeletal structure upon which everything else relies. From the tagines of North Africa to the tapenades of provincial France, they lend, in sum or in part, the unmistakable characteristics we taste as "Mediterranean." This particular tapenade with its bright flavors and rich texture uses all of these components. It is as easy and delicious a history lesson as you are likely to find. And one, as portions of history often are, that will bear repeating.

3 tablespoons olive oil
1/2 cup sliced onion
1 small red bell pepper, roasted, peeled, seeded and diced, or 1 (2-ounce) jar diced pimento, drained
2 cups cooked chick-peas (garbanzo beans), rinsed and drained
2 garlic cloves, minced
6 medium green olives, pitted
6 kalamata olives, pitted
1 serrano chile, seeded and minced
Grated zest and juice of 1 orange
Grated zest and juice of 1 lemon
Grated zest and juice of 1 lime
2 tablespoons chopped fresh parsley
2 tablespoons chopped cilantro leaves
1/2 teaspoon ground cumin
1/2 teaspoon salt

Heat 1 teaspoon of the olive oil in a sauté pan over medium heat. Add the onion and cook, stirring occasionally, until lightly caramelized. Place the remaining olive oil, roasted bell pepper, chick-peas, garlic, green and kalamata olives, chile, orange, lemon and lime zest and juice, parsley, cilantro, cumin and salt in a food processor. Pulse to coarsely chop the mixture. Transfer the tapenade to a serving dish. Serve with pita crisps (Page 29) and/or vegetable sticks. *Yield: 56 (1-tablespoon) servings*

Nutrients Per Serving: Cal 20; Prot 1 g; Carbo 2 g; Fat 1 g; 46% Cal from Fat; Sod 40 mg

Hummus

Along with tabouli, hummus is probably the Middle East's most famous food export, and deservedly so. It is, quite simply, "sustenance" in the most positive sense of the word. Tahini (sesame seed paste) is now available in many American grocery stores or at any Mediterranean specialty food store. Stir the tahini before using it and store it as you would peanut butter. The amounts of lemon, garlic, and spice are a highly individual matter. Feel free to adjust them to your taste.

15 ounces cooked chick-peas (garbanzo beans)
2 tablespoons tahini (sesame seed paste)
1/2 cup water
1/4 cup lemon juice
2 garlic cloves, minced
2 tablespoons minced fresh parsley
1/8 teaspoon cayenne pepper

Place the chick-peas, tahini, water, lemon juice, garlic, parsley and cayenne pepper in a food processor. Process until smooth. Transfer to a serving bowl and chill. Serve with wedges of pita bread and/or raw vegetable sticks. *Yield: 48 (1-tablespoon) servings*

Nutrients Per Serving: Cal 19; Prot 1 g; Carbo 3 g; Fat 1 g; 26% Cal from Fat; Sod 1 mg

Fava Bean and Spinach Dip

Fresh fava beans are very popular in Europe, but not as widely available in the United States. If you can find them, they're wonderful. But frozen baby lima beans, cooked according to package directions, are also delicious in this very Mediterranean-style legume spread.

1/4 cup extra virgin olive oil
1 cup sliced onions
4 garlic cloves, minced
2 serrano chiles, seeded and chopped
1 tablespoon ground cumin
1 cup packed fresh spinach leaves
1/4 cup fresh mint leaves and/or cilantro leaves
3 cups cooked fava beans or baby lima beans
1 teaspoon salt
1/2 teaspoon pepper
2 to 3 tablespoons lemon juice

Heat 1 tablespoon of the olive oil in a heavy skillet over medium heat. Add the onions and cook, stirring occasionally, until caramelized. Add the garlic, chiles and cumin; stir and cook for about 1 minute. Add the spinach and mint; cook just long enough to wilt the spinach. Transfer the mixture to a food processor. Add the beans, salt, pepper, lemon juice and the remaining olive oil. Purée until smooth. Transfer the dip to a serving bowl and serve at room temperature with pita crisps (Page 29) or bread rounds. *Yield: 72 (1-tablespoon) servings*

Nutrients Per Serving: Cal 16; Prot 1 g; Carbo 2 g; Fat 1 g; 44% Cal from Fat; Sod 34 mg

Skordalia

Some things satisfy in direct proportion to their simplicity. This tasty, highly nutritious legume spread from Greece needs no adornment, but if you like, you might finish it with an additional drizzle of good olive oil and a sprinkling of freshly chopped parsley.

1 1/2 cups dried white lima beans
6 cups water
5 garlic cloves, minced
1/2 cup extra virgin olive oil
1/4 cup lemon juice
1 tablespoon grated lemon zest
2 tablespoons white wine vinegar
1 teaspoon minced fresh rosemary leaves
1 teaspoon salt
1/8 teaspoon cayenne pepper
3 tablespoons grated Parmesan cheese

Place the beans and water in a 3-quart saucepan over medium-high heat. Once the water begins to boil, reduce the heat and gently simmer the beans until very tender. Remove from the heat; drain, reserving 1 cup of cooking liquid to thin the skordalia, if necessary. Place the cooked beans, garlic, olive oil, lemon juice, lemon zest, vinegar, rosemary, salt, cayenne pepper and cheese in a food processor and purée until smooth. Transfer the mixture to a serving bowl and serve with pita crisps (Page 29) or bread rounds. *Yield: 88 (1-tablespoon) servings*

Nutrients Per Serving: Cal 24; Prot 1 g; Carbo 2 g; Fat 1 g; 49% Cal from Fat; Sod 30 mg

attitude is everything

How is your attitude these days? Is it in a good, positive place or could it be time for an attitude adjustment? With the constant demands of daily living, it is important to take time to rest, reflect and refocus to maintain a positive attitude.

At Lake Austin Spa Resort, we encourage our guests to find an activity they enjoy that will recharge their batteries and give them a daily dose of appreciation. Whether you take a walk by the lake, enjoy a yoga class or just take some private time for yourself, be sure to maintain perspective. Each day, we have a choice: we can wake up and decide that the world is against us and that it's going to be a difficult day, or we can make the decision to handle what comes our way to the best of our abilities and with a positive attitude. What choice will you make today?

WELL BEING

Muhammara

Often featured on the resort's dinner menu, is an appetizer called the Mediterranean Sampler. Three spreads — Hummus, Green Olive and Artichoke, and Muhammara are dolloped onto a plate with a small cube of feta cheese and pita bread triangles. All of the spreads are delicious and universally well received, but it is invariably the tantalizingly rich, sweet-and-sour, spicy, dark red Muhammara from Turkey that elicits calls for seconds. The relatively high-fat content of this spread comes from healthy monounsaturates found in walnuts and olive oil. And finally, it's worth the trouble to search for pomegranate molasses with its citrusey, berry-like quality. It's available in Mediterranean specialty stores. American molasses is not a substitute.

4 large red bell peppers
1 cup coarsely ground walnuts
1/2 cup wheat cracker crumbs or melba toast crumbs
1 tablespoon ground cumin
3/4 teaspoon salt
1/4 teaspoon cayenne pepper
1/2 teaspoon sugar
1 tablespoon lemon juice
1 tablespoon olive oil
3 tablespoons pomegranate molasses

Place the bell peppers on a baking sheet and roast them at 450 degrees, turning them until they are charred and thoroughly blistered, about 15 to 20 minutes. Transfer the blackened peppers to a paper bag; close the bag tightly and allow the peppers to steam for 10 to 15 minutes. Remove them from the bag, peel and seed them. Place the roasted peppers, walnuts, cracker crumbs, cumin, salt, cayenne pepper, sugar, lemon juice, olive oil and pomegranate molasses in a food processor. Process until smooth. Transfer to a serving bowl and serve at room temperature with pita crisps (Page 29).

Note: Some grocery stores have pepper and olive bars that sell good quality, preprocessed red bell peppers. Feel free to use them. *Yield: 64 (1-tablespoon) servings*

Nutrients Per Serving: Cal 19; Prot 1 g; Carbo 2 g; Fat 1 g; 54% Cal from Fat; Sod 33 mg

chefstip

Let's Eata Some Pita ✳ Pita crisps make some of the very best fat-free or low-fat chips for "chipping and dipping" that you will ever taste. To make your own, cut rounds of pita bread in half to make half moon shaped "pockets." Open these up and tear in half to create half moon shaped pieces of a single thickness. At this point you may either cut them into triangular chip shapes or simply bake them as is and break them up later into free-form chips. Whichever way you go, spread them onto baking sheets and bake at 300 degrees until lightly golden and very crisp (approximately 10 minutes). Store in an airtight container for up to four days.

Salsa Picante

Texans are serious about salsa. Every year one of the Austin newspapers hosts a hot sauce contest which always draws several hundred locals who plunk down cash money and a small jar of their pride and joy for a chance at bragging rights as "the best." And every one of them who doesn't win knows the dang contest was fixed! Such fervor must be infectious because commercial salsa has been the number one selling condiment in the United States for almost a decade, with over 25 million gallons consumed annually. The irony, of course — as all those contestants can attest — is that almost anybody can make better salsa than they can buy. It's inexpensive and easy to do, so try making your own. Or, while you're still working on your secret recipe, try our not-so-secret one. It's best served at room temperature the same day you make it.

1 (14-ounce) can tomatoes with juice, or 2 cups very ripe chopped fresh tomatoes
1/4 cup chopped onion
2 green onions, coarsely chopped
1 large garlic clove, chopped
1/2 cup tomato juice
3 tablespoons chopped fresh cilantro leaves
2 serrano chiles, chopped
Juice of 1/2 lime
1/8 teaspoon sugar
1/8 teaspoon salt

Place the tomatoes, onion, green onions, garlic, tomato juice, cilantro, chiles, lime juice, sugar and salt in a food processor. Pulse on and off until the desired chunky consistency is reached. *Yield: 48 (1-tablespoon) servings*

Nutrients Per Serving: Cal 3; Prot 1 g; Carbo 1 g; Fat 0 g; 6% Cal from Fat; Sod 28 mg

Pico de Gallo

Literally translated, "the beak of the rooster," and a common condiment on Southwestern tables morning, noon and night!

1 ripe medium tomato, chopped
1/4 cup chopped onion
2 tablespoons chopped cilantro
1 small serrano chile, minced

Combine all. Use the same day if possible. *Yield: 24 (1-tablespoon) servings*

Nutrients Per Serving: Cal 3; Prot 0 g; Carbo 1 g; Fat 0 g; 7% Cal from Fat; Sod 1 mg

Roasted Red Pepper Salsa

This earthy, brick-red salsa with complex flavors and sweet, smoky undertones drawn from the grilling process and the chipotle chiles is great as a simple chipper and dipper, or as a lively accompaniment to any number of Mexican, masa-based dishes. See the recipes for Bean and Masa Griddlecakes, Sopes, or Pupusas as possibilities.

1 medium red bell pepper
3 medium tomatoes
1 small onion, sliced
2 garlic cloves, minced
1/4 cup fresh cilantro leaves
1 cup tomato juice
1 teaspoon adobo paste from canned chipotle chiles
Juice of 1 lime
1/2 teaspoon sugar
1/2 teaspoon salt

Roast the bell pepper over hot coals, turning until it is thoroughly blistered, about 5 to 10 minutes. Transfer the blackened bell pepper to a paper bag; close the bag tightly and allow it to steam for 10 to 15 minutes. Remove from the bag, peel and seed. Grill the tomatoes and onion over hot coals until softened and the outsides are charred. Combine the bell pepper, tomatoes, onion, garlic, cilantro, tomato juice, adobo paste, lime juice, sugar and salt in a food processor. Process until the desired consistency is reached. *Yield: 80 (1-tablespoon) servings*

Nutrients Per Serving: Cal 3; Prot 1 g; Carbo 1 g; Fat 1 g; 7% Cal from Fat; Sod 26 mg

Smoked Trout Salsa

Whenever we fire up the BBQ pit (we house smoke all of our own meats), we're always mindful to add in a couple of salmon fillets (see Smoked Salmon and Chive Spread, Page 22) and some rainbow trout for this favorite. Both fish freeze well after being smoked and extras can be dished up for repeat performances. If you don't have the equipment for smoking, grilled trout makes a different but delicious alternative.

1 (8-ounce) smoked trout fillet, flaked
1 tomato, seeded and diced
1/2 cup frozen corn kernels, thawed
1/2 cup chopped zucchini
1/2 cup chopped red onion
1/2 cup cooked pinto beans, drained and rinsed
2 garlic cloves, minced
1/2 small avocado, peeled, seeded and diced
1 cup chopped cilantro leaves
3 tablespoons lime juice
1 teaspoon sugar
1 teaspoon chili powder
1/2 teaspoon salt

Combine the trout, tomato, corn, zucchini, onion, beans, garlic, avocado, cilantro, lime juice, sugar, chili powder and salt in a bowl. Stir gently to mix. Chill the mixture and serve with blue corn tortilla chips. *Yield: 96 (1-tablespoon) servings*

Nutrients Per Serving: Cal 9; Prot 1 g; Carbo 1 g; Fat 1 g; 31% Cal from Fat; Sod 60 mg

pack your bags Working out becomes easier when the things you need are convenient to you. When you know you are going to work out or do some sort of activity, set out your exercise clothes the night before, or put them in a bag to take with you in the morning. If your gym provides lockers, consider using one to store your belongings, so they're always at the ready. Or simply keep a pair of walking shoes in your car and take a walk before you go to work. If you work out in the evening, avoid going home to change - you might find other things to do and skip your workout. The better you prepare, the more likely you are to stick with your program.

FITNESS

Rainbow Trout and Shrimp Mousse

There are certain food concepts so perfect, so universal in appeal, that they transcend generational trends and cultural boundaries. The chilled seafood appetizer is an example. From pickled herring in Scandinavia to Mexican ceviche to Japanese sushi and Mediterranean escabeche, almost every culture has a lasting tradition of cold fish or crustaceans as an opening course. The ubiquitous shrimp cocktail, sweet and briny, daubed with its lemon and horseradish-spiked tomato sauce, is still one of the simplest, best eating experiences imaginable. This creamy, colorful mousse, which combines fish and shrimp with herbs and citrus, is brimming (swimming?) with flavors that belie its almost fat-free composition. Add some crackers, a sunset, and a cold drink, then settle back and become part of the tradition.

1 pound steamed rainbow trout fillets, skinned and flaked
1/2 pound small shrimp, steamed and peeled
4 ounces fat-free cream cheese, softened
1 cup fat-free sour cream
1 tablespoon capers, drained
2 tablespoons minced fresh chives
2 teaspoons dillweed
1 teaspoon salt
1/8 teaspoon cayenne pepper
1 tablespoon prepared horseradish
1 tablespoon minced fresh parsley
Grated zest and juice of 1 lemon
1/4 cup pimentos, drained and chopped

Combine the trout, shrimp, cream cheese, sour cream, capers, chives, dillweed, salt, cayenne pepper, horseradish, parsley and lemon zest and juice in a food processor. Pulse to a fairly smooth consistency. Add the pimentos and pulse just to combine. Transfer the mixture to a serving bowl and refrigerate. Serve chilled with crackers. *Yield: 128 (1-tablespoon) servings*

Nutrients Per Serving: Cal 7; Prot 1 g; Carbo 1 g; Fat 1 g; 19% Cal from Fat; Sod 30 mg

Smoked Salmon and Chive Spread

In Texas, when somebody invites you over for BBQ, accept. There will be some tasty "sides" — potato salad, pinto beans — and tangy sauce to be sure. But it is the magical marriage of meat and smoke from mesquite or oak embers that folks are particular about, and partial to. To borrow a phrase, " 'tis a consummation devoutly to be desired." Felicitously, this aromatic alchemy works not only with basic BBQ fare like beef, pork, and chicken, but also with just about anything else you put into the pit, including fish (notably salmon and trout) or even vegetables. They all take on a special depth and richness from the slow saturation in wood smoke. After smoking, we portion and freeze the salmon to be conveniently ready for this delectable dip, assembled in seconds and brightened by a few chives from our garden.

4 ounces fat-free cream cheese, softened
4 ounces reduced-fat cream cheese, softened
1/2 cup fat-free sour cream
1 tablespoon prepared horseradish
1/2 teaspoon salt
1/8 teaspoon cayenne pepper
Juice of 1 lemon
1 garlic clove, minced
6 ounces smoked fresh salmon
2 tablespoons minced chives

Combine the cream cheese, sour cream, horseradish, salt, cayenne pepper, lemon juice and garlic in a food processor. Process until smooth. Add the salmon and chives and pulse on and off until a uniform color is achieved. Transfer the mixture to a serving bowl; chill. Serve with bread rounds. *Yield 40 (1-tablespoon) servings*

Nutrients Per Serving: Cal 18; Prot 2 g; Carbo 1 g; Fat 1 g; 37% Cal from Fat; Sod 141 mg

Spice Things Up ✳ Herbs, usually the leafy part of the plant, are almost always best used fresh, although quality dried herbs can be useful. At Lake Austin Spa Resort we are blessed to have a significant portion of our gardens devoted to the organic cultivation of herbs, and for the most part we are herb self-sufficient. Even if you don't have room or time for a garden plot, you can still grow three or four favorite herbs in a small pot on the back porch. We promise it will make a positive difference in your cooking! Spices are generally the seeds or roots of plants. Whole spices that you grind just prior to using give the best flavor. Purchase a coffee grinder and dedicate it to spice grinding. For best results and longer shelf life, store your dried herbs and spices in tightly sealed containers in a cool, dark, dry location.

Yucateca Shrimp Cocktail

In this tropical twist to the traditional shrimp cocktail, the tomato base gets zinged with a triple shot of citrus and a kiss of incendiary habanero chile. Then everything is topped with a cool, crunchy slaw for contrast. Whether you enjoy yours under a shady thatched roof at an open-air bar after a day at the blast-furnace beach, or just try to beat the heat further inland, this icy alchemy of sea and spice is a breeze.

24 large shrimp, in shells
3/4 teaspoon salt
1/2 teaspoon sugar
3/4 cup ketchup
1/4 cup orange juice
1/4 cup lime juice
2 tablespoons grapefruit juice
1/8 teaspoon minced habanero chile, or 1/2 teaspoon habanero salsa
2 radishes, julienned
1/4 cup minced red onion
1/2 cup finely shredded cabbage
1/4 cup chopped fresh cilantro leaves
1 teaspoon olive oil
1 teaspoon white vinegar

Place the shrimp, salt and sugar in a saucepan. Cover with cold water. Refrigerate for 30 minutes. Place the saucepan over high heat and bring to a boil. Boil for 1 minute. Drain the shrimp, reserving the cooking liquid. Peel and chill the shrimp. Return the cooking liquid to the saucepan. Boil until the mixture is reduced to 2 tablespoons. Transfer the liquid to a bowl and add the ketchup, orange juice, lime juice, grapefruit juice and habanero chile; stir to combine. Add the shrimp. To make the slaw, combine the radishes, onion, cabbage, cilantro, olive oil and vinegar in a bowl; toss to mix. Divide the shrimp mixture into 4 portions. Top each portion with slaw and serve with corn tostados. *Yield: 4 servings*

Nutrients Per Serving: Cal 115; Prot 9 g; Carbo 18 g; Fat 2 g; 13% Cal from Fat; Sod 1053 mg

Taramasalata

This creamy, scallop-pink spread from Greece packs an assertive lemony and briny punch that belies its delicate color. You will either love it, or you will not. We do. Look for true taramas (Greek fish roe) in a Mediterranean specialty food store, or you may substitute regular red caviar.

4 ounces taramas (Greek fish roe)
6 slices white bread, crusts trimmed
Juice of 2 lemons
1/4 cup extra virgin olive oil
1/4 cup fat-free mayonnaise
1/2 cup fat-free sour cream
3/4 cup minced onion
1 cup mashed cooked potatoes

Combine the taramas, bread, lemon juice, olive oil, mayonnaise, sour cream, onion and mashed potatoes in a food processor. Process until smooth. Transfer the mixture to a serving bowl and chill thoroughly. Serve cold with bread rounds or pita crisps (Page 29). *Yield: 96 (1-tablespoon) servings*

Nutrients Per Serving: Cal 15; Prot 1 g; Carbo 1 g; Fat 1 g; 51% Cal from Fat; Sod 33 mg

Red Snapper Salpicon

Translated from the Spanish, salpicon simply means a chopped mixture, often fish, but sometimes meat or poultry, marinated in a highly seasoned vinaigrette. It is usually served chilled with corn tortillas or tostados. In this instance, we have added some warm black beans and an avocado/tomato garnish to enhance the finished dish both nutritionally and aesthetically. This is the best summertime eating imaginable; a perfect balance of sharp flavors, rich textures, crunch, and color. Any firm-fleshed fish or shrimp may be substituted for the snapper.

1 pound skinless red snapper fillets
Salt and pepper to taste
Olive oil cooking spray
1/2 cup minced onion
3 serrano chiles, seeded and minced
1 cup chopped fresh cilantro leaves
3 tablespoons extra virgin olive oil
1/4 cup lime juice
1 teaspoon Worcestershire sauce
30 small baked tostados (Page 29)
3/4 cup puréed black beans, warmed
1/2 avocado, peeled, seeded and diced
6 tomatoes, diced

Season the fish with salt and pepper. Place a heavy nonstick skillet over medium-high heat; spray with cooking spray. Gently sauté the snapper, turning to cook both sides, until the fish flakes easily with a fork. Remove from the pan and set aside to cool. Shred the fish by hand and place in a large bowl. Add the onion, chiles and cilantro. Toss to combine. Combine the olive oil, lime juice and Worcestershire sauce in a bowl and mix well. Pour the mixture over the fish and toss gently. Chill the snapper mixture until ready to serve. Top each tostado with a teaspoon of warm bean purée. Spoon a small amount of the snapper mixture over the beans and top with avocado and tomatoes. *Yield: 30 servings*

Nutrients Per Serving: Cal 49; Prot 3 g; Carbo 5 g; Fat 2 g; 38% Cal from Fat; Sod 66 mg

Tuna Pâté with Lemon Aspic

Now that the world is all about yellowfin tuna and artesian baked whole grains, this pâté is our homage to things gone by — canned tuna and white bread with mayo! Whether you're into retro or not, this is a very tasty and easy appetizer, its tangy, gelatinous layer of lemon dancing chic to chic with the creamy herbed tuna underneath.

1 (8-ounce) can solid white Albacore tuna packed in water, drained
3 slices white bread, crusts trimmed
1/3 cup minced onion
1 garlic clove, minced
Grated zest and juice of 1 lemon
1 teaspoon anchovy paste
1 teaspoon chopped capers
1/2 teaspoon chopped fresh rosemary leaves
1/4 teaspoon salt
1/8 teaspoon cayenne pepper
1/3 cup fat-free mayonnaise
2 tablespoons extra virgin olive oil
1/2 cup lemon juice
3/4 cup water
1/8 teaspoon salt
1 teaspoon unflavored gelatin

Combine the tuna, bread, onion, garlic, lemon zest and juice, anchovy paste, capers, rosemary, salt, cayenne pepper, mayonnaise and olive oil in a food processor. Process until smooth. Combine 1/2 cup lemon juice, water and salt in a glass bowl; sprinkle the gelatin on top and warm the mixture in the microwave for 10 seconds. Set aside for 10 minutes. Transfer the tuna mixture to 6 individual small crocks or 1 large one. Stir the gelatin mixture to combine; pour over the top of the tuna mixture. Chill until set. Serve with crackers or bread rounds. *Yield: 6 servings*

Nutrients Per Serving: Cal 131; Prot 10 g; Carbo 8 g; Fat 6 g; 43% Cal from Fat; Sod 443 mg

a change for the better

Often, the most difficult part about change is simply getting started. At Lake Austin Spa Resort we encourage our guests to start by making just one simple change at a time. Focusing on one particular goal for a given amount of time each day, week or month makes the change more manageable and more likely to succeed. For example, the goal of becoming more active does not mean that we want to begin by running three miles each day for the next month. If we try to achieve too much too soon, we set ourselves up for unnecessary failure. A better option would be to begin by adding a variety of achieveable physical activites to your daily routine and then gradually building upon them. Park at the back of the store parking lot instead of by the door, or take the stairs instead of the elevator. This "baby steps first" approach will help provide the foundation for further accomplishments.

WELL BEING

Country-Style Chicken and Pork Pâté

One of the most enduring rules for any successful food culture is "waste not, want not." No one takes this imperative more seriously, or is better at implementing it, than the French. One of their more elegant solutions is the country pâté. Bits of game, fowl, pork, and vegetables are ground together in varying proportions with spices and spirits (usually brandy), shaped into a loaf, larded with fat for additional richness, and then baked. The finished pâté is then chilled. A slice with some good French bread, garnishes, and a glass of wine makes for a memorable repast. Our version, while it may lack the inherent frugality of the French — we use choicer, leaner cuts — does possess an economy of its own; all of the flavor and texture at a fraction of the fat.

3/4 cup chopped onion
2 large garlic cloves
8 ounces mushrooms
1/2 teaspoon salt
3/4 teaspoon black pepper
1/4 teaspoon each thyme leaves and ground nutmeg
1/8 teaspoon each ground cinnamon and ground allspice
4 ounces chicken livers
2 tablespoons brandy
12 ounces boneless skinless chicken breasts, cut into 1/2-inch cubes
4 ounces pork tenderloin, cut into 1/2-inch cubes
4 ounces fat-free cream cheese, cubed
1 large egg white
1/2 cup fresh bread crumbs
1 tablespoon minced fresh parsley
4 ounces all-natural ham, cut into 1/4-inch cubes

Combine the onion through the allspice and pulse until the vegetables are finely minced. Spray a nonstick sauté pan with cooking spray and place over medium heat. Transfer the mushroom mixture to the pan; cook, stirring occasionally, until the mixture is dark, but not dry. Spray a second skillet with nonstick cooking spray and place over medium heat. Add the chicken livers and sauté until they are no longer pink. Add the brandy and, while tipping the pan away from you, light the brandy with a match. Carefully jiggle the pan until the flames subside. Remove the pan from the heat and set aside to cool. Return the mushroom mixture to the food processor and add the chicken livers, chicken, pork, cream cheese, egg white, bread crumbs and parsley. Pulse until fairly smooth. Transfer the mixture to a bowl and fold in the ham. Spray a loaf pan with nonstick cooking spray. Transfer the pâté mixture to the loaf pan and bake at 350 degrees for 1 hour to 1 hour and 15 minutes, or until a thermometer inserted into the center reads 170 degrees. Remove the pan from the oven; cool, then chill, covered, overnight. Serve the pâté sliced with bread rounds, cornichon pickles and Brandied Blackberry Mustard (recipe below). The pâté also freezes well. *Yield: 16 servings*

Nutrients Per Serving: Cal 78; Prot 11 g; Carbo 3 g; Fat 2 g; 22% Cal from Fat; Sod 146 mg

Brandied Blackberry Mustard

2 cups Dijon mustard
5 ounces organic blackberry jam, warmed slightly
2 tablespoons brandy

Combine the Dijon mustard, jam and brandy in a bowl; mix well. Chill until ready to use. *Yield: 40 (1-tablespoon) servings*

Nutrients Per Serving: Cal 23; Prot 1 g; Carbo 3 g; Fat 0 g; 0% Cal from Fat; Sod 289 mg

Deviled Eggs

The taste and texture of these neat, nearly fat-free little forgeries is so close to the real thing that most folks will never know the difference. Try them as part of your next BBQ or picnic. Or, present them as an after-school snack.

12 hard-cooked eggs
1 teaspoon sugar
1 tablespoon white vinegar
1 (15-ounce) can chick-peas (garbanzo beans)
2 tablespoons fat-free mayonnaise
2 tablespoons fat-free sour cream
2 tablespoons prepared yellow mustard
1/8 teaspoon cayenne pepper
2 tablespoons minced green onions
1 garlic clove, minced
1/8 teaspoon paprika

Cut the eggs into halves lengthwise. Remove and discard the yolks. Combine the sugar and vinegar in a small bowl. Stir until the sugar dissolves. Drain and rinse the chick-peas. Combine the chick-peas, vinegar mixture, mayonnaise, sour cream, mustard, cayenne pepper, green onions and garlic in a food processor. Process until smooth. Transfer the mixture to a fluted pastry bag and pipe into the depressions left by the egg yolks. Sprinkle paprika over the top, if desired. Chill until ready to serve. *Yield: 24 servings*

Nutrients Per Serving: Cal 36; Prot 3 g; Carbo 6 g; Fat 1 g; 8% Cal from Fat; Sod 108 mg

Roasted Mushrooms with Walnuts

If you've ever eaten escargots, you soon realized that it was just another example of how far people will go to get garlic butter. This mushroom recipe will remind you of the happier aspects of your snail experience, but has the added virtue of being vegetarian, with most of its fat being (the walnuts and olive oils) healthy monounsaturates.

1/2 cup packed fresh parsley leaves, minced
4 garlic cloves, minced (6 cloves if you're a garlic lover)
3 tablespoons chopped walnuts
1/8 teaspoon salt
1/8 teaspoon black pepper
1 tablespoon olive oil
18 large mushroom caps

Combine the parsley, garlic, walnuts, salt and pepper in a food processor. Pulse until the mixture has a coarse texture, adding the olive oil in a steady stream at the end. Spray the mushroom caps lightly with nonstick cooking spray. Fill with the walnut mixture. Place the caps on a baking sheet and lightly spray the tops with nonstick cooking spray. Bake at 400 degrees for 10 to 15 minutes. Serve hot. *Yield: 18 servings*

Nutrients Per Serving: Cal 19; Prot 1 g; Carbo 1 g; Fat 2 g; 71% Cal from Fat; Sod 17 mg

Shrimp Spring Rolls

These completely fresh and refreshing rolls filled with herbs, vegetables, and seafood colorfully displayed through their translucent rice paper skin, come from Thai and Vietnamese traditions. They can be a little intimidating to make for newcomers, so make sure that you have everything assembled properly before dipping your first rice sheet into water. After trying one or two to get the hang of it, you should be rolling right along. Serve them with our Ginger Sauce (Page 126) or another dipping sauce of your choice. You will find rice paper in 12- to 14-inch circles or squares in most Oriental grocery stores. See our recipe for Rice Paper Salmon (Page 126) for another use for these fanciful, edible envelopes.

12 (12-inch round) pieces rice paper
1/4 cup chopped fresh mint leaves
1/4 cup chopped fresh basil leaves
1/4 cup chopped fresh cilantro leaves
24 ounces cooked medium shrimp, peeled, deveined and cut into halves lengthwise
1 cup julienned carrots (1 1/2-inch pieces) blanched for 1 minute and drained
1 cup julienned zucchini (1 1/2-inch pieces)
1 tablespoon sugar
6 ounces rice vermicelli, cooked according to package directions
3 butter lettuce leaves, stemmed and cut into 12 strips
1 cup bean sprouts
1/4 cup pickled sliced ginger
1/2 cup cut chives, cut into 1-inch lengths

Immerse 1 piece of rice paper into a large bowl of hot water for about 15 seconds, or until completely pliable. Remove the rice paper and spread on a damp cutting board. Mix the mint, basil and cilantro in a bowl. Sprinkle about 1 tablespoon of the herbs over the rice paper. Arrange 4 or 5 shrimp pieces across the rice paper 1/3 of the way up from the bottom, leaving a 3/4-inch border on the left and right. Combine the carrots, zucchini and sugar in a bowl. Arrange some carrot mixture on top of the shrimp. Add a layer of rice vermicelli, a strip of lettuce, bean sprouts and a couple of slices of pickled ginger. Roll the bottom of the rice paper up and over the filling. Arrange a few chive spears along the unrolled portion of the rice paper. Top with 4 or 5 more shrimp halves. Fold in the left and right sides of the rice paper, then continue to roll until complete. Repeat until all 12 rice papers have been filled and rolled. Chill, covered with a damp cloth, in the refrigerator. Serve chilled with a dipping sauce. *Yield 4 servings*

Nutrients Per Serving: Cal 311; Prot 47 g; Carbo 68 g; Fat 3 g; 9% Cal from Fat; Sod 841 mg

Tostados and Pita Crisps

An indispensable part of chipping and dipping is, of course, the chip. The crunch and contrast provided (not to mention the practical point of transporting the dip) are an integral part of this eating experience. Unfortunately, from a fat content point of view, it can also be the diciest part of the equation. Many of the commercially available chips and crackers contain up to one gram of fat per piece. It adds up quickly, and most of the lower fat alternatives lack the flavor we are looking for. Here are two homemade alternatives we like very much. Both will store nicely up to four days, if kept in airtight containers.

The Tostados

12 thin yellow corn tortillas, stacked, then cut into 6 triangles

The operative word here is "thin." Corn tortillas commonly come in 2 versions -- the thicker one, for enchiladas and such, will not do for chips.

Arrange the tortilla triangles on a baking sheet in a single layer. Bake at 300 degrees for 10 to 12 minutes, or until very crisp. *Yield: 12 servings at 6 chips per serving*

Nutrients Per Serving: Cal 36; Prot 1 g; Carbo 8 g; Fat 1 g; 10% Cal from Fat; Sod 28 mg

The Pita Crisps

3 pita bread rounds

Cut each pita bread into halves, then split horizontally to form 4 single-layer pieces. Cut each piece into 3 triangles. Arrange the pita pieces on a baking sheet in a single layer. Bake at 300 degrees for 10 to 12 minutes, or until crisp and lightly browned. *Yield: 6 servings at 6 chips per serving*

Nutrients Per Serving: Cal 84; Prot 3 g; Carbo 17 g; Fat 1 g; 4% Cal from Fat; Sod 161 mg

you can't "go" without carbs

All cells need carbohydrates to function. The brain and red blood cells only use carbohydrates for energy. If you don't include carbs in your diet, or if your calorie intake is below the amount your body needs, your body will find its carbohydrates from protein by breaking down your muscles. And as you lose muscle, your body will lower its metabolic rate, which means you will need fewer calories. Your body stores carbohydrates as glycogen. When you run out of glycogen, you "hit the wall," or "bonk" - it's like trying to move your body through a thick vat of mud. After you exercise, you have a 15-minute window in which your carbohydrate consumption results in a 300% faster storage of glycogen. So enjoy a glass of juice, a banana or some pasta after your morning tennis game and you'll be able to enjoy salsa dancing that evening. What's more, even the highest quality protein - egg white - is utilized by the body more effectively when consumed with some carbohydrate, such as potato, toast or beans.

NUTRITION

salads & dressings

salads & dressings

salads & dressings

Fresh Tuna Salad Niçoise, Pg.39

salads & dressings

Bibb Lettuce with Roasted Garlic Lemon Vinaigrette, Walnuts and Roquefort Cheese

The next best thing to being an American in Paris is eating like one. Start with this salad, our bistro best, redolent of roasted garlic and extra virgin olive oil (the French make some of the world's finest) sharpened with citrus and a dab of French mustard. Add the double crunch of candied walnuts and the salty complex flavors of France's signature cheese, Roquefort. Toss everything with some fresh organic greens for the right stuff from the Left Bank.

1 large garlic bulb
2 tablespoons extra virgin olive oil (French, if you have it)
1 large lemon
1/2 teaspoon Dijon mustard
1/8 teaspoon salt
Freshly ground black pepper to taste
1/3 cup walnut halves and pieces
1 teaspoon canola oil
1/2 teaspoon salt
2 tablespoons sugar
6 cups Bibb lettuce, torn and chilled
1/4 cup crumbled Roquefort cheese

Slice the top off the garlic bulb and discard. Drizzle a few drops of the olive oil over the exposed cloves. Puncture the lemon with the tip of a sharp knife. Arrange the garlic and lemon in a small covered baking dish. Roast at 375 degrees for 35 to 40 minutes. Remove from the oven and cool. Squeeze the garlic purée from the cloves into a bowl. Squeeze the juice from the lemon into the bowl with the garlic. Whisk in the Dijon mustard, salt, pepper and remaining olive oil. Cover the walnuts in a bowl with boiling water. Set aside for 30 minutes; drain. Spread the walnuts in a single layer on a baking sheet lined with a triple thickness of paper towels. Roast at 300 degrees for 30 minutes. Reduce the heat to 250 degrees and roast for an additional 20 minutes. Toss the walnuts and canola oil in a skillet over medium heat. Add the salt and stir to mix. Add the sugar, 1 tablespoon at a time, stirring with a wooden spoon after each addition. Cook until the sugar has melted and adheres to the walnuts. Remove from the heat and spread the walnuts on waxed paper to cool. To serve, toss the garlic dressing, walnuts, lettuce and cheese in a bowl. *Yield: 4 servings*

Nutrients Per Serving: Cal 216; Prot 5 g; Carbo 15 g; Fat 17 g; 65% Cal from Fat; Sod 538 mg

head to the herb garden

Use fresh herbs to make a wonderful hair rinse. Bring two cups of water to a simmer. Add two cups of herbs (rosemary and mint to stimulate scalp, equisetum or horsetail grass to strengthen hair, sage for scalp problems) and remove from heat. Allow to cool, then strain out herbs (they make a great addition to your compost pile). Use the remaining liquid as a final herbal rinse for hair, leaving it in and then styling as usual. You can also put the mixture in a spray bottle and apply it your dog's coat for a between-bath freshener.

HOME SPA

Black Bean and Papaya Salad

Legumes (beans) are some of the world's healthiest foodstuffs. We try to present them to our guests in some form or another every day. In the fall and winter, the favorite choice is often some type of hearty bean soup — the ultimate cool weather comfort food. In warmer weather, we might offer a cool and colorful tropical salad like this one.

1/4 cup orange juice
2 tablespoons fresh lime juice
1 tablespoon cider vinegar
1/4 teaspoon salt
1/4 teaspoon chili powder
1/4 teaspoon sugar
2 garlic cloves, minced
1 (15-ounce) can black beans, drained and rinsed
3 cups peeled, seeded and diced papaya
1 medium avocado, peeled, seeded and diced
1/2 cup corn kernels, fresh or frozen and thawed
1/4 cup diced pimentos
2 tablespoons chopped fresh cilantro leaves

Combine the orange juice, lime juice, vinegar, salt, chili powder, sugar and garlic in a large bowl. Whisk until well combined. Add the beans, papaya, avocado, corn, pimentos and cilantro and toss gently. Refrigerate the salad until ready to serve. Serve chilled. *Yield: 6 servings*

Nutrients Per Serving: Cal 163; Prot 6 g; Carbo 24 g; Fat 6 g; 32% Cal from Fat; Sod 325 mg

Colcannon Potato Salad

The Irish make a warm, traditional dish with potatoes and cabbage called Colcannon, which is tasty enough in its own right. But, on hot summer picnic outings, this chilled version provides the perfect combination of cool and creamy with crunch!

8 potatoes, peeled and cut into 3/4-inch cubes
1 cup fat-free mayonnaise
1 cup fat-free sour cream
2 tablespoons Dijon mustard
1/2 cup 2% milk
2 tablespoons white vinegar
1 teaspoon salt
1/2 teaspoon sugar
1/8 teaspoon cayenne pepper
1/4 teaspoon black pepper
1 teaspoon chopped fresh dillweed
2 garlic cloves, minced
1 cup chopped onion
2 cups chopped green cabbage
2 tablespoons chopped fresh parsley

Steam or boil the potatoes until tender; cool completely. Combine the mayonnaise, sour cream, Dijon mustard, milk, vinegar, salt, sugar, cayenne pepper, black pepper, dillweed and garlic in a large bowl; mix well. Fold in the potatoes, onion, cabbage and parsley. Refrigerate until ready to serve. *Yield: 12 servings*

Nutrients Per Serving: Cal 173; Prot 5 g; Carbo 37 g; Fat 1 g; 3% Cal from Fat; Sod 431 mg

Hunter's Salad with Raspberry Vinaigrette and Candied Pecans

This is our favorite salad recipe during the fall and winter months when the gardens at Lake Austin Spa Resort are burgeoning with a variety of greens, and the pecans are falling from the trees.

2 tablespoons extra virgin olive oil
2 teapoons raspberry vinegar
1 1/2 teaspoons frozen raspberry juice concentrate or cranberry-raspberry juice concentrate
1/2 teaspoon Dijon mustard
1/4 teaspoon salt
Freshly ground black pepper to taste
9 cups mixed field greens
6 tablespoons crumbled feta cheese
3/4 cup thinly sliced red onion
2/3 cup candied pecans

Combine the olive oil, vinegar, juice concentrate, Dijon mustard, salt and pepper in a bowl. Whisk vigorously until well mixed. Combine the greens, cheese, onion and pecans in a serving bowl. Pour the dressing over the mixture and toss to coat the greens. Serve immediately. *Yield: 6 servings*

Nutrients Per Serving: Cal 185; Prot 4 g; Carbo 8 g; Fat 16 g; 76% Cal from Fat; Sod 279 mg

The Candied Pecans

2 teaspoons egg white
2 teaspoons sugar
1/4 teaspoon salt
1/4 teaspoon cinnamon
1/8 teaspoon cayenne pepper
1 1/2 cups pecan pieces

Whisk the egg white, sugar, salt, cinnamon and cayenne pepper in a bowl until slightly frothy. Add the pecans and toss to coat well. Spray a baking sheet lightly with nonstick cooking spray. Spread the pecans in a single layer on the baking sheet. Bake at 275 degrees for 30 minutes, turning the pecans every 10 minutes. Remove from the oven and cool completely. Crumble the mixture into separate pieces. Set aside 2/3 cup of the pecans. Store the remaining pecans in an airtight container in the refrigerator. *Yield: 6 servings*

Nutrients Per Serving: Cal 53; Prot 1 g; Carbo 1 g; Fat 5 g; 85% Cal from Fat; Sod 25 mg

Playing the Percentages ✳ One approach to monitoring your daily intake of fat that can be useful, is to calculate the percentage of calories in your diet that are derived from fat. We (and the American Heart Association) would recommend that no more than 30% of your daily caloric intake come from fat. The total number of fat grams will vary, depending upon how many calories you are consuming, and similarly, the 30% figure is derived from all of the foods you consume. In other words, not every item you choose to eat will have 30% of its calories from fat. Some will be higher, some will be lower. It's the total effect that counts. So a simple leafy salad made with a vinaigrette dressing containing a teaspoon of oil may look to have an alarmingly high percentage of fat, but only accounts for about 4 grams of total fat, a small percentage when incorporated into the overall picture of a healthy diet.

Papaya, Strawberry and Spinach Salad

We are forever extolling the virtues of balance in life, and this multicolored jewel exhibits just the three-pronged equilibrium we are looking for. It tastes as good as it looks; it looks as good as it sounds; and it sounds as good as it tastes. Did we mention that it's good for you? Substitute mango or even cantaloupe for the papaya, and always try to buy the freshest fruit in season.

6 tablespoons organic raspberry preserves
1/4 cup raspberry vinegar
2 tablespoons grapeseed oil or extra virgin olive oil
1/2 teaspoon salt
1/4 teaspoon freshly ground black pepper
4 cups peeled, seeded and cubed papaya
4 cups quartered strawberries
2 cups fresh baby flat-leaf spinach, rinsed and dried
1/2 cup thinly sliced red onion
1/4 cup fresh mint leaves

Combine the preserves, vinegar, grapeseed oil, salt and pepper in a bowl; whisk to mix. Combine the papaya, strawberries, spinach, onion and mint in a separate bowl. Drizzle the raspberry dressing over the fruit and greens; toss to coat well. Serve immediately. *Yield: 8 servings*

Nutrients Per Serving: Cal 129; Prot 2 g; Carbo 23 g; Fat 4 g; 27% Cal from Fat; Sod 162 mg

Spinach and Citrus Salad

The inspiration for this salad comes from sunny Spain — a country known for its almonds, oranges, and olive oil. It is also known for world-famous sherries, some of which are distilled into vinegars of unsurpassed depth and character. The relatively high fat content in this salad is offset by its reliance upon healthy monounsaturates as the source — the olives, nuts, and seeds.

2 tablespoons extra virgin olive oil
2 teaspoons Spanish sherry vinegar
1/4 teaspoon sugar
1/8 teaspoon salt
1/8 teaspoon dry mustard
Freshly ground black pepper to taste
1/2 teaspoon dried leaf oregano
2 garlic cloves, minced
2 oranges
1 tablespoon sesame seeds
1/4 cup slivered almonds
1/4 cup thinly sliced red onion
9 cups fresh spinach leaves, rinsed and dried

Combine the olive oil, vinegar, sugar, salt, dry mustard, pepper, oregano and garlic in a bowl. Whisk vigorously until well mixed. Segment the oranges by cutting a thin slice from the top and bottom of the fruit. Carve away the peel, including the white pith. Hold the orange over a bowl to collect the juice and slice the orange segments from between the membranes. Spread the sesame seeds and almonds in a single layer on a dry baking sheet; bake at 350 degrees for 5 to 10 minutes or until golden. Combine the orange segments, sesame seeds, almonds, onion and spinach in a serving bowl. Pour the dressing over the salad and toss to coat. Serve immediately. *Yield: 6 servings*

Nutrients Per Serving: Cal 129; Prot 5 g; Carbo 10 g; Fat 9 g; 57% Cal from Fat; Sod 117 mg

Fattoush

Fattoush is the Lebanese equivalent of the Italian panzanella, or bread and tomato salad. It is my idea of a perfect summer lunch. The sumac called for in the dressing can be found in Mediterranean specialty food shops, or you could substitute a few additional drops of fresh lemon juice.

1 **cup plain fat-free yogurt**
2 **tablespoons fresh lemon juice**
1 **tablespoon dried leaf oregano**
3 **garlic cloves, minced**
1 **teaspoon ground sumac**
1/2 **teaspoon sugar**
6 **medium tomatoes, diced**
1 **teaspoon red wine vinegar**
2 **teaspoons extra virgin olive oil**
Salt and freshly ground black pepper to taste
3 **pita bread rounds**
1 **cup cooked chick-peas (garbanzo beans), drained and rinsed**
1 **green bell pepper, seeded and chopped**
1 **red bell pepper, seeded and chopped**
1 **small red onion, thinly sliced**
4 **green onions, chopped**
6 **cups mixed field greens (with arugula and purslane, if possible)**
3/4 **cup chopped fresh Italian parsley**
1/4 **cup chopped fresh mint leaves**
2 **ounces crumbled feta cheese**

Combine the yogurt, lemon juice, oregano, garlic, sumac and sugar in a bowl. Whisk until mixed well. Refrigerate until chilled completely. Place the tomatoes in a large bowl and mash them lightly with the back of a large spoon. Add the vinegar, olive oil, salt and pepper and mix well; set aside. Cut the pita rounds into halves, then tear the pockets open to create 4 pieces. Arrange the pita pieces in a single layer on a dry baking sheet and toast at 325 degrees for about 10 minutes or until very crisp. Remove from the oven and cool completely. Break the pita toasts into random pieces. Combine the dressing, pita pieces, chick-peas, bell peppers, red and green onions, greens, parsley and mint in a large serving bowl; mix well. Scatter the tomato mixture over the top and sprinkle the feta cheese over the tomatoes. Serve immediately. *Yield: 8 servings*

Nutrients Per Serving: Cal 183; Prot 8 g; Carbo 31 g; Fat 4 g; 19% Cal from Fat; Sod 241 mg

Tabouli

Ripe summer tomatoes make a tabouli suitable for a sultan, but the year-round availability of fresh parsley and mint in our garden allows us to enjoy this refreshing Middle Eastern dish even when other vegetables are in seasonal transition. Add some cold cooked shrimp or chicken, or a crumbling of feta cheese, to make a complete one-dish meal.

1 cup cracked bulghur wheat (available in health food stores)
1 teaspoon salt
1 1/2 cups boiling water
1/4 cup fresh lemon juice
2 tablespoons extra virgin olive oil
2 teaspoons minced garlic
1/4 cup minced fresh chives
1/4 cup minced red onion
2 medium tomatoes, diced
2 tablespoons chopped fresh mint leaves
1/2 cup chopped fresh parsley
Salt and freshly ground black pepper to taste

Combine the bulghur and salt in a large bowl. Pour the boiling water over the bulghur; stir once with a fork. Cover the bowl with plastic wrap and set aside for 15 to 20 minutes. Remove and discard the plastic wrap. Add lemon juice and olive oil; stir lightly with a fork to combine. Chill, uncovered, in the refrigerator for 3 hours. Remove from the refrigerator and add the garlic, chives, onion, tomatoes, mint, parsley, salt and pepper to taste. Toss with a fork to combine. *Yield: 8 servings*

Nutrients Per Serving: Cal 106; Prot 3 g; Carbo 17 g; Fat 4 g; 31% Cal from Fat; Sod 299 mg

journal your progress

Journaling is an insightful way to discover your innermost feelings. It can also help motivate the mind to promote change or meet specific goals. Some ideas for journals include:

Nutrition- Jot down the foods you've eaten, your hunger level and emotional setting
Creative Writing- Write your own life stories and poems
Memory – Record special events and vacations
Gratitude- Remember great experiences and happy moments
Exercise- Keep track of your workout program and performance

Allowing time for journaling in the morning may help you to set a path for your day, while writing in the evening lets you recap and reflect on the day's events. Keeping a journal can be a useful and rewarding tool for managing your total wellness.

WELL BEING

Roasted Lamb Salad

Served in moderate portions, lean, naturally raised red meat can provide valuable nutrients (notably B12 and iron) and is an excellent source of protein. The boneless London broil cut is the leanest part of the lamb. With this recipe, you can turn your lamb leftovers into a delightful Mediterranean luncheon. Cold roasted chicken works deliciously, too.

1 pound boneless lamb London broil (shoulder)
4 garlic cloves, cut into slivers
1/8 teaspoon each: salt, cayenne pepper, black pepper and granulated garlic
1 red bell pepper
15 mushrooms, cut into halves
1 cup cooked chick-peas (garbanzo beans), drained and rinsed
1 cup pita crisp pieces (Page 29) or broken bagel chips
3 ounces feta cheese, crumbled
8 cups mixed salad greens
2 tablespoons extra virgin olive oil
2 teaspoons red wine vinegar
1/2 teaspoon Dijon mustard
2 shallots, minced
2 garlic cloves, minced
1 teaspoon dried leaf oregano
1/4 teaspoon each: salt, black pepper, sugar
2 tablespoons chopped fresh parsley

Pierce the lamb in several places with a sharp thin-bladed knife; insert the garlic slivers into the openings. Combine the salt, cayenne pepper, 1/8 teaspoon black pepper and granulated garlic in a small bowl; mix well. Sprinkle the seasoning mixture all over the lamb. Spray the lamb lightly with nonstick cooking spray and arrange on a baking sheet. Roast at 325 degrees for 45 to 55 minutes or until medium-rare to medium (internal temperature from 145 to 155 degrees). Remove from the oven, cool, then refrigerate for 3 hours, or until chilled completely. Remove from the refrigerator and cut into 3/4-inch cubes. Roast the bell pepper at 425 degrees for 15 minutes, or until charred all over. Remove from the oven and place in a small paper bag; seal the bag and set aside for 10 minutes. Remove the bell pepper from the bag; peel, seed and dice. Spray the mushroom halves with nonstick cooking spray. Arrange in a single layer on a baking sheet and roast at 425 degrees for 15 minutes. Remove from the oven and cool. Combine the cubed lamb, bell pepper, mushrooms, chick-peas, pita crisp pieces, feta cheese and salad greens in a large bowl; toss to mix. Whisk the olive oil, vinegar, Dijon mustard, shallots, garlic, oregano, salt, 1/4 teaspoon pepper, sugar and parsley in a small bowl until well combined. Pour over the salad mixture and toss thoroughly. Serve immediately. *Yield: 6 servings*

Nutrients Per Serving: Cal 283; Prot 22 g; Carbo 18 g; Fat 14 g; 44% Cal from Fat; Sod 401 mg

chefstip

We Love Olive Oil ✳ By now most of us have heard of the potential health benefits of cooking with olive oil (because of its highly monounsaturated profile) but with so many options, choosing the right bottle can be a bit confusing. In general you want "extra virgin" (from the first pressing, and the highest quality), and "cold pressed" (no solvents used in processing). Buy a couple of small bottles in your price range and try them. Like wines, olive oils come in a wide range of flavor intensities, ranging from delicately floral to rich, full bodied and raucous. A little experimentation will help you to decide which ones you prefer. Store your oils in a cool, dry, dark place, as light and heat diminish the quality.

Fresh Tuna Salad Niçoise

This take on a classic French entrée salad, served with some good bread and iced herbal tea, has been a favorite picnic luncheon with our spring wildflower bikers. A high quality canned, white Albacore tuna, packed in spring water and well drained, may be substituted for the fresh tuna steak.

Poaching Liquid: 1 1/2 cups water, 3/4 cup white wine, 1/2 lemon, 1/4 cup each sliced carrot, onion and celery, 1 bay leaf, 2 peppercorns-all combined in a stainless steel saucepan

12 ounces Albacore tuna steak
4 steamed new potatoes, cut into quarters or halves
1/2 cup (3/4-inch) peeled carrot strips, steamed until tender
1 cup (1 1/2-inch) green beans, steamed until tender
1 small red bell pepper, roasted, peeled, seeded, diced
8 pitted black olives, cut into halves
1/2 cup diced red onion
2 green onions, minced
2 tablespoons olive oil
1 tablespoon white wine vinegar
1/2 teaspoon anchovy paste
2 garlic cloves, minced
1 teaspoon Dijon mustard
1 1/2 teaspoons fresh thyme leaves, or 1/4 teaspoon dried thyme
1/8 teaspoon each: salt and freshly ground black pepper

Bring the poaching liquid to a simmer and add the tuna; gently poach for 10 minutes. Remove from the heat and allow the tuna to cool to room temperature in the poaching liquid. Remove the tuna to a large bowl; flake. Add the potatoes, carrot strips, green beans, bell pepper, olives, red onion and green onions; mix well. Whisk the olive oil, vinegar, anchovy paste, garlic, Dijon mustard, thyme, salt and pepper in a small bowl. Pour over the tuna and vegetables; mix well. *Yield: 4 servings*

Nutrients Per Serving: Cal 312; Prot 25 g; Carbo 30 g; Fat 8 g; 23% Cal from Fat; Sod 316 mg

Shrimp and Nopal Cactus Salad

As a way of helping you to meet your daily cactus requirements, we offer this absolutely delicious and completely refreshing salad inspired by the cooking of coastal Mexico. Cactus paddles are available in Latin or Mexican specialty grocery stores.

1 pound fresh cactus paddles or fresh green beans
1 cup thinly sliced onion
2 garlic cloves, minced
2 medium tomatoes, diced
3 radishes, julienned
1/4 cup chopped fresh cilantro leaves
3 tablespoons extra virgin olive oil
1 tablespoon each: white vinegar and fresh lime juice
2 teaspoons dried leaf oregano
1 teaspoon salt and freshly ground black pepper to taste
1/4 cup crumbled queso fresco or feta cheese
2 pounds small cooked, peeled and deveined shrimp

Pare the spines from the cactus; trim the base and around the edge. Cut into 3/4 x 1/4-inch pieces. Blanch in boiling water for 5 to 7 minutes or until tender. Drain and rinse thoroughly. Combine with the remaining ingredients in a large bowl. Chill in the refrigerator for 3 hours or until cold. Serve cold with corn tostados (Page 29). *Yield: 16 (1-cup) servings*

Nutrients Per Serving: Cal 100; Prot 12 g; Carbo 4 g; Fat 4 g; 66% Cal from Fat; Sod 286 mg

Avocado Vinaigrette

For cool with a kick, zig this zippy emerald salsa across anything hot off the grill — from fish to fajitas — or drizzle it over sliced fresh tomatoes. Ease it onto eggs or even eggplant. Squirt it onto squash or ripple it over rabbit. Before long, your mantra may be Veni, vidi, verdi (I came, I saw, I made green).

1 medium avocado, peeled and seeded
Juice of 1 lime
1 tablespoon white wine vinegar
2/3 cup vegetable stock
1/4 teaspoon salt
1 1/2 tablespoons chopped fresh cilantro leaves
1/4 teaspoon minced, seeded serrano chile
1 garlic clove, minced
1 green onion, minced

Combine the avocado, lime juice, vinegar, vegetable stock, salt, cilantro, serrano chile, garlic and green onion in a food processor. Process until smooth. Pour the dressing into a squeeze bottle, if you like, or any covered container. Refrigerate for up to 5 days until serving time. *Yield: 32 (1-tablespoon) servings*

Nutrients Per Serving: Cal 11; Prot 1 g; Carbo 1 g; Fat 1 g; 73% Cal from Fat; Sod 25 mg

Bleu Cheese Dressing

Hardly anyone seems to drink buttermilk any more, but it definitely lends its special and naturally low-fat tang to this house favorite. Use any leftover buttermilk to make corn bread or pancakes, or as part of the breading process for a number of dishes in this book. In addition to being a dandy dressing, this recipe can also serve as a delightful dunk for raw vegetables or for oven-roasted potato spears.

1 cup fat-free mayonnaise
1 cup fat-free sour cream
1/4 cup fresh lemon juice
1/2 teaspoon dried dillweed
1/2 teaspoon garlic powder
1/2 teaspoon black pepper
1/8 teaspoon cayenne pepper
1/2 teaspoon salt
4 ounces (about 1 cup) crumbled bleu cheese
1 cup buttermilk
1 tablespoon minced garlic

Whisk the mayonnaise, sour cream, lemon juice, dillweed, garlic powder, black pepper, cayenne pepper and salt in a bowl until well mixed. Combine the cheese, buttermilk and garlic in a food processor; process for 30 seconds. Add to the mayonnaise mixture and mix well. Chill the dressing until serving time. *Yield: 64 (1-tablespoon) servings*

Nutrients Per Serving: Cal 15; Prot 1 g; Carbo 2 g; Fat 1 g; 34% Cal from Fat; Sod 76 mg

Caesar Salad Dressing

Purportedly, the world's first Caesar salad was concocted by Caesar Cardini, a Tijuana hotel maître d' looking to please the hungry Hollywood types who came South to party during prohibition. If there had been an applicable patent, it would have made Mr. Cardini richer than his namesake; for to this day, Caesar salad is still the world's most enduringly popular and widespread specialty salad. Various interpretations grace tables from Denny's to Delmonico's, Los Angeles to London. The original recipe begins by creating a classic mayonnaise (copious amounts of olive oil emulsified into raw eggs), and tasty though this might be, it poses two potential hazards: high fat content and bacterial contamination. Happily, both of these concerns can be eliminated by substituting commercial fat-free mayonnaise. Now, I know you're thinking, "How good could fat-free mayonnaise taste, compared to the real thing?" And, the answer is, who cares? By the time you've finished adding lemon juice, mustard, garlic, Worcestershire sauce, etc. — all really dominant flavors — the mayonnaise simply becomes the medium, not the message. The results, which will keep in the refrigerator for days, are delicious.

- 1/2 **cup fat-free mayonnaise**
- 1/2 **cup water**
- 4 **teaspoons extra virgin olive oil**
- 1 **teaspoon anchovy paste**
- 1 **teaspoon Worcestershire sauce**
- 1/4 **teaspoon dry mustard**
- **Juice of 1 medium lemon**
- 3 **garlic cloves, minced**
- 1/4 **cup grated Parmesan cheese**
- **Freshly ground black pepper to taste**

Whisk the mayonnaise and water in a stainless steel bowl. Add the olive oil, anchovy paste, Worcestershire sauce, dry mustard, lemon juice, garlic, cheese and pepper; mix well. Refrigerate until serving time. Serve tossed with chilled Romaine, croutons and additional grated Parmesan cheese for a neoclassic Caesar salad. *Yield: 24 (1-tablespoon) servings*

Nutrients Per Serving: Cal 16; Prot 1 g; Carbo 1 g; Fat 1 g; 62% Cal from Fat; Sod 53 mg

the language of herbs and flowers

For centuries, symbolism and mythology have surrounded the meaning of plants. In the 1700's the language of flowers, floriography, was introduced in England and was dutifully studied by young men and women as a means of communicating their feelings. In the streets, people carried small, hand-held arrangements of herbs and flowers called "tussie mussies" to sniff whenever they encountered unpleasant street odors. Entire gardens were devoted to the cultivation of flowers and herbs to be included in these small bouquets. The next time you make a bouquet or send flowers, consider using their "language" to express your feelings. For example, to express love and good wishes, include some basil in your arrangement. For encouragement, try goldenrod. And, of course, to communicate your love and joy, give roses. To find out more about the meanings of specific herbs and flowers, check out some of these books: **Flora's Dictionary: The Victorian Language of Herbs and Flowers** by Kathleen M. Gips, **The Meaning of Herbs: Myth, Language and Lore** by Gretchen Scoble and **The Language of Flowers** by Kate Greenaway.

GARDENING

Creamy Goat Cheese Dressing

When we make this dressing at the resort, we use artisanal Texas chèvre cultured from local goat's milk. But the French, I'm told, also make a fair version available in most supermarkets. This dressing is great on salads or as a dunk for raw vegetables.

2 ounces reduced-fat goat cheese
4 ounces fat-free cream cheese
1 1/4 cups buttermilk
2 garlic cloves, minced
1/4 teaspoon dry mustard
1 teaspoon dried leaf oregano
1/8 teaspoon salt
Freshly ground black pepper to taste

Combine the goat cheese, cream cheese, buttermilk, garlic, dry mustard, oregano, salt and pepper in a blender or food processor. Process until smooth. Remove to a covered container and refrigerate until ready to use. *Yield: 32 (1-tablespoon) servings*

Nutrients Per Serving: Cal 10; Prot 1 g; Carbo 1 g; Fat 1 g; 30% Cal from Fat; Sod 47 mg

Greek Island Salad Dressing

By now, most Americans have at least heard of the healthy virtues of eating a Mediterranean-style diet, even if they're not sure exactly what that means. There are several components to the picture (smaller portions, fresh and minimally processed foods, lots of grains and legumes, and moderate consumption of wine among them). But perhaps the single most important and interesting difference between American and Mediterranean eating is not so much the amount of fat consumed, but the type. Mediterranean people consume considerably less saturated fat (think meat) and considerably more monounsaturated fat (think olive oil). My sister-in-law, who once vacationed in Greece, returned to say that the country was very well named indeed because everything she ate there was swimming in it — in the form of olive oil. This dressing is particularly good on a Greek-style salad of mixed greens, chopped cucumber, tomatoes, and bell pepper, topped with kalamata olives, additional feta cheese, and (if you like) a couple of chilled anchovy fillets.

9 tablespoons extra virgin olive oil
3 tablespoons red wine vinegar
4 garlic cloves, minced
1/4 teaspoon dry mustard
1/2 teaspoon salt
1/2 teaspoon freshly ground black pepper
1/4 teaspoon sugar
1 teaspoon dried leaf oregano
1/2 cup plain fat-free yogurt
3 tablespoons crumbled feta cheese

Combine the olive oil, vinegar, garlic, dry mustard, salt, pepper, sugar, oregano, yogurt and cheese in a blender or food processor. Process until smooth. Remove to a covered container and refrigerate until ready to serve. *Yield: 16 (1-tablespoon) servings*

Nutrients Per Serving: Cal 81; Prot 1 g; Carbo 1 g; Fat 8 g; 91% Cal from Fat; Sod 97 mg

Rémoulade Dressing

This dressing is the quintessential accompaniment to chilled, grilled, or fried (all right, oven-fried) seafood of any kind. Any shortcomings you might anticipate in the fat-free sour cream or mayonnaise are simply overwhelmed by the other spicier ingredients. This dressing makes an excellent all-purpose sandwich spread, too.

1 cup fat-free sour cream
1/2 cup fat-free mayonnaise
2 tablespoons Creole mustard or another whole grain mustard
1 teaspoon anchovy paste
2 tablespoons prepared horseradish
1 garlic clove, minced
1 teaspoon minced capers
1 tablespoon minced fresh parsley
1 tablespoon dill pickle relish
1 teaspoon chopped fresh dillweed
Zest and juice of 1 lemon
1 teaspoon Worcestershire sauce
1/4 teaspoon salt
1/8 teaspoon cayenne pepper

Combine the sour cream, mayonnaise, Creole mustard, anchovy paste, horseradish, garlic, capers, parsley, relish, dillweed, lemon zest and juice, Worcestershire sauce, salt and cayenne pepper in a bowl. Whisk until well mixed. Remove to a covered container and refrigerate until ready to serve.
Yield: 32 (1-tablespoon) servings

Nutrients Per Serving: Cal 13; Prot 1 g; Carbo 2 g; Fat 1 g; 3% Cal from Fat; Sod 81 mg

chefstip

The Well-Dressed Salad ✳ In cooking, as in life, it's the little things that make a difference. Using sea salt or kosher salt instead of ordinary table salt, or grinding black pepper fresh instead of using pre-ground, can make a world of difference in the finished product. Similarly, your choice of oils and vinegars will have a dramatic impact on the flavor of your salad dressings. Extra virgin olive oil is always a good choice, but walnut, grapeseed, and avocado oils also offer excellent flavor and health benefits. And the right vinegar isn't so much a matter of type as it is buying a quality product. Spending even just a dollar or two more per bottle will make your salads sing instead of screech. Buy small, decent bottles of white wine, red wine, balsamic, and our favorite, sherry vinegars, then mix and match to create your own favorite vinaigrettes.

soups

soups

soups

Golden Gazpacho, Pg.46

soups

Golden Gazpacho

Culinarily speaking, if you want to improve your Spanish, this is the perfect summer refresher course. Peeled, fresh yellow tomatoes work wonderfully of course, but good quality canned tomatoes make an excellent — and much easier — soup. Substitute the red variety for a more traditional version. Add a couple of cooked, peeled, and chilled shrimp to make a "souper" shrimp cocktail.

1 roasted yellow bell pepper, peeled and seeded (see Chefs Tip Page 50)
1 cup minced onion
3/4 cup diced, seeded and peeled cucumber
2 garlic cloves, minced
1 (30-ounce) can yellow tomatoes
1/2 cup cold water
1 teaspoon each: fresh dillweed and sea salt
2 tablespoons cider vinegar
1 tablespoon extra virgin olive oil
1/2 teaspoon Tabasco sauce

Combine the pepper, onion, cucumber, garlic and tomatoes in a blender or food processor; purée. Add the water, salt, dillweed, vinegar, olive oil and Tabasco sauce; pulse until well mixed. Remove the soup to a covered container. Refrigerate until completely chilled. Serve cold in chilled soup bowls. *Yield: 8 servings*

Nutrients Per Serving: Cal 50; Prot 1 g; Carbo 8 g; Fat 2 g; 32% Cal from Fat; Sod 451 mg

Asparagus, Potato and Leek Soup

Easy emerald elegance. A simple but sophisticated dinner party soup that can make an ordinary meal special, and a special meal extraordinary.

3 leeks, split vertically and rinsed, then sliced (white part)
1 teaspoon olive oil
Salt and freshly ground black pepper to taste
4 cups vegetable stock or chicken stock
1 medium potato, peeled and chopped
1 pound asparagus
1/2 cup minced fresh parsley
1 1/2 cups 2% milk
1/4 cup flour
1 ounce reduced-fat cream cheese
2 ounces fat-free cream cheese

Heat the olive oil in a 3-quart saucepan over medium heat. Add the leeks; sauté until soft, but not browned. Add the salt, pepper and stock; bring to a boil. Add the potatoes and reduce the heat to a simmer; cook for 10 minutes. Cut 1-inch tips off the asparagus; blanch the tips for 2 minutes in boiling water in a saucepan. Drain and reserve the tips. Trim and discard the tough ends from the remaining asparagus stalks. Peel each stalk with a swivel vegetable peeler. Cut stalks into 2 or more pieces and add to the potato mixture. Cook over medium heat for 10 minutes or until the asparagus is tender. Remove the mixture to a blender or food processor; add the parsley and purée. Purée in batches, if necessary. Combine the milk and flour in a 3-quart saucepan over medium heat; whisk until a smooth paste forms. Cook until the mixture is slightly thickened, stirring constantly. Add the cream cheese; stir until the cheese is melted and well combined. Add the potato-asparagus purée and heat thoroughly. Serve hot, garnished with the reserved asparagus tips. *Yield: 10 servings*

Nutrients Per Serving: Cal 97; Prot 5 g; Carbo 15 g; Fat 2 g; 20% Cal from Fat; Sod 175 mg

Smoky Louisiana Red Bean Soup

Let me tell you something — people in the South do know beans about beans. They know good value and they know good food. Beans (or peas) provide both. The crowders, purple hulls, limas, pintos, black-eyeds, butter beans, and others that grace so many Southern tables in the form of soups, stews, and side dishes are as indispensable a part of the culinary landscape as fried chicken or sweet potato pie. In fact, the alchemy of these humble legumes, slow simmered with spices and vegetables, produces such complexly flavored and deeply satisfying dishes that they are quite commonly and quite appropriately referred to as "soul food." And why not? For if ever there was a foodstuff meant to represent the soul, it would be soup — bean soup, Louisiana style.

1 teaspoon olive oil
1 cup minced onion
1 rib celery, chopped
1/2 cup diced green bell pepper
1/2 cup chopped carrot
3 garlic cloves, minced
1 tablespoon paprika
1/2 teaspoon thyme
1/2 teaspoon dried leaf oregano
1/2 teaspoon garlic powder
1/4 teaspoon onion powder
1/4 teaspoon freshly ground black pepper
1/8 teaspoon cayenne pepper
1 cup crushed tomatoes
4 cups vegetable stock
2 cups cooked red beans
1 teaspoon liquid smoke
2 tablespoons chopped fresh parsley
2 tablespoons chopped green onions
Salt to taste

Heat the olive oil in a large soup pot over medium heat. Add the onion, celery, bell pepper and carrots. Sauté until the vegetables are soft, but not browned. Add the garlic, paprika, thyme, oregano, garlic powder, onion powder, black pepper and cayenne pepper. Cook for 2 to 3 minutes, stirring constantly. Add the tomatoes and stock; bring to a simmer and cook for 15 minutes. Transfer 1 cup of the mixture to a blender. Add 1 cup of the beans and purée. Return the bean purée to the soup pot; stir to mix well. Add the remaining beans, liquid smoke, parsley and green onions. Season with salt. Serve hot. *Yield: 10 servings*

Nutrients Per Serving: Cal 70; Prot 4 g; Carbo 12 g; Fat 1 g; 13% Cal from Fat; Sod 131 mg

calm yourself with chamomile

Herb-scented water is the ultimate calming substance. You can add it to a bath or splash it on afterwards. Just fill a jar with fresh or dried chamomile flowers, then pour in boiling water to cover them. After the water cools slightly, add two tablespoons of 100 proof vodka and one cup of water. Then cover with a cloth and allow the mixture to cool completely. Strain, pour into stopper bottles, and be sure to use often.

HOME SPA

Black Bean Soup with Jalapeño Sherry

This soup, despite its rather menacing moniker, is not really all that spicy. The chile peppers are strained out, leaving just a trace of heat along with the sherry's subtle, nutty sweetness. Like most bean soups, it freezes well.

- 1 **teaspoon olive oil**
- 1 **cup chopped onion**
- 2 **garlic cloves, minced**
- 2 **teaspoons cumin**
- 1/2 **pound dried black beans, picked over for dirt and rocks**
- 4 **cups water or chicken stock**
- 1/2 **cup sherry**
- 1 **fresh jalapeño chile, seeded, or 3 fresh serrano chiles**
- 1/2 **teaspoon salt**
- 1 **cup fat-free sour cream (optional)**

Gently sauté the onion with the olive oil until softened in a large, covered soup pot. Add the garlic, cumin, beans and water to the onion mixture. Bring to a boil, then reduce to a simmer. Partially cover the pot and simmer until the beans are tender. Remove two-thirds of the beans with a slotted spoon to a blender with about 1 cup of the cooking liquid; purée until smooth. Pour the bean purée back into the soup pot; mix well. In a small saucepan over medium-low heat simmer the sherry and jalapeño chile for 5 minutes. Strain the mixture into the soup; discard the jalapeño chile. Add salt and additional water, if needed; mix well. Serve hot, garnished with a dollop of sour cream, if desired. *Yield: 10 servings*

Nutrients Per Serving: Cal 128; Prot 5 g; Carbo 26 g; Fat 1 g; 6% Cal from Fat; Sod 124 mg

White Bean and Greens Soup

This is a straightforward, unpretentious, Southern-style vegetable soup that gives a good accounting of itself with every spoonful. When we're not preparing it in a strictly vegetarian style, we like to take the bones from our house-smoked turkeys and use them to create a particularly rich and rustic foundation for the stock.

- 1 **teaspoon olive oil**
- 1 **cup each: onion and leek, chopped**
- 1 **large carrot, chopped**
- 1 **rib celery, chopped**
- 1 **garlic clove, minced**
- 1 **cup cooked navy beans, drained**
- 1 **red potato, chopped**
- 1 1/2 **cups diced fresh tomato or 1 cup canned with purée**
- 2 **cups finely shredded collard, mustard or turnip greens**
- 2 **tablespoons minced fresh parsley**
- 1/2 **teaspoon each: thyme and dried leaf oregano**
- 1/8 **teaspoon cayenne pepper**
- 6 **cups vegetable (or turkey) stock**
- 2 **drops of liquid smoke**
- 4 **ounces shredded smoked turkey breast (optional)**

Gently sauté the onion, leek, carrot, celery and garlic with the olive oil in a large soup pot for 2-3 minutes. Add the remaining ingredients and simmer until the potatoes are tender. Serve hot, garnished with shredded turkey. *Yield: 12 servings*

Nutrients Per Serving: Cal 54; Prot 2 g; Carbo 10 g; Fat 1 g; 14% Cal from Fat; Sod 156 mg

White Bean, Tomato and Lamb Soup

This Middle Eastern-inspired soup, with its subtle and exotic fennel and orange seasonings, may be our very favorite soup for early fall when the evenings turn cool, and there is still fresh basil in the garden. Since it is a bit of trouble to make, we encourage you to make a double batch, then freeze the leftovers for later enjoyment.

1 **(1-pound) lamb shank, seasoned with salt and pepper to taste**
1/2 **teaspoon olive oil**
6 **cups chicken stock**
5 **Roma tomatoes, split lengthwise**
1 **small onion, thickly sliced**
1 **carrot, peeled and chopped**
1/2 **cup tomato purée**
1/8 **teaspoon cayenne pepper**
1 1/2 **teaspoons fennel seeds**
Grated zest of 1 small orange
1 **cup cooked white beans, drained and rinsed**
1/4 **cup shredded fresh basil leaves**

Brown the lamb with the olive oil in a nonstick skillet over medium heat. Transfer the lamb to a small ovenproof pot. Add 1 cup of the stock to the skillet. Bring to a boil and scrape with a wooden spoon to incorporate any brown bits. Pour the mixture over the lamb. Cover and braise at 325 degrees for 1 1/2 to 2 hours or until tender. Remove from the oven and cool. Shred the meat (discard bone); reserve the liquid. Spray the Roma tomatoes, onion and carrot lightly with nonstick cooking spray. Arrange on a baking sheet in a single layer and roast at 400 degrees for 30 minutes. Remove the vegetables to a food processor. Add the reserved lamb stock. Pulse until the vegetables are finely chopped. Remove the mixture to a soup pot and add the remaining chicken stock, tomato purée, cayenne pepper, fennel and orange zest. Bring to a simmer and cook for 15 minutes. Add the beans, shredded lamb, basil and salt; mix well. Heat thoroughly; serve hot. *Yield: 10 servings*

Nutrients Per Serving: Cal 106; Prot 9 g; Carbo 9 g; Fat 4 g; 32% Cal from Fat; Sod 483 mg

Cream of Broccoli Soup

Okay, okay. So, it's not the Gucci of soups (more like the Hush Puppy), but it's delicious and very simply made with very accessible ingredients. We probably receive more requests for this recipe than many of our more intricate concoctions. Maybe that's why.

6 **cups water or vegetable stock**
2 **pounds broccoli, stalks trimmed**
1/2 **cup flour**
2 **ounces each: reduced-fat and fat-free cream cheese**
1/2 **cup each: evaporated skim and 2% milk**
Salt and freshly ground black pepper to taste

Bring the water to a boil in a large soup pot over medium-high heat. Add the broccoli and cook just until tender enough to purée. Drain the broccoli, reserving the liquid. Purée the broccoli in a blender or food processor, using as much of the cooking liquid as needed. Cool 1/2 cup of the cooking liquid. Combine the cooled liquid and flour in a bowl; whisk until the mixture is smooth. Bring the remaining cooking liquid to a simmer in a large soup pot over medium heat. Whisk in the flour mixture. Cook until the mixture thickens, stirring constantly. Add the cream cheeses, stirring until the cheese melts. Add the puréed broccoli, skim milk and 2% milk. Cook until the soup is heated through, stirring constantly. Add salt and pepper to taste. Serve hot. *Yield: 10 servings*

Nutrients Per Serving: Cal 83; Prot 6 g; Carbo 12 g; Fat 2 g; 17% Cal from Fat; Sod 93 mg

Bangkok Carrot Soup

Most of the world's major cuisines have an identifiable flavor profile — a set of ingredients and/or spices used in combination and with enough frequency to provide a distinctive "taste." We may not always be able to pinpoint what's in something, but we know where it came from. This soup — a Lake Austin Spa Resort favorite — is a great example. The uniquely Asian blend of ginger, chili paste, peanut, and sesame transforms what would otherwise be a rather ordinary carrot purée into a somehow familiar, yet still exoticly elusive, pot of gold, rich with all the mystery and intrigue commonly associated with its city namesake.

1 medium onion, chopped
1 rib celery, chopped
2 garlic cloves, minced
1 1/2 pounds carrots, peeled and chopped
2 tablespoons minced fresh gingerroot
1/2 teaspoon Asian chili paste
2 cups chicken stock
1 1/2 tablespoons light soy sauce
1/4 cup reduced-fat all-natural creamy peanut butter
2 teaspoons sugar
1 1/2 teaspoons roasted sesame oil
2 cups 1% milk

Combine the onion, celery and garlic in a heavy soup pot lightly sprayed with nonstick cooking spray. Cook, covered, over low heat just until the vegetables are tender. Add the carrots, gingerroot, chili paste and stock; bring to a simmer and cook until the carrots are very tender. Add the soy sauce, peanut butter, sugar and sesame oil; mix well. Purée the mixture in a blender or food processor, in batches if necessary. Pour the purée back into the soup pot and add the milk; mix well. Cook until heated through. Serve hot. *Yield: 12 servings*

Nutrients Per Serving: Cal 85; Prot 4 g; Carbo 12 g; Fat 3 g; 31% Cal from Fat; Sod 255 mg

chefstip

Hot Today, Chiles Tomorrow ✳ All members of the chile family - sweet, hot, large or small - have a shiny exterior surface created by a thin cellulose skin that covers the flesh of the chile. When we consume chiles in a raw state, we usually just consume this skin as well. It's harmless, but it really has no nutritional or flavor benefits, so when we process peppers, we try to eliminate the skin. The best way, by far, is to blister it off, placing the chile over an indoor or outdoor grill, onto an open gas burner, or on a baking sheet under a broiler (gas or electric). Char the chile fairly completely, then drop it into a closed container (we like a pot with a lid) to cool. Later, peel off the skin, split the chile open and rinse out the seeds which also contain few eating pluses. Now you are ready to proceed with your recipe.

Fresh Corn and Green Chile Soup

For pure and simple eating pleasure, few culinary experiences can surpass fresh corn on the cob. Lightly steamed or roasted in the shuck, dressed with a bit of butter and salt (although the best ones are perfectly delicious and deliciously perfect unadorned), the estimable ear has few equals. At the beginning of the season, the temptation is to eat a couple of ears every day, prepared just this simply, and grinning from ear-to-ear (as it were). Only gradually does one consider other recipes, and when the time is right, this delicious Mexican-style soup provides a perfect point of departure. The freshly cut kernels, paired with green chiles, lend crunch, color, and character to the soup. Even the cobs are useful, steeped in the stock, to provide additional body and flavor.

1 large onion, chopped
3 garlic cloves, minced
6 cups chicken stock (or vegetable stock)
6 cups fresh corn kernels (about 9 to 10 ears)
9 to 10 corn cobs
1 (15-ounce) can yellow hominy, drained and rinsed
1 teaspoon adobo paste from canned chipotle chiles, or 1 teaspoon Tabasco sauce
1 large carrot, chopped
2 poblano or New Mexican green chiles, roasted, peeled, seeded and diced
1 cup 2% milk
1 (12-ounce) can evaporated skim milk
2 corn tortillas
2 ounces queso fresco or crumbled feta cheese
2 tablespoons chopped fresh cilantro leaves

Spray the bottom of a heavy soup pot lightly with cooking spray. Add the onion and cook over low heat just until tender. Add the garlic and cook, covered, for 1 minute longer. Combine the stock and corn cobs in a large saucepan over medium heat. Simmer for 15 minutes. Strain the liquid into the onion mixture; discard the cobs. Add 5 cups of the corn kernels, the hominy and adobo paste; mix well. Cook for 10 minutes. Purée the mixture in a blender or food processor, in batches if necessary. Place a fine-mesh conical strainer or sieve over a soup pot. Pour the purée through the strainer, pushing on the solids to force as much as possible through the strainer and into the pot; discard the solids. Add the carrot, chile peppers, remaining corn kernels and 2% milk to the purée; bring to a simmer. Cook just until the carrots are tender. Add the evaporated skim milk; mix well. Cut the tortillas into thin strips. Arrange on a baking sheet. Bake at 350 degrees for 10 minutes or until crisp. Serve the soup hot, garnished with tortilla strips, cheese and cilantro. *Yield: 16 servings*

Nutrients Per Serving: Cal 118; Prot 6 g; Carbo 22 g; Fat 2 g; 13% Cal from Fat; Sod 368 mg

French Green Lentil Soup

We certainly owe a debt of gratitude to whoever invented the pot. For soon after the pot came soup, a concept that definitely caught on. What other foodstuff (with the possible exception of bread, which is often soup's companion) has fed so many people in so many places for so long? Everyone has soup. And whether it's humbly constructed from catch-as-catch-can or artfully wrought from rare, refined ingredients, soup feeds us well. Even when condensed and put into cans for convenient mass consumption, soup suffices. So, if you're not a soup maker already, you should be. Start with this humble, but nourishing French potage made with Le Puy green lentils and a touch of crisp, chemical-free pork. Because it's soup you can, of course, substitute another legume if you choose. And you may omit the pork altogether for a vegetarian version (although this would not be very "French"). Make a large batch; it freezes well.

As an historical note, it is reported that certain Aboriginal groups, who couldn't wait for the pot, made soup by putting heated stones into leather bags with water, meat, and vegetables. No doubt this method must have presented certain challenges when it came time to serve.

1 gallon water
1 1/2 cups Le Puy green lentils, rinsed
2 strips nitrate-free bacon
2 teaspoons olive oil
3/4 cup chopped carrot
1/2 cup chopped celery
1 cup chopped onion
3 cups chopped Swiss chard
1 tablespoon minced garlic
3/4 teaspoon salt
1/4 teaspoon freshly ground black pepper

Combine the water and lentils in a large heavy soup pot over medium heat. Partially cover and bring to a simmer. Cook for 25 to 30 minutes or until the lentils are tender. Remove half the lentils and some of the cooking liquid to a blender or food processor and purée. Return the purée to the soup pot. Sauté the bacon in a heavy skillet until tender-crisp. Remove the bacon to paper towels to drain. Crumble into the soup. Discard the drippings and add the olive oil to the skillet. Add the carrot, celery and onion and sauté over medium heat until the vegetables are softened. Add the chard and garlic and cook for 5 minutes, stirring occasionally. Pour the chard mixture into the soup pot with the lentils. Add the salt and pepper; mix well. Simmer for 10 minutes. Serve hot. *Yield: 10 servings*

Nutrients Per Serving: Cal 122; Prot 8 g; Carbo 20 g; Fat 2 g; 13% Cal from Fat; Sod 243 mg

hydration is cool

Water is one of the most essential components of the human body. It is important because it keeps the body temerpature regulated, protects the vital organs, and aids the digestive system. Lack of water can sometimes be a main contributor to fatigue. Carry a bottle of water with you during exercise. For activities lasting longer than 90 minutes, add a small amount of juice to your water to increase endurance. And although it may seem more refreshing, cold (or hot) water is not as easily absorbed as cool water. So keep your cool during exercise and drink your water.

FITNESS

Red Lentil Soup

The diminutive, disc-shaped lentil — more prized in the United States for its solid nutritional profile than for its sex appeal — actually comes in a profusion of colors. In addition to the common brown lentil, some European versions sport racier hues like black, gold, green, and even crimson or red. Consequently, a soup like this one from the Eastern Mediterranean not only displays substance and sensibility, it's also a "looker." Find red and other brightly colored lentils at your favorite health food store.

1/2 cup red lentils
1/4 cup uncooked white rice
4 cups water
1/2 cup each: onion, celery and carrot, chopped
1 Anaheim chile, seeded and chopped
2 tablespoons tomato purée
2 teaspoons paprika
1/8 teaspoon each: cayenne pepper and powdered saffron
1/2 cup cooked chick-peas (garbanzo beans), drained and rinsed
Salt to taste
Chopped fresh basil and mint leaves for garnish

Combine the lentils, rice and water in a heavy soup pot over high heat; bring to a boil. Skim and discard the froth that rises to the top. Once the froth ceases to appear, add the onion, celery, carrot, chile, tomato purée, paprika, cayenne pepper and saffron. Reduce the heat and simmer for 1 1/2 hours. Add the chick-peas; mix well. Season with salt. Serve hot, garnished with fresh basil and mint leaves. *Yield: 10 servings*

Nutrients Per Serving: Cal 70; Prot 4 g; Carbo 14 g; Fat 1 g; 4% Cal from Fat; Sod 24 mg

Butternut Squash and Coconut Soup

The dense, intensely golden flesh and mild sweetness of butternut squash make it a natural for puréed soups. This dramatic coupling with coconut milk and Asian spices is one of our favorite winter warmers.

1 tablespoon roasted peanut oil or sesame oil
2 garlic cloves, minced
2 tablespoons minced fresh gingerroot
2 pounds cubed, seeded and peeled butternut squash
1 small onion, peeled and chopped
4 cups vegetable stock
1 (13-ounce) can light coconut milk
1/2 teaspoon powdered turmeric
1 teaspoon Asian chili paste
3/4 teaspoon salt
1 teaspoon grated lime zest
Lime wedges, cubed tofu, chopped fresh cilantro and/or basil for garnish

Heat the peanut oil in a 3-quart saucepan over medium heat. Add the garlic and gingerroot; sauté until golden. Add the squash, onion, stock, coconut milk, turmeric, chili paste, salt and lime zest; mix well. Bring to a simmer and cook until the squash is very tender. Purée the mixture in a blender or food processor, in batches if necessary. Return the purée to the saucepan and cook until hot. Serve hot with lime wedges, cubed tofu, chopped cilantro and/or basil leaves as garnish. *Yield: 8 servings*

Nutrients Per Serving: Cal 124; Prot 2 g; Carbo 16 g; Fat 6 g; 45% Cal from Fat; Sod 377 mg

Roasted Butternut Squash and Apple Soup

When frost first finds your morning windshield, it falls upon the pumpkin as well. And, when cheeks turn russeted in the chilly air, so too are apples. So, fire up the hearth (or your convection oven) to roast these fruits of the season and transform them, tempered with spice and cream, into steaming cups of kindness. This is our favorite fall and winter soup, and an homage to all things autumnal.

3 cups chopped, seeded and peeled butternut squash
1 cup chopped onion
1 baking apple, cored and quartered (Macintosh, Jonathan or Granny Smith)
1/2 teaspoon canola oil
1 tablespoon minced fresh gingerroot
1 garlic clove, minced
6 cups vegetable stock
1 tablespoon cornstarch
1 tablespoon curry powder
1/8 teaspoon cayenne pepper
Salt and freshly ground black pepper to taste
1/2 cup evaporated skim milk
2 ounces reduced-fat cream cheese, cubed

Combine the squash, onion, apple and canola oil in a bowl. Toss to coat the vegetables. Arrange the vegetables in a single layer on a baking sheet. Bake at 400 degrees for 30 minutes. Remove the roasted vegetables to a blender or food processor and add the gingerroot, garlic and about 1 1/2 cups of the stock. Purée, adding more stock if necessary. Use a little of the remaining stock to deglaze the baking sheet; pour into a large soup pot over medium heat. Combine 2 tablespoons of the stock with the cornstarch in a bowl and whisk until smooth. Toast the curry powder in a dry skillet until it begins to give off a nutty fragrance. Add the cornstarch mixture, curry powder, remaining stock, cayenne pepper, salt and pepper to the soup pot. Cook until slightly thickened, stirring frequently. Reduce the heat to a simmer and cook for 20 minutes. Add the milk and the cream cheese; heat through until the cheese melts. Correct the seasoning. Serve hot garnished with minced chives, if desired. *Yield: 12 servings*

Nutrients Per Serving: Cal 59; Prot 2 g; Carbo 10 g; Fat 2 g; 22% Cal from Fat; Sod 165 mg

Herb Roasted Tomato Cream Soup

Roasting the vegetables for this wonderful summer soup intensifies their flavors and caramelizes their natural sugars for added depth. Serve the soup either hot or chilled. For a more whimsical, but equally tasty version, garnish this soup with a toasted bread crouton, some crisp bits of all-natural bacon, and a chiffonade of lettuce for a liquid version of the BLT sandwich.

8 Roma tomatoes
1 large onion, peeled
5 garlic cloves, peeled
5 cups vegetable juice cocktail (or tomato juice)
2 tablespoons cornstarch
1 ounce reduced-fat cream cheese
1 ounce fat-free cream cheese
1/2 cup evaporated skim milk
1/2 cup 2% milk
1 tablespoon chopped fresh parsley
1 tablespoon chopped fresh oregano leaves
1 tablespoon chopped fresh basil leaves
1/8 teaspoon cayenne pepper
Freshly ground black pepper to taste

Spray the tomatoes, onion and garlic with cooking spray. Wrap the garlic in foil. Arrange the vegetables on a baking sheet and roast at 400 degrees for 20 minutes, or until the tomatoes begin to brown. Remove the vegetables from the oven; unwrap the garlic. Purée the vegetables in a blender or food processor with a little of the vegetable juice cocktail. Strain the purée into a soup pot over medium heat. Mix the cornstarch with 2 tablespoons of the vegetable juice cocktail in a bowl. Add to the puréed vegetables; bring to a simmer. Add the cream cheese; cook, whisking, until the cheese melts. Add the skim milk and 2% milk, parsley, oregano, basil, cayenne pepper and black pepper; whisk until mixed well. Cook until heated through; do not boil. Serve hot or chilled. *Yield: 10 servings*

Nutrients Per Serving: Cal 73; Prot 4 g; Carbo 14 g; Fat 1 g; 13% Cal from Fat; Sod 377 mg

chefstip

Roasted and Rustic ✳ Summers in Texas, we try to keep the heat out of the kitchen by getting out and barbecuing in the backyard. But in the fall and winter, firing up the oven provides a welcome warmth, so we turn to roasting as a preferred cooking method. Not just for meats, poultry and fish, but also for vegetables. Root vegetables, already identified with the season, do particularly well, and we regularly roast carrots, onions, turnips, rutabagas, potatoes and sweet potatoes for soups, sauces and simple side vegetables. Hard or winter squashes like butternut or acorn also respond well to this method. Even tomatoes, a summer vegetable out of season, do well for two primary reasons. First, the roasting process is a dry heat method of cooking (no water added), and as such it concentrates flavors. Second, roasting caramelizes the natural sugars present in many vegetables and fruits, bringing an additional depth of flavor to the finished product.

Eggdrop Soup with Lemon, Basil and Tofu

This simple yet striking soup derives much of its goodness from the double strength stock, brightened with fresh gingerroot and lemon. The richness from the oil and the textural interest provided by the egg and garnishes finish the soup in fine fashion.

12 cups chicken stock
1 small whole chicken
1/3 cup peeled and sliced fresh gingerroot
Zest and juice of 3 lemons
1/3 cup egg whites
1 tablespoon light soy sauce
2 teaspoons roasted sesame oil

The Garnish

Sliced water chestnuts
Cubed tofu
Frozen green peas, thawed
Thinly sliced green onion
Chopped fresh basil leaves

Combine the stock, chicken, gingerroot and lemon zest in a large soup pot over medium heat. Bring to a simmer and cook for 45 minutes, skimming the froth as necessary. Remove from the heat and allow the chicken to cool in the stock. Remove the chicken, reserving the stock. Remove and discard the skin from the chicken. Shred the breast meat; set aside. Strain the stock into a clean soup pot over medium heat; discard the solids. Remove the fat from the stock and bring to a simmer. Remove from the heat and immediately swirl in the egg whites, soy sauce, lemon juice and sesame oil. Divide the garnishes and shredded chicken among 10 bowls; add the soup. Serve hot. *Yield: 10 servings*

Nutrients Per Serving: Cal 102; Prot 14 g; Carbo 3 g; Fat 3 g; 31% Cal from Fat; Sod 837 mg

eat like a thin person

Advice concerning the newest takes on good nutrition abounds these days. The "hot tips" of the week provide headlines for nearly every magazine on the shelves, and the best seller lists are filled with books touting their particular fabulous weight loss scheme. Nevertheless, it seems that the best solution is just around the corner (or cash register). At Lake Austin Spa Resort we like to think we have a more sensible approach. We encourage you to keep healthy living and nutrition simple: incorporate more movement into your daily life and eat like a thin person. (more, but smaller meals throughout the day rather than a few large ones.) Make healthy selections, eat more slowly, and eat only when you are hungry. The Japanese have a word for this, "hara-hachibu" which when translated means "eating until you are 80% full." With a little mindful application of these simple principles, you will soon be on your own path to wellness, instead of following the pack.

WELL BEING

Sopa Tlalpena

This soup, a version of the classic Mexican tortilla soup, is a perennial favorite of our guests. The whole chicken, coupled with the chicken stock, gives an important dimension and depth to the broth. You may omit the chipotle chiles, which are smoked jalapeños, for a milder version. We like to pass the garnishes with the soup and let each person select his or her own; however, a squeeze of fresh lime juice is considered mandatory.

The Stock

1 small all-natural chicken, cut up
12 cups chicken stock
1 teaspoon adobo paste from canned chipotle chiles
1/2 cup chopped carrot
1/2 cup chopped celery
1/2 cup chopped onion
1 bay leaf
6 black peppercorns
8 cilantro stems
4 garlic cloves, minced

Combine the chicken, chicken stock and adobo paste in a large soup pot over medium heat. Add the carrot, celery, onion, bay leaf, peppercorns, cilantro stems and garlic. Bring to a simmer and cook for 1 hour, skimming as necessary. Remove the chicken from the pot. Shred and reserve the breast meat for the soup; discard the remaining chicken meat and bones. Strain and reserve the liquid; discard the solids. Serve hot. *Yield: 12 servings*

The Soup

10 cups chicken stock
1/2 cup chopped carrot
1/2 cup chopped celery
1 cup diced onion
1 teaspoon ground cumin
1/2 teaspoon dried leaf oregano
1/2 cup corn kernels
1/2 cup cooked canned hominy, drained and rinsed
10 canned chipotle chiles, rinsed and seeded

The Garnish

Avocado slices
Toasted tortilla strips
Radish slices
Chopped fresh cilantro leaves
Shredded queso fresco
Lime wedges

Prepare the stock. Combine the carrot, celery and onion sprayed lightly with nonstick cooking spray in a large soup pot over medium heat. Sauté the vegetables until soft. Add the reserved stock, reserved chicken breast meat, cumin, oregano, corn and hominy. Cook until heated through. Ladle the soup into 12 bowls and evenly distribute the chipotle chiles. Pass the garnish assortment. *Yield: 12 servings*

Nutrients Per Serving: Cal 44; Prot 4 g; Carbo 8 g; Fat 0 g; 4% Cal from Fat; Sod 1252 mg

Portuguese Red Bean and Sausage Soup

This wonderfully robust and remarkably easy soup is proof that anyone can cook — all it takes is the right "cans." At Lake Austin Spa Resort, we use a locally raised venison sausage for this soup, but other low-fat varieties will work well also.

1	**teaspoon olive oil**
1/2	**cup chopped onion**
1	**garlic clove, minced**
3	**cups canned chicken or beef stock or a mixture of both**
1/2	**pound reduced-fat sausage, cooked and sliced**
1	**cup chopped cabbage**
1/3	**cup ketchup**
5	**medium new potatoes, quartered**
1	**cup canned kidney beans, drained**
2	**tablespoons brown sugar**
2	**tablespoons cider vinegar**
	Salt and freshly ground black pepper to taste

Heat the olive oil in a soup pot over medium-low heat. Add the onion and garlic. Cover the pot and gently sweat the vegetables until softened. Add the stock, sausage, cabbage, ketchup and potatoes. Bring to a simmer and cook until the vegetables are tender. Add the beans, brown sugar, vinegar, salt and pepper; mix well. Cook until heated through. *Yield: 10 servings*

Nutrients Per Serving: Cal 136; Prot 9 g; Carbo 24 g; Fat 2 g; 10% Cal from Fat; Sod 765 mg

chefstip

A Sense of Well Bean ✳ Called legumes in proper parlance, beans are one of the healthiest foods you can put in your mouth. They are an excellent source of nutrition and fiber, and combined with any grain they form a complete protein. To cook your beans from scratch, just take your favorite variety, (no need to soak) pick through for rocks, rinse and put in a pot with enough water to cover by 3 inches. Add a little minced garlic, some herbs, bring to a boil, reduce to a simmer and in less than two hours they're done. Smaller, softer legumes like lentils, split peas, black-eyed peas and garbanzos actually cook much more quickly (20-45 minutes). To test for doneness take one out and bite into it. Add salt as needed just before the beans are done. If you don't have time to make your beans from scratch, feel free to use frozen or canned (drain and rinse) varieties for a good start on a quick healthy meal.

Neo-Nantucket Clam Chowder

"Call me E-mail." There's no telling, of course, how Mr. Melville's oceangoing classic might have begun if it had been written today. But, we can tell you that this updated Eastern seaboard favorite is every bit as tasty as the ones served in chowder houses at the turn of the nineteenth century — and a whole lot better for keeping your keel trimmed!

1 teaspoon olive oil
1 cup chopped onion
1 rib celery, chopped
3/4 cup chopped carrot
1 garlic clove, minced
1/2 teaspoon dried thyme leaves
1/8 teaspoon cayenne pepper
1 1/2 cups peeled and diced potatoes
1 1/2 cups clam juice
2 (6-ounce) cans minced clams with juice
1 1/2 cups evaporated skim milk
3/4 cup 2% milk
3/4 cup skim milk
1/4 cup cornstarch
3/4 cup frozen corn kernels, thawed
Salt and freshly ground black pepper to taste
24 tablespoons oyster crackers
Chopped fresh parsley for garnish

Heat the olive oil in a heavy soup pot over medium-low heat. Add the onion, celery, carrot and garlic and a spritz of nonstick cooking spray; mix well. Cook, covered, until the onions are softened, stirring occasionally. Add the thyme, cayenne pepper, potatoes and clam juice; mix well. Bring to a boil, then reduce to a simmer and cook for 5 minutes. Add the clams, evaporated skim milk and 2% milk; bring to a simmer. Combine the skim milk and cornstarch in a bowl; whisk until smooth. Pour into the clam mixture; cook until the mixture thickens, stirring constantly. Add the corn, salt and black pepper. Serve hot, garnished with 2 tablespoons of oyster crackers per serving and some chopped parsley. *Yield: 12 servings*

Nutrients Per Serving: Cal 155; Prot 9 g; Carbo 24 g; Fat 2 g; 14% Cal from Fat; Sod 311 mg

Sherried Crab Bisque with Wild Mushrooms

Steaming bowls of bisque — those heady shellfish-based soups with the velvet complexions and symphonic complexities — have been warming the hearts and souls (not to mention the bellies) of satisfied diners for centuries. Wherever you find a coastline, you will most likely find this happy coupling of crustacean and cream. In the north, lobster reigns, and lobster bisque is arguably the most elegant, and certainly the most renowned, of the genre. Further South, the crustacean of choice becomes the lobster's diminutive nephew, the crawfish, or the stately sidestepping blue crab. They're all delicious. This "enlightened" recipe, with its scattering of mushrooms providing both taste and textural interest, remains a worthy successor — a warming and hospitable beginning to any meal.

2 cups chicken stock
4 cups clam juice
Any available shellfish shells (shrimp, crab or lobster)
1/2 cup chopped carrot
1 rib celery, chopped
1 cup chopped onion
1 bay leaf
3 parsley stems
1/2 cup minced onion
1/4 cup minced celery
1 cup thinly sliced shiitake mushrooms
1 tablespoon canola oil
1/2 teaspoon dried thyme leaves
1/4 cup sherry
1/2 cup flour
1 1/4 cups 2% milk
1 cup evaporated skim milk
2 tablespoons minced pimento
2 tablespoons light butter
1 1/2 cups lump crabmeat
Salt to taste
Tabasco sauce to taste
Chopped parsley for garnish

Combine the stock, clam juice, shellfish shells, carrot, celery, onion, bay leaf and parsley stems in a large soup pot over medium heat. Simmer for 20 minutes; strain, reserving the liquid and discarding the solids. Combine the minced onion, minced celery, mushrooms and canola oil in a soup pot lightly sprayed with nonstick cooking spray and over medium heat. Cook, stirring, until the vegetables are softened. Add the thyme and all but 1/2 cup of the reserved liquid. Bring to a simmer. Combine the remaining liquid, sherry and flour in a bowl; whisk until well combined. Pour into the soup pot; cook until the mixture thickens, stirring constantly. Add the 2% milk and skim milk, pimento, butter and crabmeat; stir to combine. Cook until heated through. Add salt and Tabasco sauce to taste; mix well. Serve hot garnished with parsley. *Yield: 10 servings*

Nutrients Per Serving: Cal 133; Prot 7 g; Carbo 18 g; Fat 4 g; 25% Cal from Fat; Sod 456 mg

Crawfish Bisque

So entwined is the crawfish with Louisiana culinary culture that there are restaurants whose entire menu (or so it seems) is devoted solely to the various means of preparing these tasty crustaceans. You can get them simply boiled (to be peeled and eaten with spicy cocktail sauce), plumped up in pies, fried into fritters, bound into étouffées, gumbos, and jambalayas, or served up cold in a salad. The possibilities are endless, but certainly one of the most satisfying and simplest ways to experience crawfish (now that you can buy processed meat) is in soup. In this case, the choice is a savory, delicately rich bisque. It is elegant enough for your next dinner party; or hearty and humble enough to be thermosed up for your next pre-game tailgate gathering.

2 cups chicken stock
4 cups clam juice
1/2 cup each: carrot and onion, chopped
1 rib celery, chopped
1 bay leaf
3 parsley stems
2 fresh thyme sprigs
1/2 cup each: onion and celery, minced
1/4 cup sherry
3/4 cup flour
3 tablespoons tomato purée
2 cups 2% milk
1 1/2 cups evaporated skim milk
1 tablespoon light butter
1 pound frozen crawfish meat, thawed, and coarsely chopped with juices retained
Salt and Tabasco sauce to taste
Chopped parsley for garnish

Combine the chicken stock through the thyme sprigs in a large soup pot over medium heat. Bring to a simmer and cook until the vegetables are softened. Strain, reserving the liquid and discarding the solids. Sweat (low heat) the minced onion and celery in a soup pot until softened, using non-stick cooking spray. Add all but 1 cup of the reserved liquid. Bring to a simmer. Combine the remaining stock, sherry and flour in a bowl; whisk to form a slurry. Pour into the simmering soup; cook until the mixture thickens, stirring constantly. Add the tomato purée; whisk to mix. Simmer, stirring frequently, for 15 minutes. Strain the soup into a clean soup pot over medium heat. Add the 2% milk and skim milk, butter, crawfish, salt and Tabasco sauce; mix well. Cook until heated through, but do not boil. Serve hot, garnished with parsley. *Yield: 10 servings*

Nutrients Per Serving: Cal 164; Prot 14 g; Carbo 22 g; Fat 2 g; 13% Cal from Fat; Sod 478 mg

have some respect

Your body is an amazingly efficient and effective machine. By paying close attention to your body's signals, you can become proactive (instead of reactive) about your own health care. Your body can express an imbalance in many ways, including pain, stress, anxiety, insomnia, fatigue, dizziness, hunger, headaches, even dry skin. To maintain a healthy body and lifestyle, be sure to respect and listen to your body's signals and practice good preventive care - get proper nutrition, regular exercise, adequate sleep, and utilize relaxation techniques.

Salmon and Leek Chowder

Big, balanced flavors, beautiful color, and a rich, creamy texture that belies the reduced-fat content make this chowder a winning choice. Serve it with warm bread and a winter greens salad. It's just the stuff to put the glow back into the cheeks of your favorite lumberJack — or Jill.

- **1 leek, split, washed and white part chopped**
- **1 garlic clove, minced**
- **6 cups clam juice**
- **1 teaspoon chopped fresh thyme leaves**
- **1 teaspoon chopped fresh dillweed**
- **1 medium potato, peeled and cubed**
- **1/4 cup flour**
- **1 1/2 cups 2% milk**
- **3/4 cup evaporated skim milk**
- **8 ounces salmon fillet, cooked or uncooked**
- **2 ounces reduced-fat cream cheese, cubed**
- **1/8 teaspoon cayenne pepper, or to taste**
- **Salt and freshly ground black pepper to taste**
- **Minced fresh chives for garnish**

Place the chopped leeks into a soup pot. Spray with nonstick cooking spray and sauté over medium heat until tender. Add the garlic and cook for 30 seconds, stirring frequently. Add the clam juice, thyme, dillweed and potato; bring to a boil. Immediately reduce the heat to a simmer and cook just until the potatoes are tender. Combine the flour and 2% milk in a bowl; whisk until smooth. Pour into the stock mixture and whisk to mix. Cook for 5 minutes, stirring frequently. Add the skim milk, salmon and cream cheese. Cook, stirring, until the cheese melts. Add the cayenne pepper, salt and black pepper; mix well. Serve hot, garnished with chives. *Yield: 10 servings*

Nutrients Per Serving: Cal 117; Prot 9 g; Carbo 12 g; Fat 4 g; 28% Cal from Fat; Sod 380 mg

chefstip

Taking Stock ✳ The very best stocks, it goes without saying, are long-simmered, homemade affairs, and we encourage you to make them just so whenever possible. This is the 21st century, however, and most of you don't (or think you don't) have time for such leisurely renderings. Here are some alternatives:

Some upscale grocery stores make homemade-like stocks which they sell. Many others carry frozen stocks, generally of good quality. Many gourmet or health food stores carry all-natural, or even organic, stocks in shelf-stable containers. And, of course, canned stocks with reduced fat and sodium contents are now readily available. Bottled clam juice, which makes a passable seafood stock, is improved, as are canned stocks, by a brief simmering with a few stock-worthy vegetables and appropriate meat or seafood trimmings.

Bouillon cubes (some are better than others) should be used with caution, primarily because of fat and sodium content.

Shrimp, Sweet Potato and Pineapple Soup

This is a festive, slightly spicy, slightly sweet soup inspired by the cooking of coastal Mexico. We like the idea that anyone can customize this soup to his or her specifications — but the fresh pineapple is mandatory!

30 small shrimp
4 Roma tomatoes
1 teaspoon canola oil
1 cup chopped onion
4 garlic cloves, minced
2 cups chicken stock
2 cups seafood stock or clam juice
Shrimp shells
1/2 cup peeled and diced potatoes
1 cup peeled and diced sweet potatoes
1/2 cup diced chayote squash or zucchini
1/2 teaspoon dried leaf oregano
1 teaspoon sugar
1 tablespoon pure coconut extract
1 teaspoon adobo paste from canned chipotle chile peppers or Mexican hot sauce
1/2 cup frozen pineapple juice concentrate or 2 cups fresh pineapple juice reduced to 1 cup
1 cup canned yellow hominy, drained
Salt to taste

The Garnish

Finely diced fresh pineapple
Finely chopped radishes
Shredded toasted corn tortillas
Chopped fresh cilantro leaves
Queso fresco
Lime wedges

Peel the shrimp; reserve the shells and set aside. Cut an X in the bottom of each tomato. Plunge into boiling water in a saucepan for 30 seconds; drain, peel and chop. Heat the canola oil in a large soup pot over medium heat. Add the onion and garlic and sauté for 2 to 3 minutes. Remove the onions to a food processor or blender, add the chopped tomatoes and purée. Combine the chicken stock and seafood stock in a heavy soup pot over medium heat. Add shrimp shells and simmer for 10 minutes. Strain into a clean soup pot, discarding the shells. Add the tomato mixture, potato, sweet potato, chayote squash, oregano, sugar, coconut extract, adobo paste, pineapple juice concentrate and hominy. Simmer until the potatoes are tender. Add salt to taste; mix well. Add the shrimp and cook for 2 minutes. Serve hot with any of the garnishes. *Yield: 10 servings*

Nutrients Per Serving: Cal 92; Prot 4 g; Carbo 17 g; Fat 1 g; 10% Cal from Fat; Sod 309 mg

vegetarian

vegetarian

vegetarian

Chimayo Tortilla Stack with New Mexican Red Chile Sauce, Pg.79

vegetarian

Crispy Falafel Cakes

In much of the Middle East, crispy falafel, wrapped in warm pita bread with tomato, chopped pickle, and tahini, are as common (although a darn sight healthier) as hamburgers are here. And you can enjoy this recipe in just that fashion. Or, you can serve them, as we do here, on top of a simple salad as a summer dinner entrée. You'll want to use dried chick-peas (or garbanzo beans, which are the same thing) for this recipe. The canned version will not have the same texture.

1 cup dried chick-peas (garbanzo beans), soaked for 6 hours or overnight in the refrigerator
1/4 cup minced onion
2 garlic cloves, minced
2 tablespoons chopped fresh cilantro leaves
2 teaspoons curry powder
2 teaspoons ground cumin
1/8 teaspoon cayenne pepper
1 teaspoon paprika
1/2 teaspoon dried leaf oregano
1/2 teaspoon salt
1/2 teaspoon baking powder
1/2 cup cornmeal
3 tablespoons flour
1 tablespoon olive oil
3 tablespoons tahini (sesame seed paste)
3 tablespoons water
1 tablespoon lemon juice
1/8 teaspoon salt
4 cups fresh spinach leaves, rinsed and dried
2 medium tomatoes, cut into wedges

Drain the chick-peas; blanch in boiling water in a saucepan for 5 minutes; drain. Process the chick-peas, onion, garlic, cilantro, curry powder, cumin, cayenne pepper, paprika, oregano and salt in a food processor until a coarse paste forms. Remove the mixture to a bowl and add the baking powder, cornmeal and flour; mix thoroughly. Add a little water, if needed, to make the dough adhere when pressed. Shape the mixture into eight 1/2-inch-thick disks. Heat the olive oil in a nonstick skillet. Sauté the falafel cakes over medium heat for 6 to 8 minutes, turning to crisp both sides. Meanwhile, whisk the tahini, water, lemon juice and salt together in a bowl. To serve, arrange the spinach and tomatoes on 4 plates. Top with 2 falafel cakes and drizzle tahini sauce over all. *Yield: 4 servings*

Nutrients Per Serving: Cal 391; Prot 16 g; Carbo 56 g; Fat 13 g; 30% Cal from Fat; Sod 497 mg

a grain of truth

Whole grains are rich in fiber and minerals. The bran and germ of grains contain active elements, such as phytochemicals, which fight cancer and heart disease by many different methods. Refining grains removes almost all the phytochemicals, so be sure to read labels and select whole-grain food products.

NUTRITION

Bean and Masa Griddle Cakes with Roasted Pepper Salsa and Fresh Corn/Green Chile Relish

These tasty little masa cakes (although a bit of a geometry lesson in the making) are emblematic of everything we hold high in the resort's kitchen — excellent nutrition (the masa and beans combine to form a complete protein), and pure eating pleasure with a variety of colors, flavors, textures, and even temperatures that come together to create a unified, but multilayered eating experience.

2 teaspoons flour
1 cup masa harina de maiz
3/4 cup warm water
1/4 teaspoon sea salt
1 tablespoon light butter, softened
1 cup cooked white beans or chick-peas (garbanzo beans) drained and rinsed
1/8 teaspoon sea salt
2 tablespoons minced onion
1 garlic clove, minced
4 teaspoons olive oil
2 tablespoons Roasted Red Pepper Salsa (Page 20)
1 tablespoon Fresh Corn/Green Chile Relish
1/2 tablespoon crumbled queso fresco or feta cheese

For the dough, combine the flour, masa harina, water and salt in a large bowl. Work the ingredients into a smooth dough, then fold in the butter. Set the dough aside, covered with a damp cloth, for 30 minutes.

For the filling, purée the beans and salt in a food processor. Spray the onion and garlic with nonstick cooking spray in a nonstick skillet, then sauté over medium heat until the onion is soft. Add the bean purée; cook, stirring, for 2 to 3 minutes. Set aside to cool.

Remove the masa dough from the bowl. Form eight 1-inch diameter balls, then pat them into 2-inch disks. Spoon a small amount of the bean filling into the center of each disk. Fold the dough over to make a half-moon shape. Pinch the edges together to seal. Roll the cakes gently between the palms of your hands until the dough is cylindrical. Flatten to a 1/2-inch thickness. Heat the olive oil in a nonstick skillet over medium heat. Sauté the griddle cakes, turning as needed, until cooked and slightly crisp. To serve, pool the Roasted Red Pepper Salsa on each of four plates. Arrange 2 griddle cakes in the salsa; top with the relish and cheese. *Yield: 4 servings*

The Fresh Corn/Green Chile Relish

Kernels from 1 ear fresh corn
1 tablespoon minced poblano chile
2 tablespoons minced onion
1 garlic clove, minced
1 teaspoon fresh lime juice
1/8 teaspoon salt

Combine the corn, poblano chile, onion, garlic, lime juice and salt in a bowl; mix well.
Yield: 4 (2-tablespoon) servings

Nutrients Per Serving: Cal 241; Prot 8 g; Carbo 38 g; Fat 8 g; 28% Cal from Fat; Sod 261 mg

Corn Tortillas and Quesadillas

Corn is a native American plant, and corn tortillas have provided the daily bread for many of its peoples for literally thousands of years. In fact, before the arrival of the Europeans, there was no wheat here; all of the baking was corn-based. If you are the sort of person who would consider making a quick bread for a meal — cornbread, muffins, or biscuits — then you are a prime candidate for making your own corn tortillas. You will need a tortilla press, two pieces of plastic cut to mimic the shape of the press (the gauge of plastic that bread comes wrapped in works well or plastic bags), and a nonstick skillet.

1 1/2 cups masa harina de maiz
1 cup water

Combine the masa harina and water in a large bowl; mix well. Divide the dough into 8 balls. Preheat a nonstick skillet over medium-high heat. Place one sheet of plastic on the open tortilla press. Center a ball of dough on the plastic; top with the second piece of plastic. Close the press with even pressure to flatten the dough. Open the press and carefully peel the top sheet of plastic away from the flattened dough. Lift the tortilla out of the press and invert it onto the palm of your hand. Peel away the second piece of plastic. Place the tortilla in the skillet and cook for 30 seconds; flip it over and cook for 30 seconds. Flip it again, and after a few seconds, give the center a firm tamp-and-release with a bunched-up cloth dish towel. This helps the dough to separate — the tortilla should puff. If it doesn't puff, it is still a useable tortilla, just not quite as light. Stack the cooked tortillas on a warm plate and cover with a clean cloth. Repeat the procedure until all the tortillas are cooked. *Yield: 8 servings*

Once you've learned to make these homemade tortillas, the next logical step is making quesadillas. Although the direct Spanish translation for quesadilla is "little cheese thing," these delightful little turnovers can be filled with almost anything you have on hand, using only a few simple guidelines — no raw products and nothing too damp.

Quesadillas

Masa and water as for tortillas
1 cup (4 ounces) shredded reduced-fat Cheddar or Monterey Jack cheese
1 tablespoon chopped fresh cilantro leaves
1 tablespoon canola oil
1 cup Salsa Picante (Page 19)

Begin as for tortillas, but this time after peeling off the top sheet of plastic, lift the tortilla from the press and place on a work surface, keeping the plastic piece in place on the bottom. Place 2 tablespoons of the Cheddar cheese and a pinch of cilantro on the bottom half of each circle of dough. Using the plastic as a guide, fold the top half of the dough over the bottom half, enclosing the cheese mixture. Pinch the open edges of the dough together to seal. Gently peel away the plastic and set the quesadilla aside. Heat the canola oil in a heavy nonstick skillet over medium-high heat. Cook each quesadilla for 2 minutes on each side, or until golden. Serve hot with salsa, sour cream and pico de gallo, if desired. *Yield: 4 (2-quesadilla) servings*

Nutrients Per Serving: Cal 233; Prot 10 g; Carbo 27 g; Fat 11 g; 39% Cal from Fat; Sod 185 mg

Filling Variations

Diced and sautéed potatoes with cheese and/or chorizo sausage and Avocado/Tomatillo Salsa (Page 70)
Cooked and chopped poultry or shrimp with chipotle chile salsa
Cooked beans and/or chopped vegetables with Salsa Picante (Page 19)

Chilaquiles Verdes

Living in a country that dispenses literally millions of tortillas as daily bread, enterprising Mexican cooks learned long ago to make good use of the stale and uneaten ones, turning vice into virtue with chilaquiles. This casserole, for which there are countless variations (see Chilaquiles de Estudiante, Page 159), takes advantage of the tortillas' dryness by allowing them to rehydrate in sauce and develop a wonderfully chewy texture. Add beans and a salad and you have a complete meal.

8	**white corn tortillas, cut into 1/2-inch strips**
1	**cup chopped onion**
2	**cups (1/4-inch) cubed zucchini**
2	**garlic cloves, minced**
2	**cups Tomatillo Salsa (Page 104)**
1	**small poblano chile, roasted, seeded, peeled and cut into thin strips**
3/4	**cup fat-free sour cream**
1	**cup (4 ounces) shredded reduced-fat white or yellow Cheddar cheese**

The Garnish

Fat-free sour cream
Chopped fresh cilantro leaves
Queso fresco or feta cheese

Arrange the tortilla strips in a single layer on a baking sheet. Bake at 250 degrees until almost crisp. Set aside. Spray the onion with nonstick cooking spray in a nonstick pan, then sauté over medium heat until soft. Add the zucchini and garlic; sauté for 1 minute. Add the salsa, poblano chile and crisped tortilla strips. Cook until the tortillas begin to soften. Remove the skillet from the heat and add the sour cream and 3/4 of the Cheddar cheese; stir to combine. Pour the mixture into a casserole dish and sprinkle the remaining Cheddar cheese on top. Bake at 375 degrees until the Cheddar cheese melts and the chilaquiles is hot. Serve garnished with a dollop of sour cream, pinch of cilantro leaves and some crumbled queso fresco or feta cheese, if desired. *Yield: 4 servings*

Nutrients Per Serving: Cal 418; Prot 17 g; Carbo 55 g; Fat 7 g; 15% Cal from Fat; Sod 422 mg

chefstip

Sweating It Out ✳ Many recipes start off something like this: "Heat two tablespoons of vegetable oil in a skillet, adding the vegetables and sauté until the onions are translucent . . ." Those two tablespoons of oil represent 28 grams of fat! However, using just a little patience and a fraction of that fat, we can get to the same place in the recipe. Instead of sautéing which requires more fat, we "sweat" the vegetables – using less fat (nonstick spray), lower heat, and a covered pot or skillet – a technique which "steam-sautés" the vegetables, bringing them to the same stage as the first recipe, but using just 8 grams of fat.

Mushroom Enchiladas with Avocado/Tomatillo Salsa

Believe it or not, mushrooms are very much a part of Mexican cuisine, and a very tasty filling for enchiladas, too. Topped with a cool and creamy green salsa, and finished with a crunchy, colorful salad, they are just the boleta (ticket) for your next summer fiesta.

The Salsa

1 1/2 cups fresh husked tomatillos
1/2 cup chopped onion
2 garlic cloves, minced
1 serrano chile, chopped
1/2 cup packed fresh cilantro leaves
1/2 medium avocado, peeled and seeded
1/4 teaspoon salt
1/4 teaspoon sugar
1/4 tablespoon fresh lime juice

Combine the tomatillos, onion and garlic with enough water to cover in a large saucepan over medium heat. Simmer for 5 minutes. Drain the tomatillos, reserving the cooking liquid. Combine the tomatillo mixture, serrano chiles, cilantro, avocado, salt, sugar and lime juice in a blender or food processor. Process until smooth, thinning with reserved cooking liquid as needed. Chill the salsa in the refrigerator until ready to serve. *Yield: 4 (1/4-cup) servings*

The Enchiladas

1 teaspoon olive oil
6 cups chopped fresh mushrooms
1/2 cup diced onion
2 garlic cloves, minced
1 small poblano chile, roasted, peeled, seeded and diced
2 tablespoons chopped fresh cilantro leaves
Salt and freshly ground black pepper to taste
3/4 cup shredded Chihuahua cheese or reduced-fat Cheddar cheese
8 corn tortillas, softened
1 cup Avocado/Tomatillo Salsa
1/4 cup crumbled queso fresco or feta cheese

The Garnish

Thinly sliced onion
Thinly sliced radish
Shredded lettuce

Heat the olive oil in a nonstick skillet over medium-high heat. Add the mushrooms and sauté for 5 minutes. Add the onion and garlic; mix well. Cook until the mushrooms are fairly dry. Add the poblano chile, cilantro, salt and pepper; mix well. Remove from the heat and set aside to cool. Stir in the cheese and place equal amounts of the mixture in the middle of each tortilla. Roll the tortillas, enclosing the mushroom mixture, and place, seam side down, in a covered baking dish. Bake, covered, at 375 degrees for 10 minutes. Remove from the oven and place 2 enchiladas on each of 4 plates. Top each serving with salsa and 1 tablespoon crumbled cheese. Garnish with sliced onion, radish and lettuce, if desired. *Yield: 4 servings*

Nutrients Per Serving: Cal 339; Prot 16 g; Carbo 49 g; Fat 15 g; 32% Cal from Fat; Sod 541 mg

why chiles are hot

Hot chile peppers are a rich source of folic acid, vitamins C, A, E and potassium. The fat soluble phytochemical, capsaicin, is concentrated in the ribs where the seeds are attached. Capsaicin helps protect your DNA and inhibits mutations by metabolizing hydrocarbons. It also opens congested bronchial tubes in the lungs. The capsaicin stimulates release of digestive juices and tears and may even rev up the metabolism. So eat your chile pepperss and breathe easy about your health.

NUTRITION

Buckwheat Soba Noodle Salad

Asians love noodles of all types, but few are as distinctive or nutritious as the buckwheat soba noodle — a traditional favorite in Japan for hundreds of years. Serve them at room temperature or slightly chilled with crispy, colorful vegetables moistened with a bit of the slightly sweet, slightly spicy marinade. Combined with tofu, they are a delicious summer repast with complete protein value. You may substitute boneless skinless chicken breast for the tofu, treating it in the same manner. However, separate out some of the marinade to douse the noodles before marinating the chicken. Do not use the marinade with noodles after the chicken has been removed.

1 (12-ounce) package extra firm tofu
1/3 cup hoisin sauce
1 teaspoon roasted sesame oil
1/3 cup mirin (Japanese rice wine)
3 tablespoons light soy sauce
1 1/2 tablespoons brown sugar
1/4 cup tomato sauce
3 garlic cloves, minced
1 1/2 tablespoons minced fresh gingerroot
1 teaspoon Asian chile paste
1 large red bell pepper, roasted, peeled, seeded and sliced
1 (12-ounce) package buckwheat soba noodles, cooked according to package directions
1 bunch green onions, thinly sliced
1 cup grated carrot
1 cup julienned water chestnuts
1/4 cup chopped fresh cilantro leaves
2 tablespoons toasted sesame seeds

Drain the tofu and dry on paper towels. Cut into 3/8-inch slabs. Combine the hoisin sauce, sesame oil, mirin, soy sauce, brown sugar, tomato sauce, garlic, gingerroot and chile paste in a bowl; mix well. Add the tofu and marinate in the refrigerator for 4 to 12 hours. Remove the tofu from the marinade, reserving the marinade. Grill the tofu over medium-hot coals or sear in a skillet over medium heat. Combine the bell pepper, soba noodles, green onions, carrot, water chestnuts, cilantro and sesame seeds in a bowl. Pour half of the reserved marinade over the vegetables and toss to coat. Arrange 1/4 of the noodle mixture on each of 4 plates. Top each with a slab of grilled tofu. *Yield: 4 servings*

Nutrients Per Serving: Cal 569; Prot 23 g; Carbo 106 g; Fat 7 g; 10% Cal from Fat; Sod 1589 mg

Mediterranean Vegetable Sandwich with Basil/Feta Pesto

This is our idea of a truly great summertime sandwich — fresh vegetables from our garden straight off the grill, singed with smoke, and stacked on a whole wheat bun. Pile on the tomatoes and lettuce and finish everything off with a delicious dollop of our fresh, bright green basil pesto (another gift from the garden). Sink your teeth into the season. If he could, Dagwood would.

The Pesto

- **1** **cup packed fresh basil leaves**
- **1** **tablespoon minced garlic**
- **3** **tablespoons crumbled feta cheese**
- **1/8** **teaspoon salt**
- **1/8** **teaspoon freshly ground black pepper**
- **1 1/2** **teaspoons white wine vinegar**
- **2** **tablespoons extra virgin olive oil**
- **8** **kalamata olives, pitted and chopped**

The Sandwich

- **2** **portobello mushroom caps, stemmed and sliced into 1/2-inch-thick vertical slices**
- **1** **red bell pepper, quartered and seeded**
- **1** **red onion, sliced**
- **1** **small eggplant, sliced into 8 1/2-inch-thick horizontal slices**
- **1** **large zucchini, sliced into 1/4-inch vertical slices**
- **Salt and freshly ground black pepper to taste**
- **2** **medium tomatoes, sliced**
- **1** **cup shredded lettuce**
- **4** **whole wheat hoagie buns, split**

Combine the basil, garlic, cheese, salt, pepper, vinegar and olive oil in a blender or food processor; purée. Add the olives and pulse until combined. Set aside. Spray the mushrooms, bell pepper, onion, eggplant and zucchini with nonstick cooking spray; season with salt and pepper. Grill the vegetables over medium-hot coals until soft and slightly charred. Remove from the grill and layer the vegetables on 1 half of each hoagie bun. Top each with sliced tomatoes, lettuce and pesto. *Yield: 4 servings*

Nutrients Per Serving: Cal 550; Prot 22 g; Carbo 84 g; Fat 14 g; 23% Cal from Fat; Sod 784 mg

Vegetable Matter * Even if you're not a vegetarian and have no intention of ever becoming one, you should remember mom's advice and eat your vegetables. All of the world's healthiest (and most interesting) cuisines rely heavily upon vegetables, legumes and grains for their foundations, with animal protein playing a relatively minor role. Believe it or not, one of the easiest and tastiest ways to incorporate this philosophy into your own daily diet is Mexican food. Enchiladas, quesadillas, sopes and other masa-based dishes lend themselves readily to this treatment; coupled with beans, they provide both substance and excellent protein value, and topped with crisp, colorful salads and bright, spicy salsas they make for some of the best eating you can imagine. We promise, no one will miss the meat!

Gorditas

Mexico's version of the pita pocket, these "little pigs" are as messy to eat as the name implies — but muy rica (very tasty)! Stuff them with shreds of cooked meat or poultry in addition to the beans for a non-vegetarian version. Spoon on plenty of salsa and dig in! You will want to split these masa cakes as soon as they come out of the skillet and are still hot. You may then keep them covered with a warm cloth until ready to fill.

3 cups masa harina de maiz
2 1/2 cups water
1/2 teaspoon salt
1 1/2 cups cooked, mashed, pinto beans, seasoned with a good pinch of cumin, warmed
1 cup Pico de Gallo (Page 19)
1 cup shredded lettuce
3/4 cup shredded reduced-fat Cheddar cheese
1/2 cup Guacamole (Page 144)
1/3 cup Salsa Picante (Page 19)

Combine the masa, water and salt in a bowl; mix well. Divide the dough into 6 balls. Pat each ball into a 4-inch disk. Cook 1 or 2 at a time in a heavy dry nonstick skillet over medium-high heat for 2-3 minutes; turn and cook the other side for an additional 2 minutes. Remove the gorditas from the skillet. Use a sharp knife to split each gordita horizontally about halfway around. Hollow out the insides. Fill each gordita with some of the bean mixture, Pico de Gallo, shredded lettuce, shredded Cheddar cheese, Guacamole and Picante Salsa. *Yield: 6 (1-Gordita) servings*

Nutrients Per Serving: Cal 349; Prot 13 g; Carbo 62 g; Fat 7 g; 18% Cal from Fat; Sod 632 mg

Papacitas

These tasty potato and masa pockets can be filled with just about anything (try sautéed mushrooms or bits of chopped cooked meat or poultry) and served just about anytime. They make a wonderful alternative breakfast or brunch item and shine as a light lunch or dinner entrée. Serve with any of the salsas in this book — we especially like the Roasted Red Pepper or Avocado/Tomatillo salsas — and, perhaps, some Pico de Gallo and fat-free sour cream. Serve one Papacita as an appetizer, or two as an entrée.

1 cup each: minced onion and fresh corn kernels
1 small poblano chile, roasted, peeled, seeded and minced
1 1/2 cups masa harina de maiz
1 cup water
1 teaspoon salt
1/2 teaspoon baking powder
3 cups cooked and mashed potatoes
3 tablespoons canola oil

Using nonstick cooking spray, gently sauté the onion and corn until softened in a nonstick pan. Add the poblano chile. Combine the masa harina, water, salt and baking powder in a bowl; mix well. Add the mashed potatoes and stir to mix well. Divide the mixture into 12 balls. Place a 6-inch square of plastic cut from a baggie on a work surface and top with 1 of the dough balls; press it into a 4-inch circle. Scoop 2 to 3 tablespoons of the corn mixture onto the bottom half of the dough circle. Use the plastic as a guide and fold the top half of the dough circle over the filling completely enclosing it. Crimp the edges to seal. Repeat the process until all dough balls have been filled. Heat the canola oil in a nonstick skillet over medium heat. Sauté the filled Papacitas until crisp and golden on both sides. Serve warm with the salsa of your choice. *Yield: 12 (1-Papacita) servings*

Nutrients Per Serving: Cal 153; Prot 3 g; Carbo 25 g; Fat 5 g; 28% Cal from Fat; Sod 354 mg

Pupusas

Corn masa plays an integral part in the daily cooking of the peoples of Mexico, Central and South America, and each region has its own particular method of using it. Here, it is bound up with mashed potatoes, tomatoes, cheese, and seasonings to make a dish that is one of the national treasures of San Salvador, the pupusa. This is a versatile dish that lends itself to improvisation. Feel free to substitute different vegetables or another bean. The brands of masa harina de maiz that we use most often are Maseka (very popular in Mexico) and Quaker, widely distributed in the United States.

1 cup masa harina de maiz
3/4 cup water
1 medium potato, peeled, boiled, drained and mashed
1/4 cup finely chopped tomato
1/2 teaspoon salt
1/2 teaspoon chili powder
2 tablespoons shredded reduced-fat Cheddar cheese
1 tablespoon olive oil
1 small onion, sliced
1 cup cooked pinto beans, drained
1 cup Salsa Picante (Page 19)
1 Anaheim or poblano chile, roasted, peeled, seeded, cut into 8 strips
2 cups Cabbage Slaw

The Garnish

2 tablespoons chopped fresh cilantro leaves
4 radishes, sliced
1/2 cup fat-free sour cream
4 lime wedges

Combine the masa harina and water in a bowl; mix and knead until of uniform consistency. Add the potato, tomato, salt, chili powder and Cheddar cheese; mix well. Form the mixture into four 1/2-inch-thick patties. Heat the olive oil in a skillet over medium heat. Sauté the patties until crisp on both sides; remove and set aside. Sear the onions sprayed with nonstick cooking spray, over medium heat. Arrange 1 Pupusa on each of 4 plates. Top each with 1/4 cup pinto beans, 1/4 cup salsa, 2 strips poblano chile and 1/4 of the seared onion. Arrange 1/2 cup Cabbage Slaw over the top and garnish with cilantro, radish slices, sour cream and a lime wedge. *Yield: 4 servings*

The Cabbage Slaw

2 tablespoons red wine vinegar
1 tablespoon fresh lime juice
1 teaspoon each: sugar and salt
1 1/2 cups shredded cabbage
1/4 cup julienned carrot
1/4 cup thinly sliced red onion
1 serrano chile, seeded and julienned

Heat the vinegar, lime juice, sugar and salt in a small saucepan set over medium-low heat. Cook until the sugar dissolves. Combine the cabbage, carrot, onion and serrano chile in a bowl. Pour the vinegar over the cabbage mixture; toss to combine. Chill in the refrigerator, tossing occasionally. *Yield: 4 (1/2-cup) servings*

Nutrients Per Serving: Cal 364; Prot 11 g; Carbo 60 g; Fat 5 g; 13% Cal from Fat; Sod 1042 mg

Grilled Portobello and Provolone Burgers

These giant fungi are actually overgrown crimini mushrooms. They have become a favorite of vegetarians and carnivores alike in recent years, prized both for their firm texture and versatility in cooking. They are especially good grilled, developing a delightfully smoky flavor and the pleasantly chewy, but juicy, bite burger lovers look for. Omit the provolone and substitute a seasoned reduced-fat mayonnaise for the barbecue sauce and you have the "P.L.T." sandwich — also a Lake Austin Spa Resort favorite.

1 medium onion, sliced
4 large portobello mushrooms, stems removed
Salt and freshly ground black pepper to taste
4 (1-ounce) slices reduced-fat provolone cheese
4 onion Kaiser rolls, split
1/2 cup hickory-flavored barbecue sauce, warmed
8 tomato slices
1 cup shredded lettuce

Sauté the onion until golden brown, using nonstick spray in a nonstick skillet. Remove from the heat; set aside. Spray the mushroom caps lightly with nonstick cooking spray. Season with salt and pepper and grill over hot coals for 5 to 7 minutes, turning occasionally. Just before removing the mushroom caps from the grill, turn them so that the gills are facing up. Top each with a slice of cheese to melt slightly. Remove the mushrooms from the grill. Toast the rolls and dab each with 2 tablespoons barbecue sauce. Top each roll bottom with a mushroom cap, some caramelized onions, 2 tomato slices and 1/4 cup lettuce. *Yield: 4 servings*

Nutrients Per Serving: Cal 338; Prot 25 g; Carbo 55 g; Fat 7 g; 16% Cal from Fat; Sod 850 mg

invite a martin to your garden

The purple martin's cheerful singing, vibrant blue black color, and acrobatic flying are reasons enough to provide them housing, but they also eat an amazing number of flying insects, including flies and mosquitoes. Purple martins are one of the few birds that appreciate shelter provided by humans. The birds prefer light-colored wood or aluminum houses (and, of course, gourds) with small openings in them. The most important factor in locating a martin house is to avoid placing it too near large trees. Martins prefer a minimum of 20 tree-free feet around their houses. To prevent heat buildup inside the house, position the opening to take advantage of the prevailing winds. Martins can be fussy about the cleanliness of their homes, so take the houses down, wash and rinse them well and apply a light dusting of sulfur powder to control mites. Martins are very social birds and they spend a lot of time together on the houses, chattering to each other.

Chicken-Fried Portobello Mushroom Steak with Roasted Garlic Mashers and Cream Gravy

There are some folks in the Southwest who believe you could chicken-fry your wristwatch, and if you had some cream gravy to go with it, you'd have something worth eating. And, while admittedly, there is something universally appealing about the crackling crisp crust of a good chicken fry, hold onto your timepiece. Try a mushroom instead. Our version, made with that meatiest of mushrooms, the portobello, gets its crunch from toasted bread crumbs, and "fries" in the oven. Make your own crumbs by thoroughly drying out some slices of whole wheat bread in a 275-degree oven for a couple of hours, then grinding them in a food processor.

2 large portobello mushrooms, stemmed and sliced into 1/2-inch-thick vertical slices
1/2 cup buttermilk
1 egg white
1 cup whole wheat bread crumbs
1/4 cup flour
1 teaspoon paprika
1/4 teaspoon black pepper
1/8 teaspoon cayenne pepper
1/2 teaspoon each: garlic powder and onion powder
1/4 teaspoon each: dried thyme and dried leaf oregano

Whisk the buttermilk and egg white in a large bowl. Combine the bread crumbs, flour and spices in a separate bowl. Dip each mushroom piece first into the buttermilk mixture, then into the seasoned bread crumbs. Spray each piece lightly with nonstick cooking spray and arrange in a single layer on a nonstick baking sheet. Bake at 400 degrees for 12 to 15 minutes or until crisp. Serve hot with mashed potatoes and cream gravy. *Yield: 4 servings*

The Roasted Garlic Mashers

2 roasted garlic bulbs (see Roasted Garlic Vinaigrette, Page 32)
4 medium Yukon Gold or Idaho potatoes
1/2 cup skim milk
2 tablespoons light butter
Salt and freshly ground black pepper to taste

Peel and slice the potatoes. Place them in a saucepan with enough cold water to cover. Bring to a boil over high heat; cook until tender. Drain and place the potatoes in a large bowl, then immediately combine them with the garlic pulp, milk, butter, salt and pepper. Mash with a hand masher until smooth. *Yield: 4 (1/2-cup) servings*

The Cream Gravy

1/2 cup 1% milk
1/4 cup evaporated skim milk
1/2 chicken bouillon cube, or 1/4 teaspoon salt
2 tablespoons flour dissolved in 1/4 cup 1% milk
1/8 teaspoon black pepper

Combine the 1% milk and evaporated skim milk in a saucepan over medium heat. Add the bouillon cube; bring to a simmer. Whisk in the flour and milk mixture; season with the pepper. Cook, stirring constantly, for 2 minutes. Thin the gravy with additional 1% milk, if necessary. *Yield: 4 (1/4-cup) servings*

Nutrients Per Serving: Cal 362; Prot 18 g; Carbo 67 g; Fat 5 g; 11% Cal from Fat; Sod 523 mg

Mediterranean Garden Pizza with Roasted Vegetables

Somehow, somewhere, either on its ocean-crossing voyage or in the passing of generations, the real essence of pizza has been lost. Pizza was always supposed to be about the bread and the tomatoes, not about the cheese and meat! But in America today, all too often tasteless, sodden cardboard crusts slathered with a too-sweet canned sauce buckle under the flaccid weight of double mozzarella and double meat. The good news? You can make your own "scratch" pizza with a delightfully light and crispy crust in about the amount of time to takes to have one delivered.

The Crust

Follow the recipe for the Pizza Verde crust on the next page (78) but add, as you knead:

2 teaspoons extra virgin olive oil
1 garlic clove, minced
1 teaspoon each: freshly ground black pepper and dried leaf oregano

The Toppings

1 small onion, peeled, cut into 3/4-inch-thick slices
1 red bell pepper
2 tablespoons roasted garlic purée from 1 garlic bulb
1 small zucchini, split lengthwise
1/2 small eggplant, cut into 4 3/4-inch-thick slices
2 tablespoons cornmeal
4 ripe tomatoes, sliced
1 cup (4 ounces) shredded part-skim mozzarella or provolone cheese
6 imported pitted black olives, sliced
2 tablespoons golden raisins
1 teaspoon crushed fennel seeds
1 teaspoon dried leaf oregano
1/2 teaspoon crushed red pepper flakes

Preheat the oven to 400 degrees. To make the pizza topping, spray a large baking sheet with-nonstick cooking spray. Spray all of the vegetables with nonstick cooking spray. Arrange the onion slices and bell pepper in a single layer on the baking sheet. Slice and discard the top from the garlic bulb. Spray the exposed cloves with nonstick cooking spray. Wrap the bulb in foil and add it to the baking sheet. Roast these vegetables for 20 minutes. Add the zucchini and eggplant to the baking sheet and roast for an additional 10 minutes. Remove the vegetables from the oven. Remove the garlic from the foil; allow to cool, then squeeze 2 tablespoons of garlic purée onto a small saucer; set aside. Reserve the remaining garlic purée. Peel, seed and cut the pepper into 1/2-inch cubes. Cut the zucchini and eggplant into 1/2-inch cubes. Separate the onion into rings. Increase the oven temperature to 500 degrees. Spray an 11 x 17-inch baking sheet with nonstick cooking spray, then evenly sprinkle the cornmeal over the surface; set aside. Punch the dough down, then remove it to a floured surface and roll out with a rolling pin into a large flat piece that just fits the prepared baking pan. Partially drape the dough back over the rolling pin, then gingerly arrange it on the prepared baking sheet. Cover the dough and set aside to rise in a warm place for 10 minutes. Prick all but 1 inch of the outer rim of the crust with a fork. Bake for 3 minutes. Remove the crust from the oven and spread the surface with the reserved garlic purée. Top with overlapping tomato slices, the mozzarella cheese, cubed vegetables, onion rings, olives and raisins. Sprinkle the fennel seeds, 1 teaspoon oregano and red pepper flakes over the top. Bake at 500 degrees for 8 to 10 minutes or until the cheese is melted. Remove the pizza from the oven and cut in half lengthwise, then into thin strips. *Yield: 4 servings*

Nutrients Per Serving: Cal 455; Prot 20 g; Carbo 74 g; Fat 10 g; 19% Cal from Fat; Sod 804 mg

Pizza Verde

Kermit's lament notwithstanding, it is easy being green — at least when it comes to pizza. In fact, it's an almost mandatory response to the exuberance of summer basil in our gardens. If your garden, too, threatens to be overrun with this seasonal surfeit, fight back with pesto and pizza!

1 tablespoon dry yeast (1 envelope)
1 teaspoon sugar
1 teaspoon salt
1 cup water
3 cups flour
3 tablespoons cornmeal
1 pound fresh spinach, cleaned and stemmed
1 1/2 cups packed fresh basil leaves
6 green onions, cleaned and sliced
4 garlic cloves, minced
1/8 teaspoon black pepper
1/8 teaspoon salt
2 tablespoons extra virgin olive oil
4 medium tomatoes, peeled, seeded and chopped
8 kalamata olives, pitted and chopped
1/2 cup crumbled feta cheese

Combine the yeast, sugar, salt and water in a medium bowl; set aside for 10 minutes until very foamy. Add the flour and mix until a soft dough forms. Remove the dough to a floured surface and knead for 5 minutes. Or, you can place the dough in a food processor and pulse a few seconds at a time for 1 minute. Gather the dough into a ball; spray lightly with nonstick cooking spray and place in a large bowl. Cover with plastic wrap and set aside to rise until doubled in bulk. Spray an 11 x 17-inch baking sheet with nonstick cooking spray and sprinkle with cornmeal. Punch the dough down, remove it to a floured surface and roll it to roughly match the size of the baking sheet. Arrange the dough on the baking sheet and prick all over with a fork. Set aside and let rise for 5 minutes. Bake at 450 degrees for 5 to 7 minutes. Steam the spinach in a colander set over boiling water for 30 seconds or until wilted. Cool, then squeeze out all the moisture. Combine the spinach, basil, green onions, garlic, pepper, salt and olive oil in a food processor; purée. Spread the spinach mixture evenly over the surface of the crust and top with the tomatoes, olives and feta cheese. Return to the oven and bake for 5 minutes longer. *Yield: 4 servings*

Nutrients Per Serving: Cal 724; Prot 31 g; Carbo 114 g; Fat 16 g; 20% Cal from Fat; Sod 1147 mg

score some major relaxation

To relax and soothe muscles, pour a capful of therapeutic sports massage oil into a warm bath. These oils are especially formulated to promote circulation, relieve respiratory congestion and help soothe sore, aching muscles. For an extra treat, massage the oil onto your skin after the bath. Finally, for a restful night's sleep, put a few drops of inhalation oil (eucalyptus) on a tissue and place inside your pillowcase to relieve respiratory congestion.

HOME SPA

Chimayo Tortilla Stack with New Mexican Red Chile Sauce

Chimayo is a small town just north of Santa Fe, New Mexico. It's famous for its high-quality, hand-woven Indian rugs and excellent New Mexican-style food, much of it based on red chiles, squash and beans. If you can find blue corn tortillas (available in some health food stores), they would make the most authentic tortilla stack.

1 cup diced butternut squash, steamed
1 cup cooked red beans, drained, or canned beans
1/2 cup each: frozen lima beans, cooked and frozen corn kernels, thawed
2 tablespoons diced pimentos
1/2 cup shredded reduced-fat Cheddar cheese
2 ounces reduced-fat cream cheese, softened
2 ounces reduced-fat chèvre (soft goat cheese)
12 corn tortillas

Combine the squash, red beans, lima beans, corn and pimentos in a bowl. Mix the Cheddar cheese, cream cheese and chèvre in a separate bowl. Spread some of the cheese mixture on each tortilla. Top 6 of the cheese-covered tortillas with some of the vegetable mixture. Cover with the remaining 6 tortillas, cheese side down. Arrange tortillas on a baking sheet and cover with foil. Bake at 350 degrees just until the cheese melts. You may wrap each tortilla in plastic wrap and microwave on high for 10 to 15 seconds or just until the cheese melts. Serve with Red Chile Sauce and a squiggle of Crème. *Yield: 6 servings*

The Red Chile Sauce

6 dried New Mexico red chiles
1 small onion, thickly sliced
4 Roma tomatoes
2 garlic cloves, minced
2 teaspoons ground cumin
1 teaspoon dried leaf oregano
1/4 cup tomato juice
2 tablespoons flour or masa harina de maiz
2 cups vegetable stock
1/2 ounce semisweet chocolate, chopped
3/4 teaspoon ground cinnamon
1/2 teaspoon salt

Lightly toast the chiles in a dry skillet over medium heat for a few minutes, turning often. Remove and discard the stem. Place the chiles in a bowl and cover with hot water; set aside for 30 minutes. Drain and reserve. Spray the onion, tomato and garlic lightly with cooking spray and arrange on a baking sheet. Roast at 375 degrees for 20 minutes. Toast the cumin and oregano in a dry skillet for 30 seconds. Combine the reserved chiles, onion, tomato, cumin and oregano in a blender or food processor; purée. Combine the purée, tomato juice, flour, stock, chocolate, cinnamon and salt in a saucepan over medium-high heat. Cook until thickened and smooth, stirring constantly. Strain and keep warm. *Yield: 6 servings*

The Crème

1/2 cup fat-free sour cream
3 tablespoons 2% milk

Mix the sour cream and milk in a bowl. Remove to a squeeze bottle and refrigerate until ready to use.

Nutrients Per Serving: Cal 323; Prot 14 g; Carbo 53 g; Fat 8 g; 21% Cal from Fat; Sod 510 mg

Spicy Udon Noodles

This recipe, an instant hit with both our guests and staff, has just enough heat to get your attention. Like so many of our Asian favorites, it's a multicolored and many-textured mosaic of quickly cooked fresh vegetables doused in a pungent and highly aromatic sauce before being tossed with fresh herbs, soft chewy noodles, and crunchy toasted peanuts.

Zest and juice of 1 orange
2 tablespoons hoisin sauce
1 tablespoon low-sodium soy sauce
1 tablesoon Asian chile paste
1 1/2 tablespoons sugar
1 1/2 tablespoons rice wine vinegar
1 tablespoon roasted sesame oil
1 tablespoon canola oil
1 1/2 tablespoons minced garlic
1 1/2 tablespoons minced fresh gingerroot
6 cups mixed cut raw stir-fry vegetables (broccoli, bok choy, zucchini, onion, green onion, red bell pepper, carrots)
3 cups cooked udon noodles
1/4 cup chopped fresh basil leaves
1/4 cup chopped fresh mint leaves
1/4 cup chopped fresh cilantro leaves
2 tablespoons chopped dry-roasted peanuts

Combine the orange zest and juice, hoisin sauce, soy sauce, chile paste, sugar and vinegar in a bowl; set aside. Combine the sesame oil and canola oil in a small bowl. Heat 2 teaspoons of the oil mixture in a skillet over high heat. Add the garlic and ginger and stir-fry until they begin to color. Add the mixed vegetables and stir-fry for 1 to 2 minutes. Add the noodles and reserved sauce. Cook for 1 minute. Add the basil, mint and cilantro; toss to mix. Serve hot; garnish with peanuts. *Yield: 4 servings*

Nutrients Per Serving: Cal 302; Prot 7 g; Carbo 46 g; Fat 10 g; 30% Cal from Fat; Sod 390 mg

Low-Fat Fettuccini Alfredo

If you've ever summoned up the courage to inspect the informational window on the back of a half-pint of heavy cream, you know that just a couple of tablespoons of this stuff registers a serious double-digit fat gram level. Classic Alfredo sauce takes this idea and runs with it by reducing the cream in a skillet, thereby further concentrating it into even more fat grams per serving before adding the pasta. Our version, while admittedly lacking in the death-defying thrill of the original, is nonetheless delightfully creamy at a fraction of the fat.

1/2 **cup evaporated skim milk**
2 **tablespoons flour**
1 **cup 2% milk**
1/4 **cup fat-free cream cheese**
1/4 **cup grated Parmesan cheese**
1/8 **teaspoon salt**
1/8 **teaspoon cayenne pepper**
6 **cups cooked fettuccini noodles**
6 **cups steamed mixed vegetables**
2 **tablespoons chopped fresh parsley**

Combine 1 tablespoon of the evaporated skim milk with the flour in a small bowl; set aside. Bring the remaining skim milk and 2% milk to a simmer in a saucepan over medium heat. Whisk in the flour mixture. Cook for 2 minutes until thickened, stirring constantly. Add the cream cheese, Parmesan cheese, salt and cayenne pepper. Cook, stirring constantly, until the cheese melts. Combine the warm fettuccini noodles and mixed vegetables in a bowl. Pour the sauce over the mixture and toss to evenly coat the noodles. Top with the chopped parsley. *Yield: 6 servings*

Nutrients Per Serving: Cal 340; Prot 18 g; Carbo 61 g; Fat 3 g; 8% Cal from Fat; Sod 272 mg

chefstip

Bringing Asia Home * In the last 25 years probably no cuisine has had more impact on American palates than the new wave of Asian recipes. These new dishes are tremendously fresh, and bursting with bright flavors and as this food is assimilated into our eating consciousness, more and more of the products used to create it are showing up in grocery stores. Most of them, if refrigerated, have excellent if not infinite shelf lives. Our short list: light soy sauce (reduced salt), teriyaki/sweet and sour glazes, hoisin sauce, Asian chile paste, roasted sesame oil, rice wine vinegar, sweet rice wine (Mirin), pink pickled ginger, wasabi, light (reduced-fat) coconut milk, fish sauce (Nam Pla), rice noodles, soba noodles, and (although it's technically a fresh ingredient) gingerroot. Not only will this pantry bring a number of Asian dishes within your grasp, you will probably also find yourself reaching for these ingredients to add interest and flavor to your Western recipes.

Penne Positano

Positano is a small picturesque village chiseled out of the high rugged cliffs along Italy's Amalfi coast where you might — should you be so fortunate as to reside there — eat like this every day. The slow roasting of the tomatoes reduces them to a remarkable intensity of flavor and smoky sweetness, which, when coupled with the meaty portobello mushrooms, wine, herbs, and briny richness of the olives and capers produce a dish of unusual depth and character. Serve with a simple green salad, some good bread, and a glass of decent wine, and you have the makings of a memorable meal.

8 Roma tomatoes, quartered
3 tablespoons good quality olive oil
1/8 teaspoon salt
1/8 teaspoon black pepper
1/8 teaspoon sugar
1 large onion, sliced
3 medium portobello mushrooms, stemmed and sliced into 1/2 x 1-inch pieces
12 garlic cloves, minced
2 tablespoons white wine
2 tablespoons capers, drained and rinsed
12 pitted kalamata olives, cut into halves
12 pitted green olives, cut into halves
1 teaspoon chopped fresh oregano leaves, or 1/2 teaspoon dried oregano
1/2 teaspoon chopped fresh rosemary leaves, or 1/4 teaspoon dried rosemary
1 teaspoon chopped fresh parsley
1/8 teaspoon red pepper flakes
Salt and freshly ground black pepper to taste
8 cups cooked penne pasta
1/2 cup grated Parmesan cheese

Arrange the tomatoes in a single layer on a baking sheet. Drizzle a little of the olive oil over the tomatoes, then sprinkle them with the salt, pepper and the sugar. Slow-roast the tomatoes at 200 degrees for 4 hours. Heat the remaining olive oil in a heavy skillet over medium-low heat. Add the onion and cook slowly, stirring, until it browns and caramelizes. Add the mushrooms and garlic. Cook, stirring occasionally, until the mixture is fairly dry. Add the roasted tomatoes, wine, capers, olives, oregano, rosemary, parsley, red pepper flakes, salt and pepper to taste and penne and mix well. Cook until heated through. Serve topped with Parmesan cheese. *Yield: 6 servings*

Nutrients Per Serving: Cal 479; Prot 15 g; Carbo 71 g; Fat 13 g; 24% Cal from Fat; Sod 631 mg

Macaroni and Cheese

Macaroni and cheese is one of the original comfort foods and a perennial kids' favorite. Our recipe, which uses some of the low-fat dairy products now readily available, is still as nurturing and robust as the old-fashioned one, but not as heavy. Try variations using cubes of zucchini, mushrooms, tomatoes, and sautéed eggplant.

1 1/2 cups diced onions
3/4 cup diced celery
2 garlic cloves, minced
1 teaspoon garlic powder
1/2 teaspoon onion powder
1/2 teaspoon dried thyme
1/2 teaspoon dry mustard
1/4 teaspoon cayenne pepper
1/2 cup vegetable stock
6 egg whites
12 ounces 1% cottage cheese
1 1/2 cups evaporated skim milk
2 cups (8 ounces) shredded reduced-fat Cheddar cheese
10 cups cooked elbow macaroni
1 1/2 cups fresh white bread crumbs
1 teaspoon paprika

Heat a skillet sprayed with nonstick cooking spray over medium heat. Add the onions and celery. Cook, covered, until the vegetables are soft, stirring occasionally. Add the garlic, garlic powder, onion powder, thyme, mustard and cayenne pepper; cook, stirring, for 30 seconds. Add the stock. Increase the temperature and cook until reduced by half. Beat the egg whites in a mixing bowl with an electric mixer until frothy. Add the cottage cheese, skim milk, half the Cheddar cheese and the vegetable stock; mix well. Fold in the macaroni. Spray an 11 x 17-inch baking dish lightly with nonstick cooking spray. Pour the macaroni mixture into the dish. Top with remaining cheese and the bread crumbs. Sprinkle the paprika over the top. Spray the top of the mixture lightly with nonstick cooking spray. Bake at 375 degrees for 35 to 40 minutes. *Yield: 12 servings*

Nutrients Per Serving: Cal 297; Prot 19 g; Carbo 43 g; Fat 5 g; 17% Cal from Fat; Sod 229 mg

become a high tech manager

Technology is great thing. Or is it? Technology offers us the ability to stay instantly connected to those we care about and to receive communication from anywhere in the world in the blink of an eye. However, technology can also bind us in its tentacles, never allowing us to escape. How many means of communication do you have today? Do you ever have a time when you are totally unreachable? Find ways to make technology a blessing and not a burden. Use messaging to ensure that special time set aside for loved ones is not interrupted. And although e-mail may be faster, don't forget the value of personal conversation in sharing feelings and emotions. Learn to manage the technology in your life so that it is an enhancement, not an intrusion.

Cheese Ravioli with Tomato Concassé

At its heart, the best Italian cooking lies not in complicated recipes or revolutionary techniques, but in the harmonious marriage of first-rate ingredients. Your very best tomatoes and fresh basil from the garden soon reveal the extraordinary nature of ordinary things. Ricotta Salata, used here to finish the dish, is a firm, gratable cheese available in better grocery stores. It provides a refreshing alternative to Parmesan or Romano cheese. Use feta cheese if Ricotta Salata is unavailable.

4 tomatoes
2 teaspoons olive oil
1/4 cup minced shallots
2 garlic cloves, minced
1/2 cup white wine
3/4 cup light vegetable stock
2 tablespoons shredded fresh basil leaves
Salt and freshly ground black pepper to taste
1/2 cup cooked cannellini beans, drained
1 (1-pound) package reduced-fat cheese ravioli
1/2 cup grated Ricotta Salata

Peel the tomatoes by cutting an X in the bottom of each and blanch in boiling water in a saucepan for 30 seconds. Remove and discard the skins. Cut the tomatoes into halves horizontally and squeeze out the seeds; cut the flesh into small dice. Heat the olive oil in a heavy skillet over medium heat. Add the shallots and sauté until the shallots begin to color. Add the garlic, tomatoes, wine and stock; mix well. Bring the mixture to a simmer and cook for 10 minutes. Add the basil, salt, pepper and beans. Cook the ravioli according to package directions. Divide the tomato concassé among 4 shallow, wide-rimmed soup bowls. Add 1/4 of the ravioli to each serving. Top with the grated Ricotta Salata cheese. Add additional shredded basil and a few drops of olive oil, if desired. *Yield: 4 servings*

Nutrients Per Serving: Cal 441; Prot 20 g; Carbo 59 g; Fat 11 g; 22% Cal from Fat; Sod 839 mg

chefstip

Bean There, Done That * One of the healthiest foods you can put in your mouth is a bean. Legumes, as they are more properly called, are low- to no-fat and an excellent source of nutrition and fiber. Add to these virtues their variety, ease of preparation, and modest price and you have one of the world's most enduring, widespread foods. And, although we do almost all of our bean work from scratch at the resort, if you want to use a canned bean in any of these recipes, feel free to do so (just rinse to freshen). We should note that from a nutritional standpoint, as good as they are for you, beans do not have available all eight essential amino acids necessary to form a complete protein. The addition of any grain to a recipe containing beans, however, quickly rectifies this shortcoming, making the protein availability complete. This happy fact works out particularly well for the inveterate snacker – the chipper and dipper – with the dip usually providing the bean and the chip providing the grain.

Lean Star Lentil Chili

As any Texan will tell you, we have the fastest horses and the prettiest women and we make the best barbecue and chili in the country. In fact, the annual world championship chili cook-off is held in Terlingua, Texas — a West Texas hamlet where the population jumps from about 16 people to 16,000 for the festivities. Mostly, the chili is made with good Texas beef, but you will also find chili made from armadillo and even rattlesnake. Here is a meatless version that ranks right up there with the best of them. We guarantee that even card-carrying carnivores will be back for seconds. So, at your next roundup, serve up a big steamin' bowl of this genuine "Texas Red," along with a salad, corn tostados, and a cold beverage.

2 teaspoons olive oil
1/2 cup minced onion
2 garlic cloves, minced
3 tablespoons chili powder
1 1/2 tablespoons ground cumin
1/2 teaspoon dried leaf oregano
1/4 teaspoon garlic powder
1/8 teaspoon cayenne pepper, or to taste
4 to 5 cups water
1 cup uncooked brown lentils, rinsed
1/2 cup tomato purée
1/2 teaspoon salt
1/4 teaspoon sugar

Heat the olive oil in a soup pot over medium heat. Add the onion and sauté for 2 minutes. Add the garlic and cook for 30 seconds. Stir in the chili powder, cumin, oregano, garlic powder and cayenne pepper; cook for 30 seconds. Add the water, lentils and tomato purée. Bring to a boil, then immediately reduce to a simmer. Simmer for 30 minutes, skimming any surface foam as necessary and stirring occasionally. Add the salt and sugar; cook for 5 to 10 minutes or until the lentils are tender. Remove half of the mixture to a blender or food processor and purée. Return the purée to the soup pot. Check seasonings, adding additional water if needed. *Yield: 6 (1-cup) servings*

Nutrients Per Serving: Cal 145; Prot 9 g; Carbo 23 g; Fat 3 g; 17% Cal from Fat; Sod 322 mg

Torta de Calabacitas

Casseroles are usually thought of as sturdy, stick-to-your-ribs comfort foods best suited for the cooler months. This one, which will also make you feel quite comfortable, takes a lighter approach, using the abundance of summer produce from the garden. Instead of pasta or potatoes, tender young zucchini are layered with fresh tomatoes and chile peppers. Everything is bound together with a little beaten egg and reduced-fat cheese to form a simple, satisfying single-dish supper. Add some black beans and warm corn tortillas to complete the meal.

1 1/2 pounds small zucchini, sliced into 1/8 rounds
1 teaspoon salt
3 poblano chiles
6 medium tomatoes
1 cup thinly sliced onion
3 garlic cloves, minced
Salt and freshly ground black pepper to taste
4 egg whites
2 egg yolks
3 tablespoons dried bread crumbs
6 ounces shredded queso Chihuahua or reduced-fat Monterey Jack cheese
1 tablespoon olive oil

Toss the zucchini with the salt in a bowl and set aside for 1 hour. Cover the squash with boiling water; cover the bowl with plastic wrap and set aside for 5 minutes. Drain, rinse with cold water and pat dry. Arrange the poblano chiles in a single layer on a baking sheet. Roast at 450 degrees, turning until blistered on all sides. Remove to a paper bag; close tightly and set aside for 10 minutes. Remove the poblano chiles; peel, seed and cut them into strips. Cut an X into the bottom of each tomato. Blanch in boiling water in a saucepan for 30 seconds. Remove, peel, seed and chop the tomatoes. Heat a nonstick skillet over medium heat. Sauté the onions until soft using a bit of nonstick cooking spray in a nonstick skillet. Add the tomatoes, poblano chiles and garlic; cook until fairly dry. Season with salt and pepper. Beat the egg whites in a bowl with an electric mixer until stiff peaks form. Add the egg yolks and beat well. Add a pinch of salt. Spray a 2-quart casserole dish with nonstick cooking spray. Add the bread crumbs and tilt the dish to evenly distribute the crumbs. Layer 1/3 of the squash over the bread crumbs. Top with 1/2 of the tomatoes, 1/3 of the cheese and 1/3 of the egg mixture. Add another layer of squash, the remaining tomatoes, 1/2 of the remaining cheese and 1/2 of the remaining egg mixture. Top with the remaining squash, cheese and egg mixture. Drizzle the olive oil over the top and bake on the top oven rack at 350 degrees for 30 minutes. *Yield: 6 servings*

Nutrients Per Serving: Cal 230; Prot 13 g; Carbo 18 g; Fat 13 g; 49% Cal from Fat; Sod 647 mg

it's soy good for you

Soy is a complete protein and also contains several phytochemicals that appear to prevent cancer. Isoflavones in soy are the subject of much research. It has been shown that 45-60 mg of soy isoflavones significantly lowers LDL (bad) cholesterol. And 90 mg raised bone density 1% in six months in a group of postmenopausal women. Soy has also been shown to decrease fat storage and increase lean muscle mass in both humans and animals. But be aware - some soy foods have had their isoflavones removed in processing. Tofu, soymilk, edamame and other whole soy foods still have their isoflavones. Be sure to read the label.

NUTRITION

Mushroom and Cheese Grits Soufflé

One winter night, not too many seasons ago, Southern Georgians were treated to a rare meteorological event — a genuine snowstorm. The following morning when folks awoke to peer sleepily out of their windows, most of them realized immediately what had happened. The grits factory had blown up! You can make this recipe, an upscale take on a decidedly homespun Southern favorite, with yellow or white grits — or even regular cornmeal. And, if shiitake mushrooms are not available, simply use all white mushrooms. Serve this soufflé as an entrée or a delicious side dish.

2 cups minced onions
6 garlic cloves, minced
1 teaspoon minced fresh thyme leaves
1 teaspoon minced fresh sage leaves
1/2 teaspoon minced fresh rosemary leaves
1 cup sliced shiitake mushroom caps
3 cups sliced white mushrooms
3 cups water
1 teaspoon salt
1 1/2 cups stone-ground grits
1 1/2 cups 1% milk, heated
2 ounces fat-free cream cheese
1/2 cup (2 ounces) shredded reduced-fat Cheddar cheese
1/2 cup grated Parmesan cheese
1/8 teaspoon cayenne pepper
2 tablespoons Dijon mustard
2 egg yolks
1/4 cup egg substitute
6 egg whites, beaten to stiff peaks
6 tomato slices, blotted dry

Spray a heavy skillet with nonstick cooking spray. Add the onions. Cook, covered, over medium heat until the onions are soft. Add the garlic, thyme, sage and rosemary. Cook, uncovered, for 1 minute, stirring frequently. Remove the mixture to a plate or bowl and set aside. Combine the shiitake mushrooms and white mushrooms in the skillet and cook over medium heat until almost dry. Bring the water and salt to a boil in a 3-quart saucepan over high heat. Whisk in the grits. Reduce the heat to medium and cook for 5 minutes, stirring frequently. Add the milk, cream cheese, Cheddar cheese, Parmesan cheese, cayenne pepper, Dijon mustard, egg yolks and egg substitute; whisk to mix well. Remove the saucepan from the heat and fold in the onions, mushrooms and egg whites. Spray 6 individual ramekins with nonstick cooking spray. Fill each ramekin 2/3 full with the soufflé mixture and top with a tomato slice. Bake at 400 degrees for 30 to 40 minutes. Serve immediately. *Yield: 6 servings*

Nutrients Per Serving: Cal 324; Prot 20 g; Carbo 42 g; Fat 8 g; 22% Cal from Fat; Sod 799 mg

Spanakopita (Spinach Pie)

With the possible exception of baklava, spanakopita is Greece's most famous phyllo export. No self-respecting Greek restaurant menu is complete without it. Fortunately, this ubiquitous spinach pie is as easy to make as it is delicious to eat, as long as you follow a few simple rules concerning the phyllo dough. Here are "the big three" rules for dealing with phyllo. First, have a large, clean, dry surface to work on. Second, keep any phyllo not being worked with, constantly covered with plastic wrap to keep it from drying out. And, third, the filling should be cool or at room temperature. Properly handled, the unused phyllo can be tightly rewrapped and refrozen for another use.

2 teaspoons olive oil
3/4 cup minced green onion
2 garlic cloves, minced
1/4 pound frozen chopped spinach, thawed and squeezed dry
2 tablespoons minced fresh dillweed
2 tablespoons minced fresh parsley
1/2 cup grated Parmesan cheese
2 teaspoons fresh lemon juice
1/8 teaspoon cayenne pepper
1/8 teaspoon salt
2 egg whites, lightly beaten
4 sheets frozen phyllo pastry, thawed
1 cup Tzatziki Sauce
1/4 cup crumbled feta cheese

Heat the olive oil in a skillet over medium heat. Add the green onion and garlic and sauté until the vegetables are soft. Remove the vegetables to a large bowl and add the spinach, dillweed, parsley, Parmesan cheese, lemon juice, cayenne pepper, salt and egg whites; mix well. Spread 1 sheet of phyllo dough on a large, flat, clean surface with the long edge facing you. Spray the dough lightly with nonstick cooking spray. Fold the dough in half from left to right. Spray the dough's surface lightly with nonstick cooking spray. Place 3/4 cup of the spinach mixture near the edge of the pastry closest to you. Roll the pastry away from you to enclose the filling, spraying the dry surfaces lightly with nonstick cooking spray as they become exposed. As soon as the filling is completely enclosed, fold the right and left ends of the pastry in toward the center. Spray with nonstick cooking spray and continue to roll and spray until complete. Repeat the process until you have completed 4 pies. Arrange the pies in a single layer on a baking sheet sprayed with nonstick cooking spray. Bake at 400 degrees for 20 to 25 minutes until golden. Serve each pie topped with a tablespoon of crumbled feta cheese and a dollop of Tzatziki Sauce on the side. *Yield: 4 servings*

The Tzatziki Sauce

1 cup plain fat-free yogurt
1/4 cup diced, seeded and peeled cucumber
1 garlic clove, minced
1 teaspoon olive oil
1 teaspoon fresh lemon juice
1 teaspoon minced fresh dillweed, or 1/2 teaspoon dried dillweed
1/8 teaspoon salt
1/8 teaspoon cayenne pepper

Drain the yogurt in cheesecloth or a fine mesh strainer over a bowl for 1 hour. Combine the drained yogurt, cucumber, garlic, olive oil, lemon juice, dillweed, salt and cayenne pepper in a bowl and mix well. Chill until ready to serve. *Yield: 4 (1/4-cup) servings*

Nutrients Per Serving: Cal 210; Prot 13 g; Carbo 20 g; Fat 10 g; 40% Cal from Fat; Sod 616 mg

Pineapple Fried Rice with Tofu

Some of the world's very best food is made from leftovers. Little bits of this and that, fashioned with care by frugal cooks near and far, magically blossom into tasty and wholesome meals. A daily staple such as wheat, rice, or corn often provides the foundation for this exercise with other ingredients being added as available to create variations upon a theme. No better example of this worthy reclamation exists than fried rice, which, depending upon the additions, can be spicy or mild, humble or highbrow, vegetarian or not. In all cases, definitely use leftover or cold rice for this dish because fresh, hot rice is prone to stick and go gummy during the first frying process. Just remember the next time you're making rice as a side dish to make extra and you'll be set for a stir-fry extravaganza.

1 cup pineapple juice
1 tablespoon soy sauce
2 garlic cloves, minced
2 teaspoons minced fresh gingerroot
1 teaspoon sugar
1 (12-ounce) package extra firm tofu, drained and cut into 8 slabs
1 1/2 tablespoons canola oil
1 cup diced onion
1 1/2 tablespoons minced fresh gingerroot
4 cups cooked rice
1 cup shredded carrot
1 cup minced pineapple, fresh or canned unsweetened
1/2 cup egg substitute
1/2 teaspoon salt
1/2 teaspoon sugar
4 green onions, chopped
1 serrano chile, thinly sliced
1/4 chopped fresh cilantro leaves
1/2 cup bean sprouts
2 tablespoons chopped fresh basil or mint leaves

Combine the pineapple juice, soy sauce, garlic, gingerroot and sugar in a bowl. Pour over the tofu in a separate bowl and marinate for 4 to 6 hours. Drain and discard the marinade; blot the tofu dry with paper towels. Heat 2 teaspoons of the canola oil in a heavy nonstick skillet over high heat. Sear the tofu on both sides. Remove to a plate, cover and set aside. Heat the remaining canola oil in the skillet, add the garlic and sauté just until it begins to color. Add the onion and gingerroot; sauté for a few seconds. Add the rice, carrot and pineapple; stir-fry for 1 minute. Add the egg substitute; do not stir. Add the salt, sugar, green onions, serrano chile, cilantro, bean sprouts and basil; mix well. Cook until hot, stirring frequently. Serve topped with reserved tofu. *Yield: 4 servings*

Nutrients Per Serving: Cal 433; Prot 17 g; Carbo 72 g; Fat 9 g; 18% Cal from Fat; Sod 747 mg

chefstip

The Phyllo File * Phyllo dough (actually finished sheets of paper thin phyllo pastry) is usually associated with Greek cooking - vegetable and meat pies, or layered pastry desserts like Baklava. You can find it in the frozen pastry section of most major grocery stores. If you have never worked with phyllo before, the delicate nature of the sheets can be intimidating, but if you read the directions carefully and give yourself some time and space to work, you will get the hang of it in no time, with spectacular results. (Note: to the best of our knowledge, phyllo is manufactured on another planet and shipped here by friendly aliens - even traditional Greek cookbooks tell you to buy it at the store!)

poultry

poultry

poultry

Pan-Roasted Chicken with Peach and Bourbon Glaze, Pg.99

poultry

Chicken Manchego with Artichoke/Olive Salad

Many of Spain's delicious regionally produced cheeses are beginning to find a wider international following. Manchego, a mellow, ivory-colored cheese made with part-skim milk, but with a rich, nutty flavor, leads the pack. Combined here with Spain's already renowned, ultra-lean serrano ham, then enveloped by juicy chicken, it provides the perfect contrast to the vibrantly sweet and tart sherry/quince glaze. Perch it on top of a cool artichoke and olive salad (also very Spanish) and you can take a tour of the country with every bite.

8 canned artichoke hearts, rinsed, drained and quartered
2 tomatoes, peeled, seeded and diced
4 pitted kalamata olives, chopped
4 pitted green olives, chopped
4 green onions, minced
2 garlic cloves, minced
1 tablespoon olive oil
2 teaspoons fresh lemon juice
2 tablespoons chopped fresh parsley
4 boneless, skinless all-natural chicken breast halves
Salt and freshly ground black pepper to taste
1/2 cup shredded Manchego cheese
1 tablespoon chopped fresh parsley
1 teaspoon fresh thyme leaves
2 teaspoons olive oil
4 paper-thin slices serrano or prosciutto ham
3/4 cup chicken stock
2 tablespoons sherry
2 tablespoons sherry vinegar
1/4 cup quince jelly

Combine the first nine ingredients together in a bowl. Chill. Butterfly the breasts by splitting horizontally most of the way through with a sharp knife. Flatten slightly between sheets of plastic wrap. Season with salt and pepper. Combine the cheese, parsley and thyme, then divide onto the breasts and re-close. Sauté the breasts in oil until browned. Wrap each with a slice of ham and finish on a baking sheet in the oven at 375 degrees for 10 minutes. Deglaze the sauté pan with the stock. Add the remaining ingredients and reduce to sauce consistency. Serve the chicken on a bed of artichoke/olive salad with a drizzle of the pan sauce. *Yield: 4 servings*

Nutrients Per Serving: Cal 381; Prot 35 g; Carbo 29 g; Fat 14 g; 33% Cal from Fat; Sod 1185 mg

good to the last drop

When you come to the end of a bottle of essential oil don't toss it yet! Remove the dropper and wash the bottle with water. Use this scented water to fill your aromatherapy diffuser. Rinse the bottle several times, adding it to the diffuser each time. You will be amazed at how much scent is recycled from the supposedly "empty" bottle. Then recycle the empty bottle with your glass recycling.

HOME SPA

Chicken Tortilla Torta with Poblano/Spinach Cream Sauce

Stacking the tortillas gives this dish a presentational panache rolled enchiladas do not achieve. You can completely assemble the tortillas and filling (without the sauce) in advance, if you choose. Simply wrap them tightly in plastic wrap and microwave until warm when you are ready to serve.

12 ounces boneless, skinless all-natural chicken breasts
1/2 cup sliced onion
1 garlic clove, chopped
6 black peppercorns
1/2 teaspoon salt
2 poblano chiles
1 medium tomato
12 ounces fresh spinach leaves, rinsed and drained
1 1/2 cups sliced onions
1 garlic clove, chopped
1 tablespoon masa harina de maiz or flour
1 ounce reduced-fat cream cheese
1 ounce fat-free cream cheese
1 teaspoon ground cumin
1/2 cup chopped fresh cilantro leaves
2 teaspoons fresh lime juice
1/3 cup fat-free sour cream
2 tablespoons skim milk
8 corn tortillas

Combine the chicken, 1/2 cup onion, 1 garlic clove, peppercorns and salt in a large saucepan over medium heat. Add enough water to cover. Bring to a simmer and cook gently, skimming as necessary, for about 20 minutes or until the chicken is cooked through. Remove the pan from the heat and allow the chicken to cool in the broth. Remove and shred the chicken; set aside. Strain the broth, reserving the liquid and discarding the solids. Return the broth to the saucepan over high heat. Boil until the stock is reduced to 1 1/4 cups. Blister the skins of the poblano chiles over an open flame or under a broiler. Place the poblano chiles in a paper bag; close tightly and set aside for 10 minutes. Remove the poblano chiles; peel, seed and cut into strips. Cut an X in the bottom of the tomato; blanch in boiling water in a saucepan for 30 seconds. Peel, seed and dice the tomato. Blanch the spinach in boiling water in a saucepan for 30 seconds; drain and squeeze dry. Sauté 1 1/2 cups sliced onions with nonstick cooking spray in a nonstick skillet until they are soft. Remove 1/2 of the onions and combine with the spinach in a blender. Add the cumin and cilantro and 1/2 of the poblano chiles. Purée and set aside. Add the tomato, 1 garlic clove, chicken and remaining chiles to the onions in the skillet. Season lightly with salt and pepper. Sauté over medium heat for 1 minute; set aside and keep warm. Combine the chicken stock and masa harina in a saucepan over medium heat. Cook, stirring constantly, until slightly thickened. Add the cream cheese; cook, stirring constantly, until the cheese melts. Pour the cheese sauce into the spinach mixture; process on slow speed until mixed. Add the lime juice; taste and correct the seasonings. Combine the sour cream and skim milk in a squeeze bottle; shake to mix well. Warm the tortillas. Place 1 tortilla on each of 4 plates. Top each with 1/4 of the chicken mixture and arrange another tortilla over the top of the chicken. Ladle the spinach sauce over the tortilla. Drizzle a design on the top with the sour cream mixture. *Yield: 4 servings*

Nutrients Per Serving: Cal 319; Prot 27 g; Carbo 43 g; Fat 5 g; 14% Cal from Fat; Sod 568 mg

Coq au Vin Sauté

In spite of the fact that it takes less than 30 minutes to cook — one-fourth of the time required for its labor-intensive, oven-bound French ancestor — this saucy, stove-top supper retains most of the rustic charm and flavor of the original. Using a lean, all-natural bacon without chemicals provides a richness and depth of flavor with considerably less fat than you might expect (2 1/2 grams of fat per slice). The cast-iron skillet, which creates all the caramelized bits of pork, chicken, and vegetables, helps give added dimension to this home-style bistro favorite.

2 strips all-natural, nitrate-free bacon
2 teaspoons olive oil
4 (4-ounce) boneless, skinless all-natural chicken breast halves
Salt and freshly ground black pepper to taste
1/2 cup minced shallots
1/2 cup diced carrot
1/4 cup diced celery
2 garlic cloves, minced
8 medium mushrooms, quartered
1/2 teaspoon minced fresh thyme leaves
1/2 bay leaf
1 1/2 cups red wine
2 cups chicken stock, or half beef and half chicken stock
2 tablespoons tomato purée
2 tablespoons flour, dissolved in stock
1/2 cup drained, bottled pearl onions
1 tablespoon chopped fresh parsley
Salt and freshly ground black pepper to taste

Slowly sauté the bacon in a cast-iron skillet over medium-low heat until tender-crisp. Remove the bacon and blot dry with paper towels; crumble and set aside. Discard the bacon grease. Return the skillet to the heat and add 1 teaspoon of the olive oil. Season the chicken with salt and pepper and sauté until browned on all sides. Remove from the skillet and set aside. Heat the remaining olive oil in the skillet. Add the shallots, carrot and celery; sauté until the vegetables are soft. Add the garlic and mushrooms; mix well. Add the thyme, bay leaf, wine, stock, tomato purée and flour mixture. Increase the heat slightly; cook, stirring frequently, until the mixture thickens and is reduced to sauce consistency. Taste and correct the seasonings. Add the chicken, bacon, pearl onions and parsley. Cook until the chicken is cooked through. *Yield: 4 servings*

Nutrients Per Serving: Cal 298; Prot 27 g; Carbo 17 g; Fat 7 g; 22% Cal from Fat; Sod 520 mg

Done For ✳ When you're cooking very lean foods in a very lean fashion, there is a definite window between "done" and "dry"; and once you cross over, there is no coming back. This idea applies equally to meats, poultry and fish. With meat, we are accustomed to gradations of doneness - rare, medium rare and so on. With poultry we know that the center shouldn't be glassy or pink. But with fish things get a bit fuzzier. Sushi fans like their fish raw; if you order a tuna steak in a restaurant, the waiter is likely to ask if you would like it "medium rare." Many Europeans routinely prefer their cooked fish with glassy centers. But even if you're one of those old-fashioned types who likes fish "cooked through," you still want it to be moist and flavorful. However you cook it, fish needs about 10 minutes per total inches of thickness to be fully cooked. As soon as it flakes, it's done.

Grilled Chicken with Spicy Peanut Sauce and Masa Potato Cakes

Peanuts are indigenous to the Americas and have played an important role as a nutritious binder for Mexican sauces and moles since pre-Columbian times. In this recipe, they are puréed with tomatoes, chipotle chiles (smoked jalapeños), lime juice, and seasonings to create a wonderfully spicy, slightly piquant salsa that adds a lively interest to the simple goodness of the chicken and masa cakes.

4 (4-ounce) boneless, skinless all-natural chicken breasts
Salt and freshly ground black pepper to taste
2 medium tomatoes
2 garlic cloves, minced
1 canned chipotle chile in adobo sauce
1 tablespoon brown sugar
1 teaspoon ground cumin
1/2 teaspoon dried leaf oregano
1/4 cup chopped fresh cilantro leaves
3 tablespoons smooth reduced-fat all-natural peanut butter
2 tablespoons fresh lime juice
Water or chicken stock as needed

Season the chicken lightly with salt and pepper. Spray each piece lightly with nonstick cooking spray, then grill over hot coals until cooked through. Grill the tomatoes, turning them occasionally, until they begin to char and soften. Remove the tomatoes from the grill and combine in a blender or food processor with the garlic, chile, brown sugar, cumin, oregano, cilantro, peanut butter and lime juice. Purée the mixture, thinning a little with water or stock as needed. Serve the chicken napped with the warm sauce and Masa Potato Cakes. *Yield: 4 servings*

The Masa Potato Cakes

1/4 cup masa harina de maiz
1/2 cup water
1 cup cooked and mashed potatoes
1 garlic clove, minced
1 tablespoon minced fresh chives
1/4 teaspoon salt
1/4 cup crumbled feta cheese
2 teaspoons olive oil

Mix the masa harina, water, potatoes, garlic, chives, salt and cheese in a bowl. Shape into four 1/2-inch-thick disks. Heat the olive oil in a heavy nonstick skillet over medium-high heat. Sauté the cakes until browned and crisp on both sides. *Yield: 4 servings*

Nutrients Per Serving: Cal 353; Prot 30 g; Carbo 27 g; Fat 14 g; 34% Cal from Fat; Sod 607 mg

Indonesian-Style Mahogany Glazed Chicken and Shrimp

Previously relegated to the beverage section of the menu, coffee, tea, and even cola are now finding their way into the skillet as chefs search for new color and flavor combinations. This time it's tea providing the mahogany color as well as an intriguing flavor that your dinner guests will most likely devour, but not be able to decipher.

1/2 cup sherry
1/4 cup strong brewed tea
1/4 cup pineapple juice
2 tablespoons light soy sauce
2 tablespoons honey
1/2 teaspoon ground cinnamon
1/2 teaspoon ground ginger
1/2 teaspoon black pepper
1/4 teaspoon salt
4 (3-ounce) boneless, skinless all-natural chicken breasts
1 1/2 tablespoons canola oil
3/4 cup sliced red bell pepper
4 green onions, sliced
2 garlic cloves, minced
12 medium shrimp, peeled and deveined
2 tablespoons toasted sliced almonds
1/4 cup chopped fresh cilantro leaves

Combine the sherry, tea, pineapple juice, soy sauce and honey in a bowl; mix well and set aside. Combine the cinnamon, ginger, pepper and salt in a bowl; mix well. Rub the spice mixture over the chicken breasts. Heat 1 tablespoon of the canola oil in a heavy skillet over medium-high heat. Sauté the chicken until cooked through; remove and set aside. Add the remaining canola oil to the skillet. Add the bell pepper, green onions, garlic and shrimp; sauté for 1 minute. Add the reserved sherry and tea mixture. Cook until the mixture is reduced by half. Return the chicken to the skillet; top with almonds and cilantro. Cook until heated through. *Yield: 4 servings*

Nutrients Per Serving: Cal 327; Prot 22 g; Carbo 40 g; Fat 9 g; 25% Cal from Fat; Sod 485 mg

stretch your flexibility

By staying flexible, you improve your ability to participate in daily activities. As we age, flexibility exercises are increasingly important, not necessarily because of the aging process, but because some of us tend to become more sedentary, which results in a loss of range of motion. Here's the good news - a simple daily stretching routine can improve the range of motion around a joint, increase blood circulation, improve posture, alleviate stress, and reduce the risk of injury. In order to improve flexibility, breathe deeply while sustaining a gentle stretch without bouncing for a minimum of 30 seconds.

Walnut and Gorgonzola Stuffed Chicken with Fig Conserve on White Beans with Prosciutto

This is just the sort of rustic Italian, down-home, comfort food that we like to offer our guests in the fall. Figs, gorgonzola, and prosciutto are always a great combination. And, even in the sparing amounts used here, they lend a lot of flavor to the dish. In spite of what might seem to be a rather imposing list of ingredients, the dish comes together in a very straightforward fashion and is easily adapted for a quick, home-cooked family dinner. A green vegetable is all that is needed to complete the meal.

4	**(4-ounce) boneless, skinless all-natural chicken breasts**
	Salt and freshly ground black pepper to taste
3	**tablespoons chopped walnuts**
3	**tablespoons crumbled gorgonzola or other bleu cheese**
1	**teaspoon olive oil**
1/2	**cup diced onion**
1/3	**cup diced celery**
1/3	**cup diced carrot**
2	**garlic cloves, minced**
1	**ounce chopped prosciutto ham**
1	**teaspoon minced fresh rosemary leaves**
2	**cups cooked white beans, drained**
1/2	**cup chicken stock**
1	**tablespoon chopped fresh parsley**
2	**teaspoons olive oil**
1/2	**cup diced onion**
1/2	**cup chicken stock**
4	**ounces fig preserves**
3	**tablespoons balsamic vinegar**
	Grated zest and juice of 1 small lemon

Season the chicken breasts lightly with salt and pepper. Cut a large slit in the side of each chicken breast. Mix the walnuts and cheese in a bowl; tuck an equal portion into each slit. Refrigerate the chicken, covered, until ready to cook. Heat 1 teaspoon olive oil in a heavy nonstick skillet over medium-high heat. Add 1/2 cup onion, celery and carrot; sauté for 1 minute. Add the garlic, prosciutto and rosemary; sauté for 30 seconds. Add the beans, 1/2 cup stock and the parsley; mix well. Taste and adjust the seasoning, if necessary. Remove the skillet from the heat; cover and keep warm. Heat 2 teaspoons olive oil in a heavy cast-iron skillet over medium-high heat. Add the chicken and sauté, covered until cooked through. Turn the chicken to sauté on both sides. Remove the chicken to a plate and keep warm. Add 1/2 cup onion to the skillet; cook for 1 minute, stirring frequently. Add 1/2 cup stock, fig preserves, vinegar, zest and lemon juice. Bring to a boil and cook until the mixture is reduced to a sauce consistency, stirring frequently. Serve the dish by dividing the bean mixture among 4 deep plates or wide-bottom soup bowls. Top each with a piece of chicken, some fig sauce and a sprinkling of chopped parsley. *Yield: 4 servings*

Nutrients Per Serving: Cal 465; Prot 36 g; Carbo 52 g; Fat 13 g; 25% Cal from Fat; Sod 462 mg

Manchamantel

This savory, slightly sweet, slightly spicy stew with the cautionary title (manchamantel means "tablecloth stainer" in Spanish) uses the poblano chile in both its fresh and dry form - ancho chile peppers are dried poblanos. Serve this dish with black beans and/or a salad, fresh corn tortillas, and our low-fat flan for a "fiesta-tive" feast guaranteed to please your dinner guests. (Or we'll pick up the linen bill.)

1 garlic bulb
1 teaspoon olive oil
1 medium onion, peeled and cut into thick slices
4 medium tomatoes
3 fresh tomatillos, husked
1 small fresh poblano chile
2 ancho chiles
1/4 teaspoon dried leaf oregano
1/4 teaspoon ground cumin
1/8 teaspoon dried thyme leaves
1/2 teaspoon ground cinnamon
1/8 teaspoon ground cloves
2 cups chicken stock
2 teaspoons olive oil
1 pound boneless, skinless all-natural chicken breasts, cubed
Salt and freshly ground black pepper to taste
1/2 pound sweet potatoes, peeled and cubed
1 tablespoon sugar
2 tablespoons raisins
1 cup peeled and cubed fresh pineapple
1 medium Granny Smith apple, cored, peeled and diced
2 tablespoons chopped fresh cilantro leaves

Slice the top off the garlic bulb. Drizzle the olive oil over the exposed cloves, wrap in foil and place on a baking sheet. Add the onion, tomatoes, tomatillos and poblano chile in a single layer. Roast at 400 degrees for 25 minutes. Toast the ancho chiles in a dry cast-iron skillet over medium heat for 1 to 2 minutes, turning often. Remove the ancho chiles from the skillet and seed the chiles. Soak the ancho chiles in hot water to cover in a bowl for 20 minutes. Combine the roasted onion, tomatoes, tomatillos and pulp squeezed from the garlic bulb in a blender or food processor; purée. Remove the roasted vegetable purée to a bowl; set aside. Combine the ancho chiles, oregano, cumin, thyme, cinnamon and cloves in the blender or food processor; purée, adding a little chicken stock if necessary. Set aside. Heat 1 teaspoon of the olive oil in a heavy skillet over medium heat. Season the chicken with salt and pepper and spray lightly with nonstick cooking spray. Add to the skillet and sauté until the meat begins to brown. Remove the chicken to a plate and set aside. Add the remaining olive oil and ancho chile purée to the skillet. Cook, stirring frequently, for 2 to 3 minutes. Add the remaining chicken stock, sweet potato, sugar, raisins, pineapple, apple, roasted vegetable purée and reserved chicken. Bring to a simmer and cook for 10 to 15 minutes. Serve hot, garnished with cilantro. *Yield: 4 servings*

Nutrients Per Serving: Cal 350; Prot 27 g; Carbo 46 g; Fat 8 g; 20% Cal from Fat; Sod 409 mg

Pan-Roasted Chicken with Peach and Bourbon Glaze

We use this recipe for a cooking class we call "20 Dishes You Can Make for Dinner in 20 Minutes." It is perfectly delicious just as written, but we would urge you to think of it not only as a single recipe, but as a template for other recipes. For example, instead of chicken breast, think salmon fillet, pork tenderloin, turkey cutlet, or tofu. Instead of bourbon, think rum, red wine, white wine, sherry, or fruit juice. Instead of peach preserves, think pineapple, black cherry, or fig preserves. The technique remains the same, but the combinations change to create different results. You'll get the idea (or 20 of them) in no time. And your family will get a different meal every week.

4 (4-ounce) boneless, skinless all-natural chicken breasts
Salt and freshly ground black pepper to taste
2 teaspoons canola oil
1/2 cup minced onion
2 tablespoons bourbon
1/4 cup chicken stock
1/2 cup all-fruit peach preserves
4 teaspoons chopped fresh mint leaves
1 tablespoon fresh lemon juice
1 tablespoon cider vinegar
1 tablespoon sugar

Season the chicken with salt and pepper. Heat the canola oil in a cast-iron skillet over medium heat. Add the chicken; cook, covered, for 3 to 4 minutes. Turn the chicken; cook, covered, for 2 minutes longer. Add the onion; cook, covered, for 2 minutes longer. Remove the chicken and onion to a plate; cover and keep warm. Return the skillet to medium-high heat and add the bourbon. Carefully flambé, tilting the pan away from you. When the flames subside add the stock, peach preserves, mint, lemon juice, vinegar and sugar. Stir with a wooden spoon, being careful to incorporate all the brown bits. Cook, stirring occasionally, until the mixture has reduced to a sauce-like consistency. Taste and adjust the seasonings. Add the reserved chicken and any accumulated juices. To serve, place 1 piece of chicken on each of 4 plates; top each with sauce.

To convert this recipe to chicken with a cream sauce, simply add 2 ounces of reduced-fat cream cheese to the skillet after adding the stock. Omit the preserves, mint, lemon juice, vinegar, and sugar. Cook until the sauce is reduced and slightly thickened. We sometimes like to add sliced mushrooms along with the onion, too. *Yield: 4 servings*

Nutrients Per Serving: Cal 260; Prot 23 g; Carbo 25 g; Fat 5 g; 18% Cal from Fat; Sod 98 mg

chefstip

The Spirits Of Cooking * We must admit, for a healthy kitchen, we have a remarkably well-stocked liquor cabinet. Not for the proverbial five o'clock "pick me up," but to add flavor and interest to recipes. In most of our finished dishes, with the exception of a few desserts, the alcohol (and calories) are completely cooked out, leaving behind just the essence of the wine, liqueur or spirit. For a well-stocked pantry we recommend: wines – a bottle of red, a bottle of white, not the cheapest but not expensive; fortified wines – one bottle each of sherry, Madeira, port; liqueurs – something orange, Grand Marnier, Cointreau or triple sec, Kahlua and Pernod; and spirits – brandy, rum and bourbon.

Panéed Chicken with Creole Mustard Sauce

Panéed is the French word for "breaded." In this case, the breading is a mixture of bread crumbs and Parmesan cheese. Make your own whole wheat bread crumbs simply by drying (really drying) some slices of whole wheat bread in a 275-degree oven, then grinding them in a food processor. For your trouble you will get a genuine "N'awlins-style" chicken dish with both better color and better nutrition. Store excess bread crumbs in a sealable plastic bag in the freezer. After all, a panée saved is a panée earned! If you do not have Creole mustard, any whole grain mustard will substitute nicely.

4 (4-ounce) boneless, skinless all-natural chicken breasts, cut into halves
1 cup buttermilk
2 egg whites
1 1/2 cups toasted whole wheat bread crumbs
1/2 cup grated Parmesan cheese

The Creole Mustard Sauce

1/3 cup evaporated skim milk
1/3 cup fat-free sour cream
1/4 cup Creole mustard
1 teaspoon Worcestershire sauce
1/2 teaspoon dry mustard
1/8 teaspoon black pepper
1/8 teaspoon white pepper
1/8 teaspoon dried basil
1/8 teaspoon cayenne pepper

To prepare the chicken, pound the chicken pieces between 2 pieces of plastic wrap, using a rolling pin, until they are 1/4-inch-thick. Beat the buttermilk and egg whites in a bowl. Combine the bread crumbs and cheese in a separate bowl. Dip the chicken pieces first into the buttermilk mixture, then into the bread crumbs, coating each piece completely. Spray a nonstick skillet with nonstick cooking spray and place over medium heat. Add the chicken and sauté until golden brown on both sides.

To prepare the Creole Mustard Sauce, combine the skim milk, sour cream, Creole mustard, Worcestershire sauce, dry mustard, black pepper and white pepper, basil and cayenne pepper in a small saucepan over medium-low heat. Cook until heated through and nap warm sauce over the chicken. *Yield: 4 servings*

Nutrients Per Serving: Cal 286; Prot 36 g; Carbo 18 g; Fat 7 g; 23% Cal from Fat; Sod 739 mg

Pistachio-Crusted Chicken with Plum Sauce

Nuts and seeds, when you stop to think about it, are simply encapsulated energy. They are the power source for the plant and its link to generational survival. These nuclear nuggets are cram-packed with essential nutrients, protein and fat. The good news, however, is that this fat is primarily the healthy monounsaturated variety that elevates your HDL (high-density lipoprotein), the cleansing side of your cholesterol. Consequently, we think nuts and seeds can, and should be, a part of a healthy diet. The slightly sweet-and-sour plum sauce that accompanies this dish is also an excellent dipping sauce for rice paper spring rolls.

4 (3-ounce) boneless, skinless all-natural chicken breasts
Salt and freshly ground black pepper to taste
4 teaspoons Dijon mustard
1/2 cup coarsely ground dry-roasted pistachio nuts
6 red plums, quartered and seeded
1/4 cup sugar
1 cup port
1 teaspoon Asian chile paste
1 teaspoon minced fresh gingerroot
1 tablespoon sherry vinegar
1/4 teaspoon salt
2 teaspoons fresh lime juice

Place the chicken between sheets of plastic wrap and pound to an even thickness with a rolling pin or the palm of your hand. Remove the plastic wrap and season the chicken with salt and pepper. Slather the top of the chicken with Dijon mustard and coat with the ground pistachios. Spray a baking sheet with nonstick cooking spray. Arrange the chicken, coated side up, on the baking sheet. Bake at 350 degrees for 15 minutes or until cooked through. Combine the plums, sugar, port, chile paste, gingerroot, vinegar and salt in a nonreactive saucepan over medium heat. Simmer for 10 minutes. Remove the mixture to a blender or food processor and purée. Strain the purée into a bowl and mix in the lime juice. Pool some of the sauce in the middle of each of 4 plates. Top with a piece of chicken. *Yield: 4 servings*

Nutrients Per Serving: Cal 481; Prot 25 g; Carbo 43 g; Fat 18 g; 32% Cal from Fat; Sod 339 mg

a bounty of basils

Basil comes in many colors, shapes and sizes, one of which is sure to fit in your herb garden. From the basketball-size spicy globe to the four-foot-tall by four-foot-wide African Blue, basil is an herb with tremendous potential as an attractive landscape annual, not to mention a boon in the kitchen. We have many varieties of basil in our gardens, including Sweet (the best-known of the basils), Cinnamon, Lemon, Lime, Spicy Globe, Holy (also known as sacred basil), Thai, Aussie Sweet, Red Rubin, Purple Ruffles, Lettuce Leaf and the enormous African Blue. Naturally, each variety of basil offers its own special taste and visual appeal.

GARDENING

Roast Chicken Three Ways

It is difficult to imagine a simpler yet more satisfying supper than an herb-roasted chicken accompanied by seasoned mashed potatoes and a green vegetable, all drizzled with a bit of reduced pan juices. Whether you're serving it for a large family gathering or as a quiet dinner for two, this humble bird, crisped to a succulent turn, unfailingly reminds us that fresh, simple foods prepared simply, but with care, can provide some of life's greatest eating pleasures. Food like this nurtures and sustains us - and has for generations. Here are three versions of this classic that our guests at Lake Austin Spa Resort have particularly enjoyed. We use an all-natural, bone-in, skin-on breast for two servings. You will want two whole breasts or four halves.

Tarragon/Dijon Roast Chicken

2 tablespoons chopped fresh tarragon
1 1/2 tablespoons Dijon mustard
1 1/2 tablespoons white wine
1 teaspoon olive oil
2 teaspoons honey
1/8 teaspoon salt
1/8 teaspoon freshly ground black pepper
4 (4-ounce) all-natural bone-in, skin-on, chicken breasts
1 1/2 cups chicken stock

Combine the tarragon, Dijon mustard, wine, olive oil, honey and salt in a blender or food processor and process until smooth. Coat the chicken with the sauce, on top of and beneath the skin. Arrange the chicken, skin side up, on a rack set over a roasting pan. Roast at 400 degrees for 20 to 25 minutes or until the internal temperature is 160 degrees. Remove the pan from the oven. Set the chicken aside and cover. Pour off any fat accumulated in the pan. Add the chicken stock to the pan. Cook over high heat until the liquid is reduced to about 3/4 cup, stirring to dislodge the brown bits. Add any juices accumulated around the chicken. Drizzle the pan juices over the chicken when serving. *Yield: 4 servings*

Nutrients Per Serving: Cal 157; Prot 23 g; Carbo 4 g; Fat 4 g; 25% Cal from Fat; Sod 520 mg

Lemon/Garlic/Rosemary Roast Chicken

Grated zest and juice of 1 lemon
2 garlic cloves, minced
2 teaspoons minced fresh rosemary leaves
2 teaspoons minced fresh parsley
1 teaspoon olive oil
1/8 teaspoon salt
Freshly ground black pepper
4 (4-ounce) all-natural bone-in, skin-on, chicken breasts
1 1/2 cups chicken stock

Combine the zest, half the lemon juice, garlic, rosemary, parsley, olive oil, salt and pepper in a blender or food processor. Process until smooth. Coat the chicken pieces with the sauce, on top of and beneath the skin. Arrange the chicken, skin side up, on a rack set over a roasting pan. Roast at 400 degrees for 20 to 25 minutes, or until the internal temperature reaches 160 degrees. Remove the pan from the oven. Set the chicken aside and cover. Pour off any fat accumulated in the pan. Add the chicken stock and remaining lemon juice. Cook over high heat until the liquid is reduced to about 3/4 cup, stirring to dislodge the brown bits. Add any juices accumulated around the chicken. Drizzle the pan juices over the chicken when serving. *Yield: 4 servings*

Nutrients Per Serving: Cal 142; Prot 23 g; Carbo 2 g; Fat 4 g; 26% Cal from Fat; Sod 385 mg

Orange/Red Chile/Cilantro Roast Chicken

2 tablespoons frozen orange juice concentrate, thawed
2 tablespoons water
1 teaspoon chili powder
1/4 teaspoon ground cumin
1/8 teaspoon cayenne pepper
2 tablespoons chopped fresh cilantro leaves
1 teaspoon olive oil
1/8 teaspoon salt
Freshly ground black pepper
4 (4-ounce) all-natural bone-in, skin-on, chicken breasts
11/2 cups chicken stock

Combine the orange juice concentrate, water, chili powder, cumin, cayenne pepper, cilantro, olive oil, salt and pepper in a blender or food processor. Process until smooth. Coat the chicken pieces with the sauce, on top of and beneath the skin. Arrange the chicken, skin side up, on a rack set over a roasting pan. Roast at 400 degrees for 20 to 25 minutes or until the internal temperature reaches 160 degrees. Remove the pan from the oven. Set the chicken aside and cover. Pour off any fat accumulated in the pan. Add the chicken stock. Cook over high heat until the liquid is reduced to about 3/4 cup, stirring to dislodge the brown bits. Add any juices accumulated around the chicken. Drizzle the pan juices over the chicken when serving. *Yield: 4 servings*

Nutrients Per Serving: Cal 152; Prot 23 g; Carbo 4 g; Fat 4 g; 25% Cal from Fat; Sod 391 mg

Kung Pao Chicken

Our knowledge of the Chinese language being limited, we're not exactly sure what "kung pao" means. But, for our money, it could be "colorfully crunchy" or "spicy-sweet" or "fresh and fast" or "can't stop," all of which would apply nicely to this emblematic Eastern specialty. The daikon radish called for in this recipe is a large, mild, white radish available in most major grocery stores.

2 teaspoons canola oil
1 pound boneless, skinless all-natural chicken breasts, cubed
1 cup diced carrot, blanched in boiling water for 2 minutes and drained
1 cup diced daikon radish, blanched in boiling water for 2 minutes and drained
3/4 cup fresh snow peas
8 green onions, cut into 1-inch lengths
1/4 cup apple jelly
1/4 cup Ginger Sauce (Page 126)
1/4 cup bottled teriyaki glaze
1 teaspoon Asian chile paste
1/2 cup dry-roasted peanuts

Heat 1 teaspoon of the canola oil in a heavy skillet over medium-high heat. Add the chicken and stir-fry for 2 to 3 minutes. Remove the chicken from the skillet and set aside. Add the remaining canola oil, carrot and radish. Stir-fry for 1 minute. Add the snow peas, green onions and reserved chicken. Stir-fry for 30 seconds. Add the apple jelly, Ginger Sauce, teriyaki glaze, chile paste and peanuts. Cook, stirring constantly, until the chicken and vegetables are evenly coated. Serve with steamed white rice, if desired. *Yield: 4 servings*

Nutrients Per Serving: Cal 405; Prot 29 g; Carbo 41 g; Fat 14 g; 32% Cal from Fat; Sod 606 mg

Enchiladas Verdes

In the hierarchy of Tex-Mex, green enchiladas (verde means green) rank second only to the ubiquitous "chili and cheese." Traditionally made with chicken or cheese or a combination of both, and topped with a feisty green tomatillo sauce, they offer a delicious (and vegetarian-friendly) alternative for all Mexican food lovers. Interestingly, the star ingredient in this sauce - even though tomatillo translates directly as "little tomato" - is not a true tomato at all, but a member of the gooseberry family. You will find fresh tomatillos wrapped in their papery green husks in the produce section of many grocery stores. Canned tomatillos may be substituted, but be leery of canned tomatillo salsas which can be quite hot.

3 cups husked tomatillos
1 small onion, peeled and quartered
3 green onions, cut into 2-inch lengths
2 large garlic cloves, minced
1 poblano chile, roasted, peeled and seeded
1/2 cup chopped fresh cilantro leaves
2 teaspoons ground cumin
1/2 teaspoon salt
1 teaspoon sugar
Juice of 1/2 lime
3/4 cup fat-free sour cream
12 corn tortillas
3/4 cup shredded reduced-fat white Cheddar or Monterey Jack cheese
1 pound shredded cooked all-natural chicken breasts

Combine the tomatillos, onion and green onions in a 3-quart saucepan over medium-high heat. Add enough water to cover and bring to a simmer. Simmer for 5 minutes; drain. Combine the tomatillo-onion mixture with the garlic, chile, cilantro, cumin, salt, sugar and lime juice in a blender or food processor; purée. Add the sour cream and pulse to mix. Soften the tortillas by either steaming them or briefly microwaving them in a plastic bag. Place a tortilla on a clean work surface and add a bit of cheese and some chicken. Roll the tortilla tightly and place, seam side down, in a baking dish. Once all tortillas are rolled and arranged in the baking dish, pour the salsa-sour cream mixture over the top. Scatter shredded cheese over the top of the enchiladas. Bake at 375 degrees until the cheese melts and the enchiladas are heated through.

Note: The tomatillo-onion purée, without the sour cream, makes an excellent salsa verde with many uses of its own. *Yield: 6 servings*

Nutrients Per Serving: Cal 332; Prot 32 g; Carbo 35 g; Fat 7 g; 20% Cal from Fat; Sod 358 mg

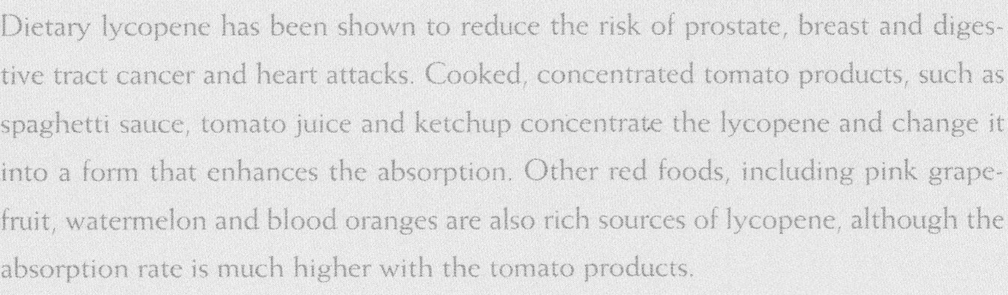

why we like lycopene

Dietary lycopene has been shown to reduce the risk of prostate, breast and digestive tract cancer and heart attacks. Cooked, concentrated tomato products, such as spaghetti sauce, tomato juice and ketchup concentrate the lycopene and change it into a form that enhances the absorption. Other red foods, including pink grapefruit, watermelon and blood oranges are also rich sources of lycopene, although the absorption rate is much higher with the tomato products.

NUTRITION

Enchiladas Rojas

In Texas, where Tex-Mex rules, enchiladas are invariably filled with cheap, processed American yellow cheese and covered with a thin, slightly greasy chili gravy. Accompanied by puréed refried pinto beans and seasoned rice, they form the "plato numero uno" in most Tex-Mex restaurants; and we eat them by the thousands every week. In Mexico proper, however, enchiladas are quite likely to be a different story altogether. Homemade corn tortillas are stuffed with stewed chicken or any of a number of tasty, unprocessed white cheeses, then dressed with a bright, spicy red or green chile sauce to be baked and served with a crisp green salad or slaw on top. The presentation and combinations of flavors and textures make for a memorable dining experience. Once you have eaten enchiladas made in this manner, you will be hard pressed to go back to your old ways. Our favorite accompaniment is whole black or pinto beans, seasoned with a bit of cumin, cilantro, onion, and garlic.

1 tablespoon canola oil
3/4 cup minced onion
3 garlic cloves, minced
2 cups tomato juice
2 teaspoons adobo paste from canned chipotle chiles
2 teaspoons brown sugar
1/2 teaspoon salt
12 white corn tortillas
2 cups shredded cooked chicken breast, or 2 cups shredded Chihuahua or reduced-fat white Cheddar cheese
3 cups shredded lettuce
3 radishes, slivered
1/2 cup finely sliced onion
1/4 cup chopped fresh cilantro leaves
1 teaspoon olive oil
2 teaspoons cider vinegar
1/2 cup crumbled queso fresco or feta cheese

Heat the canola oil in a heavy skillet over medium heat. Add the onions and sauté until soft. Add the garlic and sauté for a few seconds. Add the tomato juice, adobo paste, brown sugar and salt. Simmer until the mixture is reduced to a sauce consistency, stirring occasionally. Soften the tortillas by microwaving them in a plastic bag or by steaming them. They should be very pliant. Place about 6 tablespoons shredded chicken or Chihuahua cheese on each tortilla. Roll the tortillas tightly and place, seam-side down, in a baking dish sprayed with nonstick cooking spray. Pour the sauce over the enchiladas and sprinkle additional shredded Chihuahua cheese over the top. Bake at 400 degrees for 10 minutes. Combine the lettuce, radishes, onion, cilantro, olive oil and vinegar in a bowl; toss to mix. Place 2 enchiladas on each of 6 plates. Top with an equal portion of slaw and some crumbled queso fresco cheese. *Yield: 6 servings*

Nutrients Per Serving: Cal 289; Prot 21 g; Carbo 35 g; Fat 8 g; 24% Cal from Fat; Sod 652 mg

Chicken Chorizo and Potato Quesadillas

Quesadilla translates as "little cheese thing," and although there is a bit of cheese in this recipe, it's the substitution of lean chicken breast for pork in this warm, pungently spiced Mexican sausage filling that provides the missing link. Try one, accompanied by our bright avocado salsa and a dab of fat-free sour cream, if desired, for breakfast, lunch, or dinner.

1/2 pound ground all-natural chicken breast
2 tablespoons chili powder
1 small bay leaf, ground in a spice grinder
1/2 teaspoon ground cinnamon
1/4 teaspoon each: dried leaf oregano, dried thyme leaves and ground marjoram
1/8 teaspoon each: ground cloves and salt
1 tablespoon cider vinegar
1 cup diced and peeled potato
2 teaspoons canola oil
1/2 cup each: diced onion and shredded reduced-fat Cheddar cheese
8 corn tortillas

The Salsa

1/2 ripe avocado
1 large garlic clove, minced
1/4 cup chopped fresh cilantro leaves
1/2 serrano chile, minced
2 teaspoons fresh lime juice
1/8 teaspoon salt
1/4 cup water

Combine the chicken, chili powder, bay leaf, cinnamon, oregano, thyme, marjoram, cloves, salt and vinegar in a bowl; mix well. Set aside. Boil the potato in lightly salted water in a saucepan until tender; drain. Heat 1 teaspoon canola oil in a nonstick skillet over medium-high heat. Sauté the chicken mixture, stirring to break up the pieces, until the chicken is almost cooked through. Add the potato, onion and remaining canola oil; cook until the potatoes begin to brown. Remove from the heat and mash the mixture. Top each of 4 tortillas with an equal amount of chicken mixture. Top with shredded Cheddar cheese, then another tortilla. Spray a griddle or nonstick skillet with nonstick cooking spray. Cook the Quesadillas over medium heat until both sides are crisp, turning once. Combine the avocado, garlic, cilantro, chile, lime juice, salt and water in a blender; purée. Cut Quesadillas into wedges and serve with avocado salsa. *Yield: 4 servings*

Nutrients Per Serving: Cal 338; Prot 21 g; Carbo 38 g; Fat 13 g; 33% Cal from Fat; Sod 304 mg

Simple Salt And Pepper * Salt and pepper are the foundational seasonings of America's (and much of the world's) food and yet we too often take them for granted. Both sea salt, in particular, and kosher salt have better flavor than ordinary table salt and none of its additives. Yes, they're more expensive but we're talking about going from eighty cents to a dollar and a half for a canister that will last you more than 6 months. Regarding pepper (and most spices), freshly ground is definitely superior to pre-ground. A whole peppercorn is full of vital oils and essences that are released (and begin to dissipate) as soon as it is ground. Fresh means better flavor.

Chicken Tamale Soup

Tamales are an old food and the first ones, which date from pre-Columbian times, were probably little more than bits of meat or vegetables surrounded by a ground corn and water paste, then wrapped in a cornhusk or banana leaf. These early tamales were buried underground on a bed of coals to be steamed like a luau pig - except for the fact that there were no pigs until the Spaniards arrived with their lard-on-legs companions and put pork and pork fat into the tamale equation. Our new generation of tamales substitutes light butter for lard, poultry for pork, and foil for corn husks. The butter and poultry give us a tasty, lower fat tamale and the foil makes them easier to produce. For you purists, we would argue that early native peoples used husks and leaves because that's what was available. And, if they had had aluminum foil, they would have used it! The tamale recipe doubles and triples easily. They also freeze well (already wrapped), so make extras for future use.

1 1/2 cups masa harina de maiz
1/4 teaspoon salt
3/4 cup warm chicken stock
3 tablespoons light butter, softened
6 ounces boneless, skinless chicken or turkey breast, shredded
1/4 cup red or green salsa (commercial or homemade)
1/2 cup diced carrot
1/2 cup diced onion
1/4 teaspoon dried leaf oregano
1/2 teaspoon ground cumin
1 garlic clove, minced
3 cups chicken stock
1/2 cup undrained diced tomatoes
1/4 cup tomato purée
1/4 cup diced zucchini
1/2 cup corn kernels
1/2 cup chick-peas (garbanzo beans)
1/2 teaspoon adobo paste from canned chipotle chiles
1/4 cup chopped fresh cilantro leaves
3 tablespoons crumbled queso fresco or feta cheese
4 lime wedges

Combine the masa harina, salt and 3/4 cup stock in a large bowl. Whip the butter in a mixing bowl with an electric mixer until fluffy. Mix the butter into the masa dough. Spread a 2 1/2 x 4-inch rectangle of masa mixture onto an 8 x 10-inch piece of foil. Mix the chicken and salsa in a bowl. Place 2 tablespoons of the chicken mixture onto the 4-inch length of the masa dough. Using the foil as a guide, fold the tamale lengthwise, shaping the packet with your fingertips, until the filling is completely enclosed. Fold the foil to seal the tamale, first along the long side, then folding in the ends to form a packet. You should have enough filling for 8 tamales. Steam the tamales in a steamer set over boiling water for 1 1/2 hours.

Heat a 3-quart saucepan over medium heat. Spray the pan with nonstick cooking spray; add the carrot and onion. Cook, covered, until the onion is soft, stirring occasionally. Add the oregano, cumin and garlic; sauté for a few minutes. Add 3 cups stock and bring the mixture to a simmer; cook for 15 minutes. Add the tomato, tomato purée, zucchini, corn, chick-peas and adobo paste; simmer for 10 minutes. Unwrap the tamales and place 2 in each of 4 large wide-bottom soup bowls. Ladle some soup over the tamales. Garnish with cilantro, queso fresco cheese and a squeeze of lime juice. *Yield: 4 servings*

Nutrients Per Serving: Cal 416; Prot 22 g; Carbo 65 g; Fat 10 g; 21% Cal from Fat; Sod 1069 mg

Moo Shu Chicken Crêpes

We think of crêpes as a French invention, but the tradition of rolling savory fillings into thin pancakes occurs in several other cultures as well. The use of soy milk in this recipe, in addition to enhancing it nutritionally, makes it a dairy-free dish, common with Asian food.

12 ounces boneless, skinless all-natural chicken breasts
1/4 teaspoon salt
1/2 cup minced onion
3 garlic cloves, minced
2 tablespoons ketchup
3 tablespoons commercial teriyaki glaze (we like Kikkoman brand)
3/4 cup rice or wheat flour
3/4 cup soy milk
1 egg
1/4 teaspoon baking powder
1/8 teaspoon salt
2 teaspoons sesame seeds
2 teaspoons minced fresh chives
1/4 cup all-fruit apricot preserves
2 tablespoons hoisin sauce
2 tablespoons light soy sauce
1 tablespoon rice vinegar
1 tablespoon brown sugar
1 teaspoon Asian chile paste
1 teaspoon roasted sesame oil
2 cups shredded cabbage
1 cup shredded carrot

Combine the chicken, salt and enough water to cover in a 3-quart saucepan over medium heat. Simmer until the chicken is cooked through. Drain, reserving 3/4 cup of the cooking liquid. Shred the chicken and set aside. Spray a nonstick heavy skillet with nonstick cooking spray. Add the onion and garlic and sauté over medium heat until the onion begins to soften. Add the reserved cooking liquid, chicken, ketchup and teriyaki glaze. Simmer until liquid has reduced and mixture is moist, but not wet. Combine the rice flour, soy milk, egg, baking powder, salt, sesame seeds and chives in a mixing bowl. Beat on medium speed until mixed. Spray a 6-inch nonstick skillet with nonstick cooking spray. Pour just enough crêpe batter into the skillet to coat the bottom. Cook over medium heat until the edges begin to brown. Loosen the crêpe and slide it onto a flat plate. Invert the skillet over the plate, then carefully turn the skillet and plate over so that the crêpe falls back into the skillet with the uncooked side down. Cook for 15 to 20 seconds, slide the crêpe onto a plate, cover and keep warm. Repeat the process until all the crêpe batter has been used. Combine the preserves, hoisin sauce, soy sauce, rice vinegar, brown sugar, chile paste and sesame oil in a saucepan over medium-low heat. Cook until the mixture is hot, stirring occasionally. Remove from the heat and cool to room temperature. Place 1 warm crêpe on a flat surface. Spoon some of the chicken mixture in the center of the crêpe. Roll the crêpe, completely enclosing the filling. Serve the crêpes topped with cabbage and carrot slaw and accompany the dish with a bowl of dipping sauce. *Yield 6 servings*

Nutrients Per Serving: Cal 260; Prot 16 g; Carbo 38 g; Fat 4 g; 15% Cal from Fat; Sod 752 mg

Buffalo Hot Wings Sandwich

The city of Buffalo, N.Y., may be known to some for its football team and to others as the gateway to Niagara Falls. But, for most people, Buffalo will always be famous as the "city of hot wings." Some long-forgotten tavern owner sloshed hot sauce all over a part of the chicken that nobody ate, cooked it up, dipped it into bleu cheese dressing, and created a national phenomenon. Today, hot wings are a multi-million dollar business. Here's our version, with the flavor, but without the fat.

3 tablespoons hot pepper sauce, such as Tabasco sauce
3 tablespoons light butter, melted
1 teaspoon dried leaf oregano
1 teaspoon dried basil leaves
1/2 teaspoon garlic powder
1 tablespoon paprika
1/2 teaspoon salt
1/4 teaspoon black pepper
4 (4-ounce) boneless, skinless all-natural chicken breasts
2 teaspoons canola oil
4 whole wheat buns, split
4 leaves iceberg lettuce
8 tomato slices
1/2 cup reduced-fat Bleu Cheese Salad Dressing (Page 40)

Combine the pepper sauce, butter, oregano, basil, garlic powder, paprika, salt and pepper in a bowl; mix well. Add the chicken, turning to coat each piece, and marinate in the refrigerator for 4 to 6 hours. Drain, reserving about 1 tablespoon of the marinade. Pat the chicken dry with paper towels. Heat the canola oil in a covered cast-iron skillet over medium heat. Add the chicken and sauté, covered, removing the lid only to turn the chicken. Drizzle the reserved marinade over the chicken for the final 2 minutes of cooking. Serve hot on buns with lettuce, tomato and bleu cheese dressing. *Yield: 4 servings*

Nutrients Per Serving: Cal 314; Prot 30 g; Carbo 28 g; Fat 10 g; 29% Cal from Fat; Sod 1040 mg

brilliant broccoli

Cruciferous or brassica vegetables include broccoli, cauliflower, cabbage, brussels sprouts, collards and kale, all part of the cabbage family. All of these vegetables contain sulforaphane and isothiocynates, which trigger your immune system to help fight off cancer. Preliminary studies suggest that in order to cut the risk of cancer in half, the average person would need to eat about two pounds of broccoli or similar vegetables per week. However, the concentration of sulforaphane is much higher in broccoli sprouts than in mature broccoli, and studies are being done to verify whether a person can achieve the same reduction in risk by eating just over an ounce of broccoli sprouts per week. Caution: sulforaphane and dietary consumption of cruciferous vegetables can interact with drug detoxifying enzymes. Individuals taking these drugs should consult their doctor before taking sulforaphane or broccoli-sprout extracts.

King Ranch Casserole

The King Ranch, in South Texas, is the largest cattle ranch in the largest cattle ranching state in the country. This casserole, which was supposedly invented there, actually harks back to the chilaquiles tortilla casseroles from Old Mexico. (Check the index for other chilaquiles recipes in this book.) Make our version with as many homemade or commercial ingredients as time and your conscience will allow. We are particularly partial to fresh green chiles. Serve this casserole with pinto beans and a green salad for some of the tastiest vittles your favorite cowpokes have ever eaten.

8 corn tortillas, sliced into 1/2-inch strips
1/2 cup diced onion
1/2 cup sliced mushrooms
1/2 cup mild red salsa
1/2 cup mild green salsa
1 cup diced tomato, drained
1 1/2 teaspoons chili powder
12 ounces boneless, skinless all-natural chicken breasts, cubed
1 cup chicken stock
2 New Mexico green chiles, roasted, peeled, seeded, diced, or 1 small poblano chile, or 1 (4-ounce) can diced green chiles, drained and rinsed
3/4 cup evaporated skim milk
2 teaspoons cornstarch
1 ounce reduced-fat cream cheese
1 ounce reduced-fat processed cheese, such as Velveeta light
3 tablespoons shredded reduced-fat Cheddar cheese
4 green onions, minced
2 tablespoons chopped fresh cilantro leaves

Allow the tortillas to become stale by leaving them uncovered for 8 hours or overnight or bake on a baking sheet at 300 degrees until stiff, but not crisp. Spray a heavy, covered soup pot with nonstick cooking spray. Add the onion and mushrooms and sauté over medium heat until the vegetables are soft. Add the red and green salsas, tomato, chili powder, chicken, chicken stock and chiles; simmer for 5 minutes. Add the tortilla strips and continue cooking until the mixture thickens and the tortillas begin to soften. Whisk the milk and cornstarch in a small saucepan over medium heat. Cook, stirring constantly, until the mixture thickens slightly. Add the cream cheese and processed cheese; cook until the cheese melts. Pour the cheese mixture into the chicken and vegetable mixture; mix well. Spray a casserole dish with nonstick cooking spray and pour the cheese and chicken mixture into the dish. Top with the Cheddar cheese and bake at 350 degrees until the Cheddar cheese melts and the casserole is bubbly. Serve topped with green onions and cilantro. *Yield: 4 servings*

Nutrients Per Serving: Cal 352; Prot 30 g; Carbo 44 g; Fat 7 g; 18% Cal from Fat; Sod 819 mg

Cajun-Style Oven-Fried Chicken

A big, juicy drumstick coated with Cajun spices and a crusty, crunchy crumb crust — now that's our idea of spa food! We use a free range bird that checks in at about one gram of fat per skinless breast portion and three grams of fat for each dark meat portion. You can use commercially prepared bread crumbs, but homemade whole wheat crumbs will give better color, texture, and nutrition. Simply dry some slices of whole wheat bread in a 275-degree oven until they are very crisp; then grind them in a food processor. Accompany your chicken with Roasted Garlic Mashed Potatoes with Cream Gravy (Page 76) and a green vegetable and you've got the makings of a Southern spa Sunday supper.

1 (3-pound) all-natural chicken, skinned
2 cups buttermilk
1 tablespoon hot pepper sauce
1 1/2 cups flour
2 tablespoons blackening seasoning
2 egg whites
2 tablespoons fat-free plain yogurt
2 cups dried whole wheat bread crumbs
1 cup cornmeal
1/2 teaspoon dried leaf oregano
1/2 teaspoon salt
Freshly ground black pepper to taste

Cut the chicken into 6 pieces - 2 breasts, 2 thighs and 2 legs. Freeze the remaining parts for stock. Combine the buttermilk and hot pepper sauce in a large sealable plastic bag. Add the chicken and turn to coat all the pieces. Marinate in the refrigerator for 6 hours or overnight. Drain, discarding the marinade, and pat the chicken pieces dry with paper towels. Combine the flour and blackening seasoning in a bowl. Beat the egg whites in a mixing bowl until frothy. Add the yogurt and beat well. Combine the bread crumbs, cornmeal, oregano, salt and pepper in a bowl; mix well. Dip the chicken pieces first into the flour mixture, then the egg white mixture, then the bread crumbs. Spray the coated chicken with nonstick cooking spray and arrange in a single layer on a baking sheet. Bake at 375 degrees for 35 to 40 minutes, turning after about 20 minutes. *Yield: 6 servings*

Nutrients Per Serving: Cal 429; Prot 35 g; Carbo 52 g; Fat 9 g; 19% Cal from Fat; Sod 980 mg

chefstip

Let's Talk Turkey * Most major grocery stores now offer fresh, all-natural, minimally processed birds. If you can get organic, even better. In any case, you want to avoid birds that have been injected with saline solutions and vegetable oils. Today's birds have been carefully bred for tenderness. They don't (nor do you) need extra salt and fat. All of the poultry we use at the resort has been free-ranged, given no antibiotics or growth hormones, and fed only grain containing no animal by-products. Similar products are available to you: look for them; ask for them; become a label reader.

Thanksgiving Turkey with Fat-Free Gravy and Corn Bread Stuffing

One of the things we like most about the holidays is that they never change. In a world where products are often obsolete before they reach the end of the assembly line, where global communications zoom around the planet at the speed of light (or at least satellite), where the ability, the necessity, even the urgency to change has never been greater, days like Thanksgiving resurface with welcome predictability to reground us in a ritual. They give us a familiar, familial piece of terra firma on which to plant our feet (or put them up) out of the maelstrom of modern life. Of course, there's always the matter of the food and certainly no other holiday is so synonymous with food as Thanksgiving. Not just food in general, but specific fare — turkey and dressing, potatoes white and sweet, cranberry sauce, and pumpkin pie. And more. Lots more, because more is what Thanksgiving is all about. Somewhere down the road the line between abundance and overindulgence has gotten a little blurred. And this is further complicated by the fact that those of us who are prone to go overboard now know enough about nutrition to know exactly what we've done to ourselves. Where amnesty used to lie, now lurks angst. With just a little judicious tinkering, however, we believe you can keep both the spirit and the substance of your old Thanksgiving just the way it always was, and just the way you hope it will always be. Here's our recipe for turkey, gravy, and dressing to get you on that "new old" road again. In the end, you'll feel better about yourself, and most likely, just plain feel better. For similar treatments with potatoes and pies, check the listings in the index of this book.

1 (12-pound) fresh all-natural turkey, with parts
Salt and freshly ground black pepper to taste
2 medium carrots, chopped
2 ribs celery, chopped
1 medium onion, chopped
2 garlic cloves, chopped
6 cups beef stock
6 cups chicken stock
2 bay leaves
1 teaspoon dried thyme leaves
8 parsley stems
1/2 cup flour

Remove and reserve all parts from the turkey. You'll want the heart, giblets and neck; discard the liver. Rinse the turkey inside and out; pat dry. Season liberally inside and out with salt and pepper. Cut the wing tips — first joint — from the bird and reserve. Cut a slit entirely through the space that runs between the 2 large bones in the second joint of each wing with a chef's knife. Fold a 3-foot piece of all-cotton string in half, then poke the closed loop through one of the slits from the inside of the wing to the outside. Bring the open ends of the string up over the wing and through the loop created by the closed end on the opposite side. Cinch the string tightly, then bring the string across the breast and poke the open ends through the slit on the opposing wing, inside to outside. Loop the string over the second wing and tie it off on itself, drawing both wings up close to the body. Cross the turkey's legs at the ankles and use a 2-foot length of all-cotton string to secure them. Spray the turkey lightly with nonstick cooking spray. Place on a roasting rack set over a roasting pan. Roast at 450 degrees for 10 minutes. Reduce the temperature to 325 degrees and roast for 15 to 18 minutes per pound. Remove the turkey to a large platter, taking care to pour all juices into the roasting pan. Cover the turkey with a foil tent. Pour all the juices from the roasting pan into a large bowl. Add 1 cup of the chicken stock to the pan. Scrape up all the browned bits with a wooden spoon and add to the bowl. Place the bowl in the freezer until the fat congeals on the top of the liquid, about 15 minutes. Remove from the freezer; skim and discard the fat. Strain the remaining liquid into a bowl for use in the gravy. Add any accumulated juices from the resting turkey to the bowl.

While the turkey is roasting, heat a cast-iron skillet over medium-high heat. Spray the skillet with nonstick cooking spray and add the neck, giblets, heart and wing tips. Cook until the turkey parts are browned. Remove to a large soup pot. Add carrots, celery, onion and garlic to the skillet. Cook until the onion begins to brown. Add the vegetables to the soup pot. Pour about 1 cup of the chicken stock into the skillet. Cook, stirring with a wooden spoon, until all the brown bits are incorporated; pour into the soup pot. Add the remaining chicken and beef stock, bay leaves, thyme and parsley stems to the pot. Bring to a boil, then reduce to a simmer and cook, skimming as needed, for 2 hours. Strain the liquid into a large saucepan over medium heat. Press on the solids to extract all the juices; discard the solids. Set aside 1 cup of the stock. You should have about 7 cups of remaining stock. If you have more, bring to a boil and reduce. Add the bowl of deglazed juices and any accumulated juices from the resting turkey. Bring the mixture to a simmer. Whisk the flour into the reserved cup of stock until no lumps are visible. Pour into the simmering stock, whisking constantly. Cook, stirring, until the gravy thickens. Taste and adjust the seasonings as needed. *Yield: 16 servings*

Nutrients Per Serving: Cal 325; Prot 51 g; Carbo 7 g; Fat 9 g; 25% Cal from Fat; Sod 623 mg

The Corn Bread Stuffing

2 cups diced onions
1 cup diced celery
2 garlic cloves, minced
1 cup diced mushrooms
6 cups day-old corn bread, broken up, or 1 package of commercial unseasoned corn bread stuffing
1/2 cup chopped fresh parsley
1/8 teaspoon cayenne pepper
1/2 teaspoon black pepper
2 tablespoons minced fresh sage, or 1 tablespoon dried sage
1 tablespoon minced fresh thyme, or 1/2 tablespoon dried thyme
1 teaspoon garlic powder
1 teaspoon onion powder
3/4 teaspoon salt
1/2 cup chopped pecans
1 1/2 to 2 1/2 cups chicken stock
2 to 3 egg whites (optional)

Heat a heavy covered skillet over medium heat. Spray the skillet with nonstick cooking spray. Add the onions, celery, garlic and mushrooms. Sauté gently until the vegetables begin to soften. Combine the vegetables, corn bread, parsley, cayenne pepper, black pepper, sage, thyme, garlic powder, onion powder, salt and pecans in a large bowl; mix well. Add stock, a little at a time, stirring until the mixture is moist but not wet. For a more solid or bound stuffing, add the egg whites. Spray a baking dish with nonstick cooking spray. Add the stuffing mixture and bake at 350 degrees for 30 to 40 minutes. Moisten with additional stock as needed. *Yield: 12 servings*

Nutrients Per Serving: Cal 187; Prot 5 g; Carbo 26 g; Fat 8 g; 36% Cal from Fat; Sod 628 mg

Duck Breast À l'Orange with Rutabaga Mashers

Fast, low-fat and French! Boneless skinless duck breast has less fat than most commercial chicken breasts, and more upscale grocery stores are beginning to carry them - you'll need to remove the skin. The other good news is that our version of this provincial classic, which normally uses the whole bird, can be ready and on the table in 20 minutes. The rutabaga and potato accompaniment pairs beautifully with the duck and, as an added virtue, fills your daily rutabaga requirement in a single serving.

4 (4-ounce) boneless, skinless duck breasts
Salt and freshly ground black pepper to taste
1 1/2 teaspoons canola oil
1/4 cup minced shallots
1 1/2 tablespoons slivered orange zest
2 teaspoons slivered grapefruit zest
2 cups beef or duck stock, reduced to 1 1/4 cups
3/4 cup orange juice
1/4 cup grapefruit juice
1/3 cup orange marmalade
1 tablespoon sherry vinegar
2 tablespoons orange liqueur (like Curaçao)
1 (4-ounce) can mandarin orange segments, drained

Season the duck with salt and pepper. Heat the canola oil in a heavy covered skillet over medium-high heat. Add the duck and sauté until brown and cooked to medium-rare or medium stage. Add the shallots for the final minute of cooking. Blanch the orange and grapefruit zest in boiling water in a small saucepan for 1 minute; drain. Remove the duck to a plate and keep warm. Add the orange and grapefruit zest, stock, orange juice, grapefruit juice, marmalade, vinegar, and orange liqueur to the skillet. Cook, stirring with a wooden spoon, until the brown bits are incorporated. Continue cooking until the sauce is reduced and thickens slightly. Add the mandarin oranges and accumulated juices from the duck. Cook until heated through. *Yield: 4 servings*

The Rutabaga Mashers

1 1/2 cups cubed, peeled potatoes
1 1/2 cups cubed, peeled rutabagas
4 teaspoons light butter
3 tablespoons warm skim milk
Salt and freshly ground black pepper to taste
2 tablespoons chopped fresh parsley

Combine the potatoes and rutabagas in a large saucepan over high heat. Add water to cover. Boil until the vegetables are soft; drain. Combine the potatoes, rutabagas, butter, milk, salt, pepper and parsley in a large mixing bowl. Whip with an electric mixer on low speed until the mixture is smooth. *Yield: 4 servings*

Nutrients Per Serving: Cal 368; Prot 28 g; Carbo 52 g; Fat 6 g; 15% Cal from Fat; Sod 473 mg

Duck Breast with Fennel, Port and Cranberries on Roasted Butternut Squash Purée

Boneless, skinless duck breast makes for a great, super-lean red meat option, particularly in the fall with its natural affinity for the fruits and vegetables of the season. And it is increasingly available in American grocery stores, although you might have to remove the skin. This dish is a holiday favorite at the resort and a great way to use up that leftover Thanksgiving cranberry sauce! Sear the breast medium-rare to medium (still pink) for the juiciest, most flavorful results.

1 1/2 cups each: ruby port and cranberry juice
1 cup beef stock
2 teaspoons ground fennel seeds
1 teaspoon black pepper
1 teaspoon ground coriander seeds
1/8 teaspoon salt
4 boneless skinless duck breasts
2 teaspoons canola oil
1/4 cup minced shallots
1 cup whole cranberry sauce

Combine the port, cranberry juice and stock in a saucepan over high heat. Cook until the liquid is reduced to 1 cup. Cool and reserve. Combine the spices and rub the spice mixture into the duck breasts. Heat the canola oil in a heavy skillet over medium-high heat. Add the duck and sear on both sides until medium-rare. Remove the duck and keep warm. Add the shallots to the skillet and sauté for 30 seconds. Add the port mixture, cranberry sauce and any accumulated juices from the duck to the skillet. Stir with a wooden spoon to incorporate the brown bits and cook over medium-high heat until the mixture is reduced and slightly thickened. *Yield: 4 servings*

The Roasted Butternut Squash Purée

1 pound peeled and cubed butternut squash
Salt and freshly ground black pepper to taste
2 tablespoons light butter
1/2 cup orange juice
1/4 teaspoon each: ground cinnamon and ground nutmeg
1/8 teaspoon each: ground cloves and cayenne pepper

Spray the squash lightly with nonstick cooking spray and arrange in a single layer on a baking sheet. Roast at 350 degrees for 35 minutes. Combine the roasted squash, butter, orange juice, cinnamon, nutmeg, cloves and cayenne pepper in a food processor; purée. Divide the purée among 4 plates, fan sliced duck breast over the top and drizzle the sauce over all. *Yield: 4 servings*

Nutrients Per Serving: Cal 549; Prot 29 g; Carbo 70 g; Fat 8 g; 13% Cal from Fat; Sod 398 mg

chefstip

Time And Temperature * With the cooking of lean foods in a lean fashion, there is a definite window between done and dry. We want our food to be properly cooked, for reasons of safety and taste, but not over-cooked, which usually results in a dry, tough and tasteless product. One very good and dependable way to judge "doneness" is by reading the internal temperature with a thermometer. A simple "stick-pin" meat thermometer, or one of the digital varieties, inserted into the center of your roast, chicken, steak or turkey, will tell you when it is done to your liking. The thermometer ususally comes with a chart that delineates the proper finished temperatures.

Stuffed Quail with Bourbon and Blackstrap Sauce

Doubtless we could have worked something out with this recipe that involved just one whole chicken to feed four people. But there's something especially appealing about each person having his or her own elegant little bird. And, it's a perfectly sized serving when you add the stuffing. Many large-city grocery stores now carry quail in their frozen food department, and a few of them even offer them fresh.

1 (4-ounce) boneless, skinless all-natural chicken breast, diced
1 tablespoon minced dried fruit
2 tablespoons dried coarse whole wheat bread crumbs
1 tablespoon each: chopped toasted pecans and minced onion
1 garlic clove, minced
1 teaspoon chopped fresh parsley
1 teaspoon minced fresh sage, or 1/2 teaspoon dried sage
1/8 teaspoon each: salt and black pepper
1 1/2 tablespoons egg substitute
4 semi-boneless quail
Salt and freshly ground black pepper to taste
2 tablespoons bourbon
1 1/4 cups strong chicken stock
1 tablespoon flour
4 teaspoons blackstrap molasses

Pulse the chicken meat in a food processor until coarsely ground. Soak the dried fruit in hot water in a cup for 20 minutes; drain. Combine the chicken, dried fruit, bread crumbs, pecans, onion, garlic, parsley, sage, salt, pepper and egg substitute in a bowl; mix well. Season the quail with salt and pepper, then stuff with the chicken mixture. Arrange the birds in a single layer in a small roasting pan, making sure they do not touch each other. Roast at 450 degrees for 15 to 20 minutes. Remove from the oven. Transfer the birds to a plate and cover to keep warm. Combine the bourbon, stock and flour in a bowl and mix well. Place the roasting pan over medium-high heat, add the bourbon mixture and stir with a wooden spoon to incorporate all the brown bits. Add the molasses and any accumulated juices from the quail. Cook until the mixture is reduced and slightly thickened. Pool some sauce on each of 4 plates, top with a quail and serve immediately. *Yield: 4 servings*

Nutrients Per Serving: Cal 226; Prot 27 g; Carbo 9 g; Fat 7 g; 27% Cal from Fat; Sod 372 mg

got mulch?

Why do some summer gardens look better than others? Mulch, mulch and more mulch! Mulch is the key to a successful warm season garden. Not only does it help to conserve water, it also keeps soil temperatures much lower, sometimes as much as 20 degrees. When applying mulch, it is a good idea to work in a little organic fertilizer around the root zone of the plants and then add a half-inch or more of compost before adding the mulch. Never fertilize plants that are too dry. Water them first and then apply fertilizers. The best mulch is shredded native, mostly cedar and oak trimmings which allow water and air to enter the soil. Shredded native mulch is locally available and does not wash away or pack too densely. A three to four-inch layer is adequate for most plantings. Also, when you mow, be sure to leave the grass clippings on the lawn. The clippings act as mulch to retain moisture and add valuable nutrients.

GARDENING

Spicy Barbecue Quail on White Beans and Spinach

One of the very best ways to invent your own secret barbecue sauce is to start with someone else's secret barbecue sauce. Just purchase your favorite commercial variety and start by adding a little fruit juice, some sweetener — molasses is always good — some seasonings, and a little dark beer or distilled spirits. Before you know it, you'll be an expert and have your own closely guarded formula. Mike Conner, our sous chef and resident barbecue guru, developed this particular sweet and sassy and not-so-secret-now sauce. It's a perfect complement to the rich, smoky flavor of the quail in this delicious one-dish meal. You may substitute chicken breast for the quail, if you like, but these small game birds (now available frozen in many grocery stores) do lend something special to the finished presentation.

	Grated zest and juice of 1 orange
1	**tablespoon teriyaki glaze**
2	**tablespoons bourbon**
1	**tablespoon molasses**
2	**garlic cloves, minced**
3/4	**cup commercial barbecue sauce**
2	**strips all-natural, nitrate-free bacon**
1	**teaspoon olive oil**
1/2	**cup diced onion**
1/4	**cup diced carrot**
1/4	**cup diced celery**
1	**tablespoon diced red bell pepper**
1	**garlic clove, minced**
1	**cup chicken stock**
1/8	**teaspoon salt**
1/8	**teaspoon paprika**
1/8	**teaspoon black pepper**
1/8	**teaspoon garlic powder**
6	**semi-boneless quail, split**
8	**ounces spinach leaves, rinsed and drained**
2	**cups cooked white beans, drained**

Combine the orange zest, juice, teriyaki glaze, bourbon, molasses, garlic and barbecue sauce in a saucepan over medium heat; simmer for 5 minutes. Remove from the heat and set aside. Cook the bacon in a heavy skillet over medium-high heat until tender-crisp. Remove from the skillet, blot dry, crumble and set aside. Discard the bacon grease and add the olive oil, onion, carrot, celery and bell pepper to the skillet. Sauté over medium heat for 2 to 3 minutes. Add the garlic and stock. Cook over high heat until the liquid is reduced by half. Remove from the heat and set aside. Combine the salt, paprika, pepper and garlic powder in a bowl. Rub the spice mixture over the quail. Grill the quail over hot coals until cooked through. Spray a heavy skillet with nonstick cooking spray. Add the spinach and sauté quickly over medium heat, just until wilted. Add the bacon, beans and reserved vegetable mixture; stir to combine. Taste and adjust the seasonings as necessary. Cut the quail into halves lengthwise. Portion the spinach-bean mixture into 4 wide-bottom soup bowls. Top with 3 quail halves. Drizzle barbecue sauce over each serving. You will have extra sauce to save for another meal. *Yield: 4 servings*

Nutrients Per Serving: Cal 457; Prot 43 g; Carbo 43 g; Fat 11 g; 22% Cal from Fat; Sod 924 mg

seafood

seafood

seafood

Linguini all' Amatriciana with Clams, Pg.131

seafood

Candied Catfish with Pecans

Caution! Sweet, spicy, crunchy catfish is addictive. The Grape Nuts cereal helps to hold down the fat grams, but still contributes to the nutty texture of the topping. Try this nut-cereal mixture scattered over salads, too.

1 teaspoon egg white
1 tablespoon sugar
1/4 teaspoon salt
1/4 cup chopped pecans
1/4 cup Grape Nuts cereal
4 (4-ounce) skinless catfish fillets
Salt and freshly ground black pepper to taste
1 teaspoon canola oil
4 green onions, cut into 1-inch lengths
Juice of 1 lemon
1 tablespoon water
2 tablespoons brown sugar
1/2 teaspoon Louisiana hot sauce

Combine the egg white, sugar and salt in a bowl. Add the pecans and Grape Nuts; toss to coat. Spray a baking sheet with nonstick cooking spray and spread the nut mixture on the baking sheet. Bake at 275 degrees for 45 minutes, turning the mixture every 15 minutes. Remove from the oven and cool. Season the catfish with salt and pepper. Heat the canola oil in a nonstick skillet, spray the fish lightly with nonstick cooking spray and sear on both sides over medium-high heat. When the fish is almost cooked, remove from the skillet; set aside, cover and keep warm. Add the green onions to the skillet and stir-fry for 10 seconds. Add the lemon juice and water; stir with a wooden spoon until all the brown bits are incorporated. Add the brown sugar and hot sauce; mix well. Add the catfish along with the pecan mixture; heat until cooked through. *Yield: 4 servings*

Nutrients Per Serving: Cal 228; Prot 14 g; Carbo 12 g; Fat 9 g; 36% Cal from Fat; Sod 285 mg

Bayou Teche Redfish

This recipe offers a nostalgic nod to those wonderfully rich and decadent fish dishes so prominent on the menus and in the cookbooks of legendary New Orleans stalwarts like Brennan's and Galatoire's in the Sixties and Seventies. Those were the days before anyone had ever heard of cholesterol — or cared. Times and sensibilities are different now, but we still love those flavors. Our updated version sautés the fish in just a touch of monounsaturated canola oil instead of clarified butter. It gets its silken texture from fat-free cream cheese instead of reduced heavy cream. With a bit of crispy chemical-free bacon, fresh oysters, tomatoes, savory seasonings, and Madeira thrown in for good measure, we can recapture a lot of the goodness without the "oh my goodness gracious!"

4 (4-ounce) skinless redfish fillets or other firm-fleshed white fish
Salt and freshly ground black pepper to taste
4 teaspoons canola oil
4 garlic cloves, minced
1/2 cup minced onion
12 fresh oysters, shucked
1/2 cup diced, seeded and peeled tomato
1/4 cup crumbled cooked all-natural, nitrate-free bacon
1/2 teaspoon dried thyme leaves
1/4 cup Madeira
1 cup seafood stock or clam juice
2 ounces fat-free cream cheese
4 teaspoons chopped fresh parsley

Season the fish with salt and pepper. Heat the canola oil in a nonstick skillet. Spray the fish with nonstick cooking spray and sauté just until done. Remove the fish from the skillet; set aside, cover and keep warm. Add the garlic, onion, oysters, tomato, bacon and thyme; mix well. Cook for 1 minute. Deglaze the pan with Madeira and stock. Add the cream cheese and cook until it melts. Return the fish to the pan until heated through. Serve garnished with parsley. *Yield: 4 servings*

Nutrients Per Serving: Cal 285; Prot 28 g; Carbo 9 g; Fat 13 g; 43% Cal from Fat; Sod 350 mg

chefstip

A Proper Purée * A good blender can certainly do an adequate, and even occasionally a superior job, but day-in-and-day-out, it's hard to beat a food processor for puréeing. There are a couple of points to remember. Hot liquids expand dramatically with Vesuviual-like consequences when processed, so cool your liquids before puréeing or add lesser amounts – no more than half the container capacity - before gingerly pulsing the processor on and off until you can safely let it run. (This same approach also applies to blenders.) Another tip is to add liquid only as needed to get the job done. Most solid foods require some liquid to purée successfully, but too much liquid allows them to "swim" and not purée. And finally, occasionally pulsing the processor on and off after it has been running for a while will sometimes break up those last stubborn solids.

Apple and Ginger Glazed Salmon

For our money, the mighty salmon of the Pacific Northwest ranks as the premier eating fish in America. Prized as much for its versatility as for its flavor, the salmon's rich, dense, coral-colored meat lends itself readily to almost any preparation from sashimi to slow smoking over hardwood. You can coat it with Cajun spices and grill it, or poach it in a fumet and chill it. Try roasting it with wild mushrooms or, as we've done here, simply sear it and serve it with crunchy apple and a jazzy Asian pan glaze.

1/2 cup apple jelly, warmed to a liquid
1 small garlic clove, minced
Grated zest and juice of 1 lemon
1 tablespoon prepared horseradish
1/4 cup Ginger Sauce (Page 126)
4 (4-ounce) boneless, skinless salmon fillets
Salt and freshly ground black pepper to taste
2 teaspoons canola oil
1 large cooking apple, cored and sliced (such as Rome, Jonathan or Macintosh)

Combine the jelly, garlic, lemon zest and juice, horseradish and Ginger Sauce in a bowl; mix well. Season the salmon lightly with salt and pepper. Heat the canola oil in a nonstick skillet. Spray the salmon with nonstick cooking spray and sear just until cooked through. Add the apple slices and top with the apple-ginger glaze. Increase the heat and cook rapidly to reduce the sauce and thicken it slightly. *Yield: 4 servings*

Nutrients Per Serving: Cal 384; Prot 22 g; Carbo 48 g; Fat 11 g; 27% Cal from Fat; Sod 175 mg

snooze factor

Once you have incorporated exercise into your routine, taking time to sleep or rest is especially important because your body now requires more time to recover and recuperate in order to meet the challenges of your exercise program. If your body is not adequately rested, you will experience fatigue much more quickly during workouts, plus you'll find it takes your muscles longer to recover. Everyone has his or her own unique sleep requirements. To learn how many hours of sleep your body requires, try this simple experiment: for several days in a row, go to bed at the same time every night and see when your body naturally wakes up. Your sleep hours should become consistent. Then try to allow for this amount of rest as often as possible. Your body will thank you in the morning.

FITNESS

Blackened Salmon

Paul Prudhomme, who hails from Louisiana, is as good a regional American chef as this country has ever produced. His work has been influential in a number of ways, but the dish for which he will always be remembered is blackened redfish. Paul discovered that you could take a redfish fillet, coat it with some fairly common spices, toss it into a super-hot skillet with some clarified butter, burn the heck out of the whole thing, and it would come out tasting great! So great, in fact, that soon not only local Louisiana folk, but seemingly the entire populace of the United States could not get enough of this spicy, charred fish dish. Supply and demand, behaving as it usually does, sent redfish prices skyrocketing, and enterprising, but perhaps shortsighted, Gulf Coast commercial fishermen worked long and hard to cash in on this bonanza. So effective were their efforts that the redfish stocks in the Gulf of Mexico were depleted to a point requiring a total ban on the commercial capture of this species. Some 15 years later, the fish has still not recovered and the ban is still in effect. If you see redfish for sale in your fish market, it has been farmed, not caught in the wild. Chef Prudhomme must have been alternately delighted and dismayed at the turn of events. If there's a silver lining to this story, it's that other things besides redfish taste good blackened, too. And, you don't need all that butter to make it happen. We like salmon best, which brings its own richness to the dish and we like to grill it over coals, which is a really tasty Texas way to burn something.

1/4 cup paprika
2 teaspoons onion powder
2 teaspoons garlic powder
1/2 teaspoon cayenne pepper
1 teaspoon white pepper
1 teaspoon black pepper
1 teaspoon dried thyme leaves
1 teaspoon dried leaf oregano
2 teaspoons salt (optional)
4 (4-ounce) salmon fillets, skin removed

Combine the paprika, onion powder, garlic powder, cayenne pepper, white pepper, black pepper, thyme, oregano and salt in a medium bowl; mix thoroughly. Pat the fish fillets dry with paper towels, then dredge them in the seasonings, coating each piece thoroughly. Spray both sides of each fillet with nonstick cooking spray. Grill over hot coals, turning occasionally, until blackened and cooked through, approximately 10 minutes per inch of thickness. Serve with a lemon wedge or brush with a little melted light butter, if desired. *Yield: 4 servings*

Nutrients Per Serving: Cal 187; Prot 22 g; Carbo 4 g; Fat 9 g; 45% Cal from Fat; Sod 54 mg

Chèvre-Potato Cakes with Smoked Salmon and Yellow Tomato and Vodka Sauce

From Russia, with Love. These warm, rich, mellow potato pillows topped with coral-colored thimbles of chilled salmon are a delicious study in contrasting flavors, textures, and temperatures. Add a splash of vodka-laced tomato sauce and you have one of our favorite upscale luncheons or light suppers.

6 medium Yukon Gold potatoes
1/4 cup egg substitute
1/4 cup flour
2 ounces chèvre (soft goat cheese)
1/4 cup grated Parmesan cheese
2 tablespoons minced fresh chives
3/4 teaspoon salt
1/16 teaspoon cayenne pepper
3 tablespoons canola oil
9 ounces smoked lox-style salmon, thinly sliced into 18 pieces
2 1/2 cups Yellow Tomato and Vodka Sauce

Pierce each potato with a fork. Bake at 400 degrees for 1 hour. Remove from the oven and split with a knife; let steam-dry. Scoop out the potato flesh; discard the skins. Combine the potato, egg substitute, flour, chèvre, Parmesan cheese, chives, salt and cayenne pepper in a bowl; mix well. Shape into 18 small disks and arrange on a platter. Chill in the refrigerator until cold. Heat the canola oil in a heavy nonstick skillet over medium-high heat. Sauté the potato cakes until golden. Cook the potato cakes in 2 or 3 batches if necessary. To serve, pool 1/3 cup Yellow Tomato and Vodka Sauce in the middle of each of 6 plates. Arrange 3 potato cakes on top. Roll each salmon slice into a pinwheel roll. Arrange 1 roll on top of each potato cake. *Yield: 6 servings*

The Yellow Tomato and Vodka Sauce

1/2 cup diced onion
2 garlic cloves, minced
2 cups diced yellow tomatoes (fresh or canned)
3 tablespoons Citron vodka
1/8 teaspoon salt
1/8 teaspoon sugar
1/8 teaspoon cayenne pepper

Heat a heavy nonstick skillet sprayed with nonstick cooking spray over medium heat. Add the onion; cover and cook until onions are soft. Remove the lid and add the garlic, tomatoes, vodka, salt, sugar and cayenne pepper; mix well. Reduce the heat and simmer, uncovered, for 5 minutes. Remove the mixture to a blender or food processor and purée. *Yield: 6 servings*

Nutrients Per Serving: Cal 378; Prot 18 g; Carbo 46 g; Fat 13 g; 30% Cal from Fat; Sod 1329 mg

Coulibiac

Coulibiac is a Czarist Russian seafood classic with the traditional filling always encased in rich pie or puff pastry. The crispy, fat-free phyllo dough we have chosen makes a dandy substitution. And, speaking of substitutions, the Czar's marketing team might have come up with a more appetizing word than "groats." How about, "tasty toasted kernels of buckwheat"? Whatever you end up calling these humble whole grain nuggets, they are an essential and delicious component of the recipe. Try them cooked like rice, as a starch alternative, or as part of any number of cold weather entrées.

1 cup buckwheat groats (available in health food stores)
1 tablespoon egg white
2 1/2 cups chicken stock
1/4 cup minced onion
2 garlic cloves, minced
2 cups minced mushrooms
Salt and freshly ground black pepper to taste
2 tablespoons white wine
4 hard-cooked eggs
2 cups flaked poached salmon fillet
4 teaspoons minced fresh dillweed, or 2 teaspoons dried dillweed
6 sheets frozen phyllo dough, thawed
8 teaspoons melted light butter
1 tablespoon fresh lemon juice
1/2 cup fat-free sour cream

Toss the groats and egg white in a bowl until the groats are coated. Toast the groats in a heavy skillet over medium-high heat, stirring constantly, until the grains separate and are browned. Add to the stock in a saucepan over medium-high heat. Reduce the heat to low and cook, covered, for 12 to 15 minutes. Remove from the heat, uncover and set aside to cool. Add the onion, garlic and mushrooms to a nonstick skillet. Spray with a small amount of nonstick cooking spray and sauté over medium-high heat until the mixture is dry. Season with salt and pepper. Add the wine and cook until the mixture is dry. Remove from the heat and set aside to cool. Peel the eggs; discard the yolks and dice the whites. Place 1 sheet of phyllo dough on a clean, dry work surface with the long side facing you. Spray with nonstick cooking spray. Fold the sheet in half lengthwise. Layer the groats, mushrooms, egg whites, salmon and dillweed at one end of the dough, leaving a 1-inch border. Roll the dough once, egg roll fashion, completely enclosing the filling. Tuck in the sides after 1 roll. Continue rolling, spraying the dry dough surface with nonstick cooking spray as it is exposed. Repeat the procedure until 4 Coulibiacs are prepared. Arrange the Coulibiacs, seam side down, on a baking sheet. Bake at 375 degrees for 15 to 20 minutes or until golden. Serve hot, drizzled with melted butter, a teaspoon of lemon juice and a dollop of sour cream. *Yield: 4 servings*

Nutrients Per Serving: Cal 535; Prot 38 g; Carbo 55 g; Fat 18 g; 30% Cal from Fat; Sod 746 mg

chefstip

Save The Whales ✳ For fish entrees (and most others as well) we typically offer a four ounce portion, which we believe to be a very adequate supply of protein. We would encourage you to size similarly at home, and since fish fillets do not always come conveniently sized at four ounces, we would recommend you pare off those extra one and two ounce pieces (uncooked) and collect them in a plastic baggie in your freezer. Before you know it, you will have enough product in your collection for a ceviche, a chowder, a stew or some other equally delicious "bonus" meal.

Rice Paper Salmon

Rice papers, artfully wrought vinyl-like sheets of puréed rice, are most commonly used as the wrapping for chilled Asian spring rolls. Packages of these edible envelopes, which have an infinite shelf life, can be purchased at some upscale grocery stores or at any Asian market. The sheets come in a variety of shapes — circles, squares, triangles — and sizes. We like the 12-inch circles for most applications. In this recipe, the rice paper is used similar to the French technique of baking en papillote (in parchment paper), a technique that keeps food moist and flavorful. The difference is that in this instance the wrapper is an edible part of the dish. The accompanying Ginger Sauce is used in many recipes in FRESH. You may double or triple the sauce recipe; refrigerated it keeps practically forever.

4 (12-inch-round) pieces rice paper
2 tablespoons chopped fresh mint leaves
2 tablespoons chopped fresh basil leaves
2 tablespoons chopped fresh cilantro leaves
4 (3-ounce) skinless salmon fillets
2 cups finely shredded green cabbage
1 cup very thinly sliced red, yellow and/or green bell peppers
6 green onions, sliced
1 jalapeño chile, very thinly sliced
8 slices pink pickled ginger
4 large cooked shrimp, peeled, deveined and chilled (optional)
3/4 cup Ginger Sauce (below)

Immerse 1 sheet of rice paper into a large bowl of very hot tap water for 15 seconds, or until it is completely pliant. Remove from the water and spread it on a clean flat surface. Sprinkle 1/4 of the mint, basil and cilantro over the surface. Arrange 1 salmon fillet, skin side up, in the center. Fold the bottom of the rice paper over the fish. Fold in the sides and continue to roll and encase the salmon. Repeat the process for the remaining pieces. Spray a baking sheet lightly with nonstick cooking spray. Arrange the salmon packages, seam side down, not touching each other, on the baking sheet. Bake at 400 degrees for 12 to 15 minutes. Toss the cabbage, bell pepper, green onions and chile in a bowl. Arrange 1 salmon package in the center of each of 4 plates. Top with slaw, 2 slices of pickled ginger and 1 shrimp. Drizzle Ginger Sauce over the top. *Yield: 4 servings*

Nutrients Per Serving: Cal 312; Prot 24 g; Carbo 45 g; Fat 7 g; 20% Cal from Fat; Sod 443 mg

Ginger Sauce

1 cup light corn syrup
1/3 cup cider vinegar
2 tablespoons minced pickled ginger
2 tablespoons juice from pickled ginger
2 teaspoons Asian chile paste
1/2 teaspoon salt
2 (1/4-inch) pieces gingerroot

Whisk together the corn syrup, vinegar, pickled ginger, pickled ginger juice, chile paste, salt and gingerroot in a bowl. Chill until ready to serve. *Yield: 26 (1-tablespoon) servings*

Nutrients Per Serving: Cal 38; Prot 0 g; Carbo 10 g; Fat 0 g; 0% Cal from Fat; Sod 93 mg

Hot Sweet and Sour Snapper on Asian Slaw

It's not just for take-out anymore! Sure, the first generation of America's Chinese restaurants is still doling out a daily armada of styrofoam containers filled with egg rolls, won ton soup, fried rice, sweet and sour chicken, and the ubiquitous fortune cookie. But, in recent years, a new wave of Asian food, raucous, and even outrageous by comparison — as new generations so often are — has been clamoring for our attention. Or, maybe it is we that have been doing the clamoring, for it is said that an idea can only succeed if you are willing to receive it. In any case, where once there was only Hunan, now the culinary landscape fairly bustles with other possibilities: Chinese regional restaurants, Thai noodle bowl shops, Korean barbecue, Vietnamese seafood, and more. It's an exciting time and this is exciting food full of color, sass, and crunch. One bite of this saucy snapper dish with slaw and you will be hooked, too.

1/4 cup walnut pieces
Grated zest and juice of 1 orange
3 tablespoons all-fruit apricot preserves
1 tablespoon soy sauce
2 teaspoons Asian chile paste
3 tablespoons ketchup
2 tablespoons Ginger Sauce (Page 126)
2 teaspoons canola oil
4 (4-ounce) boneless, skinless red snapper fillets
2 tablespoons cornstarch

Arrange the walnut pieces on a baking sheet and bake at 350 degrees for 10 minutes. Remove from the oven; set aside. Combine the orange zest, orange juice, preserves, soy sauce, chile paste, ketchup and Ginger Sauce in a bowl; mix well. Heat the canola oil in a heavy nonstick skillet over medium-high heat. Dust each snapper fillet with cornstarch, then add to the canola oil. Sauté for 3 to 4 minutes, turning the fish once. Add the sauce mixture; cook until sauce reduces to a glaze. Turn the fish to coat both sides. Remove fish to a plate; cover and keep warm. Add toasted walnuts to the pan; stir to thoroughly coat the walnuts. Arrange Asian Slaw and 1 fish fillet on each of 4 plates; top with walnuts and glaze. *Yield: 4 servings*

The Asian Slaw

2 cups shredded green or napa cabbage
1 cup sliced bok choy
1/2 cup shredded carrot
1/3 cup sliced red onion
3 green onions, sliced
1/2 cup chopped fresh cilantro leaves
1/4 cup chopped fresh mint leaves
1 tablespoon roasted peanut oil
1 teaspoon roasted sesame oil
2 teaspoons rice vinegar
1 teaspoon sugar
1/2 teaspoon soy sauce
2 garlic cloves, minced

Toss the cabbage, bok choy, carrot, red onion, green onion, cilantro and mint in a large bowl. Whisk the peanut oil, sesame oil, vinegar, sugar, soy sauce and garlic in a small bowl. Pour the oil mixture over the vegetables and toss to coat the vegetables. Chill in the refrigerator until ready to serve. *Yield: 4 (1 1/4-cup) servings*

Nutrients Per Serving: Cal 268; Prot 18 g; Carbo 30 g; Fat 9 g; 29% Cal from Fat; Sod 670 mg

Jerk-Crusted Snapper with Bananas

In the Caribbean, jerk generally refers to any type of barbecued meat that has been coated in a spice mix before cooking. In this recipe we've taken the jerk spice mix and applied it as one might a blackening seasoning mix in the South to create a spicy burnt crust for the fish. To complete this tasty tropical storm of flavors, top the finished fish with cool, sweet bananas spiked up with a bit of serrano chile pepper and lime juice and accompany it with a drizzle of smacky rum-molasses glaze.

1 tablespoon black pepper
1 tablespoon coriander seeds
1 teaspoon cinnamon
1 teaspoon allspice
1 teaspoon nutmeg
1/2 teaspoon garlic powder
1/2 teaspoon onion powder
1/2 teaspoon cumin seeds
1 teaspoon dried thyme leaves
1 teaspoon salt
1/2 teaspoon ground ginger
4 (4-ounce) skinless red snapper fillets
2 teaspoons canola oil
1/4 cup dark rum
1/4 cup packed brown sugar
2 tablespoons molasses
2 tablespoons cider vinegar
1/8 teaspoon salt
3 medium slightly green bananas
1/2 serrano chile, seeded and minced
2 tablespoons chopped fresh cilantro leaves
1 tablespoon fresh lime juice
1/8 teaspoon salt

Combine the pepper, coriander, cinnamon, allspice, nutmeg, garlic powder, onion powder, cumin, thyme, salt and ginger in a spice mill and grind to a powdery consistency. Remove the spice mixture to a paper plate or piece of waxed paper. Dredge the top of the fillets in the spice mixture. Heat the canola oil in a cast-iron skillet over medium-high heat. Sear the fish, spice side down. Remove the fish and arrange, spice side up, on a baking sheet sprayed with nonstick cooking spray. Bake at 400 degrees for 5 to 8 minutes. Combine the rum, sugar, molasses, vinegar and salt in a saucepan over medium-high heat. Cook, stirring constantly, until the mixture is reduced to a syrupy glaze. Peel and dice the banana. Combine it with the chile, cilantro, lime juice and salt in a bowl; mix well. Pool some molasses glaze in the center of each of 4 plates. Top with a fish fillet and some banana salsa. *Yield: 4 servings*

Nutrients Per Serving: Cal 302; Prot 17 g; Carbo 44 g; Fat 4 g; 12% Cal from Fat; Sod 773 mg

Moroccan-Style Roasted Red Snapper

If the number of ingredients in this dish seems imposing, bear in mind that it constitutes an entire meal. Everything actually comes together quite easily with fish, potatoes, and vegetables all cooking in the same place for about the same amount of time. If you're preparing this dish for more than four people, you will probably need two ovens. The idea is to roast a sizable quantity of vegetables to pile upon the plates, and there simply isn't enough room or heat for more than the indicated amount in most home ovens. Adding additional vegetables to the tray will cause them to steam rather than roast.

1 tablespoon ground cumin seed, toasted briefly in a dry skillet
6 garlic cloves, minced
3/4 cup packed fresh parsley leaves, chopped
1/2 teaspoon salt
1/4 teaspoon pepper
Grated zest and juice of 1 large lemon
2 tablespoons olive oil divided, 2 teaspoons each
4 (4-ounce) red snapper fillets, skin scored
6 small new potatoes, sliced and blanched for 2 minutes
1 cup each: sliced carrot, sliced onion and sliced green bell pepper, seeded
1 Anaheim chile, seeded and sliced
2 medium tomatoes, cut into wedges
1 lemon, thinly sliced
Grated zest and juice of 1 orange
1 teaspoon paprika
1/2 teaspoon fennel seeds, crushed
1/2 cup hot water
8 pitted kalamata olives, cut into halves
Chopped fresh parsley

Process the the first six ingredients and 2 teaspoons olive oil in a blender to form a paste. Rub this paste onto the fleshy side of the fish. Chill for 1 hour. Toss the potatoes, carrot, onion, bell pepper, chile, tomatoes, lemon slices, orange zest, 2 teaspoons olive oil, paprika and fennel seeds in a bowl. Arrange the vegetables loosely on a baking sheet sprayed with nonstick cooking spray. Roast at 450 degrees for 25 minutes. Arrange the fish fillets on a separate baking sheet sprayed with nonstick cooking spray. Place in the oven 10 minutes after the vegetables and roast for 15 minutes. Arrange 1 fish fillet on each of 4 plates. Arrange 1/4 of the vegetables on top of each fillet. Deglaze the roasting pans with the water and orange juice, using a wooden spoon to scrape up all the brown bits. Pour the juices over the vegetables and top with 4 olive halves, 1/2 teaspoon olive oil and some chopped parsley. *Yield: 4 servings*

Nutrients Per Serving: Cal 361; Prot 23 g; Carbo 49 g; Fat 11 g; 26% Cal from Fat; Sod 507 mg

chefstip

An Avocation for the Avocado ✳ Everyone knows avocados are high in fat and everyone knows they are delicious. If you are having a love/hate affair with your favorite guacamole recipe, you may find some solace in knowing that the fat in avocados is primarily of the healthy monounsaturated variety which adds to your HDL (high density lipoprotein), the cleansing side of your cholesterol. Avocados also contain valuable antioxidants and cancer fighting phytochemicals and in moderation can be a valuable part of a healthy diet. We particularly like the Haas avocados (black, pebbled skin variety, primarily grown in California), but if you like the bright green skinned Florida avocados, note that they have about half the fat, ounce per ounce, of the Californians.

Tortilla-Crusted Gulf Snapper

Any firm-fleshed white fish fillet will substitute nicely, but if you use snapper, specify "red" or "gulf" snapper, not the less desirable western rockfish some malodorous marketing magnate misnamed "Pacific Coast Snapper." The chipotle mayonnaise, which accompanies this fish, is a nice addition. The chipotle chiles are actually smoked jalapeño chiles. They are available dried, or more commonly, canned in adobo paste. We sometimes add a dried chile to a pot of beans or use the paste from the canned version to flavor marinades and sauces. A word of caution: these little bummers are HOT! So use sparingly, gradually adjusting upwards to your own personal pain-or-pleasure level.

1/2 cup flour
2 egg whites
1 cup buttermilk
6 corn tortillas cut into paper-thin strips
4 (4-ounce) skinless red snapper fillets, no more than 1/3-inch-thick
4 teaspoons canola oil
3/4 cup Chipotle Mayonnaise

Spread the flour in a pie plate or other shallow dish. Whisk the egg whites and buttermilk in a small bowl and pour into a second shallow dish. Spread the tortilla strips in a third shallow dish. Dredge the fish first in the flour, then the egg and buttermilk mixture and then coat with tortilla strips, pressing so that the strips adhere to the fish. Spray the fillets with nonstick cooking spray. Heat the canola oil in a nonstick skillet over medium heat. Sauté the fish, turning as needed, until the tortilla strips are crisp, but not burned. *Yield: 4 servings*

Nutrients Per Serving: Cal 316; Prot 24 g; Carbo 38 g; Fat 7 g; 21% Cal from Fat; Sod 357 mg

The Chipotle Mayonnaise

1/2 cup fat-free mayonnaise
1/4 cup skim milk
1 garlic clove, minced
1/4 teaspoon ground cumin
1 teaspoon adobo paste from canned chipotle chiles
Juice of 1 lime
1 tablespoon chopped fresh cilantro leaves

Combine the mayonnaise, milk, garlic, cumin, adobo paste, lime juice and cilantro in a blender or food processor. Process for 30 seconds. *Yield: 1 cup*

Nutrients Per Serving: Cal 7; Prot 1 g; Carbo 1 g; Fat 1 g; 2% Cal from Fat; Sod 56 mg

fabulous fatty acids

Omega 3 fatty acids are essential to our diet, yet they are sadly lacking in the typical American diet. Research indicates they offer benefits for asthma, rheumatoid arthritis and menstrual cramps, enhance blood clotting and reduce blood pressure and bone loss. They have also been found to improve depression and attention deficit disorder. Experts recommend 2.2 grams of ALA (alpha linolenic acid) and .65 grams of EPA/DHA per day. There are two forms of omega 3 fatty acids, inactive and active. Flax seed, walnuts, soy, canola oil, pumpkin seeds and dark leafy greens provide an inactive form that the body can change to an active form when adequate zinc, magnesium, vitamin C and niacin are present in the diet. Fatty fish, including sardines, mackerel and salmon are excellent sources of the active forms of EPA and DHA, as are eggs from chickens fed flax seeds or marine algae. For babies, breast milk provides an essential source of active omega 3 fatty acids. Breastfed babies have been shown to have better vision and cognitive functioning. Formulas including these essential fatty acids provide comparable results.

Linguini all' Amatriciana with Clams

Bacon and clams have long been a classic combination. Here, teamed with tomatoes, wine, red pepper, garlic, fresh herbs, and a bit of grated Italian cheese, they create a dish positively bursting with flavor, but not necessarily fat. Choose a lean, all-natural bacon (the brand we use has no chemical additives and renders out at 1 1/2 grams of fat per slice).

- 4 strips all-natural bacon or lean nitrate-free pancetta
- 2 teaspoons olive oil
- 1 small onion, minced
- 2 garlic cloves, minced
- 1/4 teaspoon red pepper flakes
- 1 (28-ounce) can diced tomatoes
- 1/8 teaspoon salt
- 32 clams, scrubbed
- 1/2 cup white wine
- 1/2 cup shredded fresh basil leaves
- 12 ounces linguini, cooked according to package directions
- 1/2 cup grated Pecorino Romano cheese

Render the bacon in a heavy skillet over medium heat until tender-crisp. Remove and blot dry with paper towels; crumble and set aside. Discard the bacon drippings. Add the olive oil and onion to the skillet. Sauté until the onion begins to color. Add the garlic and red pepper; sauté for a few seconds. Add the undrained tomatoes and salt. Cook until the tomatoes are almost dry. Add the clams, wine and basil. Cover and steam for 2 minutes or until the clams open. Discard any unopened clams. Toss the mixture with hot linguini and reserved bacon in a serving bowl. Serve with grated cheese. *Yield: 4 servings*

Nutrients Per Serving: Cal 657; Prot 44 g; Carbo 65 g; Fat 11 g; 15% Cal from Fat; Sod 1005 mg

Peppered Tuna with Sherry Mustard Sauce

Few things are tastier than a peppered steak hot off the grill. Especially when it's a tuna steak! Cook it to the same degree of doneness you would a beefsteak — unless you eat your beef well done. The clean, mild flavor of the tuna coupled with the spiciness of the peppercorns and the sweet-sharp tang of the dressing are a great combination. Two ounces makes a perfectly sized first course; use four-ounce steaks for an entrée.

1/4 cup Dijon mustard
3 tablespoons honey
2 tablespoons extra virgin olive oil
2 tablespoons sherry
2 1/2 tablespoons sherry vinegar
1/2 teaspoon dry mustard
1/4 teaspoon salt
1 large garlic clove, minced
4 (4-ounce) Yellow Fin or Ahi tuna steaks
2 tablespoons coarsely ground black pepper
1/8 teaspoon salt
4 cups mixed salad greens, preferably organic

Mix the Dijon mustard, honey and 1 tablespoon of the olive oil in a bowl. Add the sherry, vinegar, dry mustard, salt and garlic; mix well. Coat the tuna steaks with pepper and salt. Grill over hot coals or pan sear using the remaining tablespoon olive oil until medium-rare. Remove from the grill or pan and slice thinly. Divide the salad greens equally among 4 plates. Fan the sliced tuna over the greens. Drizzle the mustard sauce over each serving. *Yield: 4 servings*

Nutrients Per Serving: Cal 301; Prot 29 g; Carbo 24 g; Fat 8 g; 26% Cal from Fat; Sod 641 mg

chefstip

Getting Fresh ✳ Fresh fish fillets should look, well, fresh! The flesh should be firm, slightly moist with a sort of "glow." Smell is another useful indicator: the scent should be very mild and clean, not "fishy." Whole fish should be firm, with a taut, shiny skin, the eyes should be clear, bright and not sunken. Another very good way to determine fresh fish, particularly if you're squeamish about demanding a close examination, is to buy from a reputable source – a fish market or a grocery store with a seafood department – and ask questions. When did this come in? What's your freshest fish today? Which days are the best for me to buy fish? Get to know the people behind the counter, and let them help you. In many establishments, much of the fish has been previously frozen and then thawed. This is not necessarily a sign of inferior product - if it has been done properly. Likewise, if you are not going to use fresh fish within 24 hours, you should freeze it. Thaw slowly, under refrigeration.

Grilled Tuna St. Tropez

Texas is cattle country, and we like our steak and potatoes as much as the next person. But, in the summertime, when the temperatures soar, a tuna steak and a cool, spicy Mediterranean potato salad hold a lot more appeal than the old beef and baker. If you have any leftovers, flake the tuna into bite-size pieces, add a few cherry tomatoes and a few cooked and cooled green beans for a delicious salad Niçoise.

8 new potatoes, sliced, steamed and rinsed
2 teaspoons capers, drained
8 pitted kalamata olives, chopped
2 shallots, minced
1/4 cup diced pimentos
2 anchovy fillets, chopped
2 garlic cloves, minced
2 tablespoons minced fresh parsley
1 tablespoon minced fresh mint leaves
1 1/2 tablespoons red wine vinegar
1 1/2 tablespoons extra virgin olive oil
1 teaspoon Dijon mustard
1/4 teaspoon salt
1/4 teaspoon black pepper
1/2 teaspoon sugar
1 cup canned yellow tomatoes
1 tablespoon minced fresh mint leaves
1/4 teaspoon salt
1/8 teaspoon cayenne pepper
2 teaspoons extra virgin olive oil
4 (3-ounce) Yellow Fin tuna steaks
1/2 teaspoon ground coriander
1/2 teaspoon ground fennel seeds
Salt and freshly ground black pepper to taste

Toss the potatoes, capers, olives, shallots, pimentos, anchovy, garlic, parsley and mint in a large bowl. Whisk the vinegar, olive oil, Dijon mustard, salt, pepper and sugar in a small bowl. Combine the undrained tomatoes, mint, salt, cayenne pepper and olive oil in a blender or food processor; purée. Season the tuna with coriander, fennel, salt and pepper; spray each tuna steak lightly with nonstick cooking spray. Grill over hot coals to the desired degree of doneness. Warm the tomato sauce in a saucepan over medium heat. Divide the potato salad equally among 4 plates. Top with a tuna steak and drizzle tomato sauce over each serving. *Yield: 4 servings*

Nutrients Per Serving: Cal 375; Prot 28 g; Carbo 46 g; Fat 11 g; 26% Cal from Fat; Sod 725 mg

Pan Bagnat

Throughout the French Mediterranean in general, and particularly in the city of Nice where it was born, pan bagnat — that spicy tuna sandwich on a bun — is as beloved and bragged about as any barbecue brisket sandwich in Texas or lobster roll in Maine. Every vendor has his or her special recipe. But what they all have in common is top grade tuna dressed with plenty of good olive oil and vinegar, along with olives and anchovies. No mayo here, thank you very much. It's all about the sun and the sea (and more monounsaturates for you and me), a confluence of foods and flavors, in many ways emblematic of the entire Mediterranean diet.

12 ounces solid white canned tuna, thoroughly drained
1/4 cup minced red onion
2 garlic cloves, minced
2 teaspoons minced capers
2 anchovy fillets, chopped
6 pitted kalamata olives, chopped
1 tablespoon chopped fresh parsley
1 tablespoon Dijon mustard
2 tablespoons extra virgin olive oil
1 tablespoon red wine vinegar
1 teaspoon fresh lemon juice
Salt and freshly ground black pepper to taste
8 slices fresh tomato
4 leaves green leaf lettuce
4 focaccia buns, split

Combine the tuna, onion, garlic, capers, anchovy fillets, olives, parsley, Dijon mustard, olive oil, vinegar, lemon juice, salt and pepper in a large bowl; mix well. Spread the mixture on the bottom half of each of 4 focaccia buns. Arrange 2 tomato slices and 1 lettuce leaf over each portion. Top with the remaining half focaccia and compress the sandwich by hand to more solidly mold it. *Yield: 4 servings*

Nutrients Per Serving: Cal 221; Prot 28 g; Carbo 50 g; Fat 13 g; 53% Cal from Fat; Sod 1240 mg

lovely lemon verbena

Many herbs have a hint of lemon flavor, but lemon verbena really packs a lemony punch. Native to Chile, it is a deciduous shrub that grows 10 to 15 feet tall. In most of the deep South it is semi-hardy and freezes to the ground in winter. If mulched heavily and not over-watered, it usually returns in spring. Northern gardeners may want to grow it in a large pot and take it indoors for the winter. Widely used in Europe for perfumes in the 18th century, lemon verbena makes a soothing and relaxing bedtime tea. It has also been used to treat congestion and to soothe indigestion. The leaves contain vitamin C and are said to boost the immune system. The fresh leaves are delicious when added to pineapple juice, orange juice or white wine and then refrigerated overnight. Lemon verbena is a favorite for use in herbal vinegars, cakes, muffins, puddings and homemade ice cream. The leaves also add a lovely scent to potpourris, sachets, sleep pillows and baths.

GARDENING

Caldo de Mariscos

Similar versions of this deceptively simple stew are served up and down the Mexican Gulf coast from Tampico to Veracruz. As would be customary, choose only the ripest tomatoes and freshest seafood available. Unlike many stews, this one is at its very best freshly made, not reheated or frozen. Take care not to overcook the squid — 1 minute is all it needs — or it becomes challengingly chewy. Buen provecho!

3 cups chicken stock
3 cups clam juice
1/2 cup chopped carrot
1/2 cup chopped celery
1 cup chopped onion
6 to 8 peppercorns
1 bay leaf
Shrimp shells and fish bones as available, well-rinsed
6 Roma tomatoes, coarsely chopped
1 cup chopped onion
3 garlic cloves, chopped
1 chile de arbol, stemmed, seeded and broken up or 1/8 teaspoon cayenne pepper
1/2 teaspoon ground cinnamon
1/8 teaspoon allspice
1 tablespoon extra virgin olive oil
1 medium potato, peeled and cubed
1 sprig epazote, or 2 tablespoons chopped fresh cilantro leaves
8 ounces skinless red snapper fillets, cubed or other white-fleshed fish
8 ounces medium shrimp, peeled and deveined
4 ounces squid tubes, cut into half-inch rings
1/8 teaspoon salt
1/8 teaspoon cayenne pepper
Lime wedges

Combine the stock, clam juice, carrot, celery, onion, peppercorns, bay leaf, shrimp shells and fish bones in a 3-quart saucepan over medium heat. Simmer for 15 to 20 minutes. Strain into a clean container, discard the solids. Combine the tomato, onion, garlic, chile de arbol, cinnamon and allspice in a blender or food processor; purée. Combine the purée and olive oil in a large soup pot over medium heat. Cook until most of the liquid has evaporated. Add the reserved stock, potato and epazote and simmer until the potato is tender. Add the fish and simmer, partially covered, for 3 minutes. Add the shrimp and cook for 1 minute longer. Add the squid and cook for 1 minute longer. Remove from the heat; add salt and cayenne pepper. Taste and adjust the seasonings. Serve hot with lime wedges. *Yield: 4 servings*

Nutrients Per Serving: Cal 296; Prot 28 g; Carbo 27 g; Fat 9 g; 29% Cal from Fat; Sod 1135 mg

Coconut Ceviche

As might befit a country whose longitudinal borders separate the Gulf of Mexico from the Pacific Ocean (in less than a day's drive you can plunk your pinkies into each), Mexico has an abundant legacy of seafood dishes. Classics like Shrimp in Mojo de Ajo, Red Snapper Veracruzano, and Caldo de Mariscos abound, but one of the simplest and most defining preparations is ceviche - bits of fresh fish "cooked" in a lime juice marinade, then tossed with green chiles, onion, and cilantro. Served chilled with crispy tostados and an icy cerveza (Mexican beer), a fresh ceviche provides remarkable restorative powers against the blazing equatorial heat. Toss in some cubed avocado, ripe mango, cucumber, and coconut for good measure, and you have the makings of one of the most delightfully refreshing dining opportunities you will ever experience.

16 ounces very fresh skinless fish fillets (red snapper, tuna, mahi mahi, or orange roughy would all be good choices)
1 1/2 cups fresh lime juice
2 tablespoons red bell pepper, diced
1 serrano chile, seeded and minced
1/4 cup minced red onion
1/2 cup minced, seeded and peeled cucumber
1 cup minced fresh mango
1/2 cup minced avocado
1/4 cup chopped fresh cilantro leaves
1/4 cup reduced-fat coconut milk
1 tablespoon pure coconut extract
2 tablespoons orange juice
1/2 teaspoon salt

Cut the fish into 1/4-inch pieces and arrange in a glass bowl. Reserve 2 tablespoons of the lime juice and pour the remainder over the fish. Refrigerate, covered, for 4 to 6 hours. Drain and discard the marinade. Combine the fish with the reserved lime juice, bell pepper, chile, onion, cucumber, mango, avocado, cilantro, coconut milk, coconut extract, orange juice and salt. Refrigerate until thoroughly chilled. Serve with baked tostado chips. *Yield: 4 servings*

Nutrients Per Serving: Cal 201; Prot 17 g; Carbo 21 g; Fat 5 g; 23% Cal from Fat; Sod 332 mg

Parmesan-Crusted Trout

The American rainbow trout, a native of central western United States rivers, ranks as one of the truly great game fish in the world. It's a worthy adversary of sports fishermen, wonderful eating, and nutritionally high in beneficial Omega 3 oils. Along with catfish, it's one of the most successfully aqua-farmed fish — a ready, reliable, and flavorful flash in the pan.

1/2 cup grated Parmigiano-Reggiano cheese
4 (4-ounce) boneless rainbow trout fillets
4 lemon wedges

Spread the cheese in a flat-bottomed dish large enough to hold a trout fillet. Dredge each fillet, flesh side down, in the cheese. Arrange the fillets, flesh side up, on a clean dry work surface and coat with additional cheese. Heat a heavy nonstick skillet sprayed lightly with nonstick cooking spray over medium-high heat. Arrange the fillets, flesh side down and not touching, in the hot skillet; cook for 3 minutes. Turn the fillets once; cook for 2 minutes longer. Serve hot with lemon wedges. Accompany the fish with a green vegetable, rice or potatoes for a luscious meal. *Yield: 4 servings*

Nutrients Per Serving: Cal 148; Prot 20 g; Carbo 1 g; Fat 7 g; 43% Cal from Fat; Sod 224 mg

Mixed Seafood Risotto with Roasted Tomato Broth

Arborio rice is a stubby-grained variety with a high starch content that contributes to its unique, chewy texture. If you lack Arborio, you can substitute sushi rice, which gives very similar results. Or, you can even use a good quality long grain white rice for a different, but equally delicious dish. Whichever rice you choose, the gentle stirring with each addition of liquid is important to develop the proper texture. You may choose the amount of liquid introduced in the final stage to make your risotto drier or soupier, as you please. Almost any combination of seafood will work well.

Risotto Stock: 4 cups each: clam juice and chicken stock; 1 each: small carrot, onion and celery rib, sliced; 1 bay leaf, 1/2 teaspoon fennel seeds, 4 parsley stems, any available shrimp shells

12 medium shrimp, peeled, deveined and shells reserved
4 ounces salmon fillet and 4 ounces snapper fillet or other white-fleshed fish, cut into 1/2-inch cubes
1/2 cup white wine
2 teaspoons olive oil
1/4 cup minced onion
2 garlic cloves, minced
1 cup Arborio rice
1/4 teaspoon saffron
1/2 teaspoon salt
4 ounces crabmeat (optional)
3 tablespoons Parmesan cheese
12 mussels or clams, scrubbed

Simmer the stock ingredients together for 15 minutes. Strain, reserving the liquid and discarding the solids. Return the liquid to the saucepan over medium heat. Add the fish cubes to the simmering stock; poach for 5 minutes. Strain the stock, reserve the fish and return the strained stock to the saucepan over medium-low heat. Remove 1/2 cup stock and combine it with white wine in a bowl; set aside. Sauté the onion with the olive oil in a large saucepan until softened. Add the garlic, rice, saffron and salt; sauté for 1 minute, stirring constantly. Add 1 cup of the simmering stock; stir gently until most of the liquid has been absorbed. Repeat with a second cup of stock. Taste to test the doneness of the rice. Add as much additional stock as needed, stirring after each addition, until the rice is cooked al dente. Remove the rice from the heat and fold in the reserved fish cubes, crabmeat and cheese. Combine the reserved stock and wine mixture, shrimp and mussels in a large skillet. Bring to a boil and cook, covered, for 3 minutes or until the mussels open. Discard any mussels with unopened shells. Strain, reserving the shrimp, mussels and broth. To serve, press the risotto into an 8-ounce mold, such as a cup, invert the mold into a wide-bottom soup bowl. Ladle the Roasted Tomato Broth around the rice. Arrange 3 shrimp and 3 mussels around each serving. Garnish with chopped Italian parsley and a few thawed frozen green peas, if desired. *Yield: 4 servings*

The Roasted Tomato Broth

2 large garlic cloves, peeled
1/8 teaspoon olive oil
2 large Roma tomatoes
Salt and cayenne pepper to taste
1 1/4 cups reserved shellfish broth from Seafood Risotto

Rub the garlic cloves with the olive oil. Wrap the garlic cloves loosely in foil and place on a baking sheet. Add the tomatoes and roast at 400 degrees until the tomatoes are soft and mottled brown. Remove the garlic from the foil and combine with the tomatoes, salt, cayenne pepper and shellfish broth in a blender or food processor; purée. *Yield: 1 1/2 cups*

Nutrients Per Serving: Cal 474; Prot 32 g; Carbo 54 g; Fat 10 g; 21% Cal from Fat; Sod 1737 mg

Bar Harbor Lobster Roll

Every part of the United States has its regional food favorites, and for most of us, the state of Maine is synonymous with lobster. Whether simply served whole with a side of drawn butter at the local lobster pound, its bright red shell still steaming from a boiling bath in seawater, or elegantly sauced in some tony seaside restaurant, these tasty crustaceans dominate the Northeastern food scene — along with steamed clams, of course. Even nationally franchised burger chains, which pride themselves on uniformity from coast to coast, yield to the local tastes and carry some version of Maine's favorite sandwich, the lobster roll. Try ours; it's wicked good! Serve it with baked beans and a slice of blueberry pie for dessert and you will have dined as well as if you were in "Bah Habah" itself.

3 tablespoons fat-free mayonnaise
3 tablespoons fat-free sour cream
1 teaspoon Dijon mustard
1 1/2 tablespoons 2% milk
1 teaspoon white vinegar
1/4 teaspoon dried dillweed
1/4 teaspoon salt
1/8 teaspoon freshly ground black pepper
1/8 teaspoon cayenne pepper
1/8 teaspoon sugar
1/2 garlic clove, minced
1/2 cup minced onion
1 tablespoon chopped fresh parsley
1 cup finely shredded green cabbage
12 ounces cooked lobster meat, coarsely chopped
4 whole wheat hot dog buns
4 teaspoons light butter

Mix the mayonnaise, sour cream, Dijon mustard, milk, vinegar, dillweed, salt, black pepper, cayenne pepper, sugar, garlic, onion and parsley in a large bowl. Fold in the cabbage and lobster. Chill in the refrigerator. Split the hot dog buns and spread the split sides with butter; toast lightly on a baking sheet at 400 degrees. Remove from the oven and fill with lobster salad. Serve immediately. *Yield: 4 servings*

Nutrients Per Serving: Cal 245; Prot 22 g; Carbo 29 g; Fat 5 g; 17% Cal from Fat; Sod 823 mg

step to it

Ten thousand steps is a fun, easy way to gauge your daily activity level. Research shows that walking 10,000 steps a day helps with weight control, improves cholesterol, lowers blood pressure, and decreases your risk of cancer, diabetes, osteoporosis and heart disease. The typical office worker averages 2,500 to 5,000 steps a day in routine activity. You can measure your steps with a pedometer called a "step counter," available at your local sporting goods store or at Lake Austin Spa Resort's boutique, Natural Expressions. Opportunities to take 10,000 steps each day might include walking while talking on the phone; taking the stairs, planning a "walking" meeting, changing the television channels manually, dancing while cooking, window shopping, or visiting an art museum. Carrying a pedometer can be a great motivator - when you see the pedometer or feel it on your waistband you are reminded to get moving!

Mediterranean Fish Casserole

This is a dish for all seasons, particularly in Texas where we share the Mediterranean's abundance of sunshine. The casserole is light enough for summer, yet substantial enough for the fall when we still have great tomatoes and eggplant from the garden and we're looking to combine them in heartier meals. The salting and draining of the eggplant is to remove any potential bitterness. We like to leave the skin on, but you may peel it, if you wish. If possible, grind your spices from whole seeds. The flavor will be much better and a twenty-dollar coffee grinder (a.k.a. spice grinder) is all that you need to put you in business for years.

1 small eggplant, sliced into 1/4-inch rounds, salted
2 medium potatoes, peeled, sliced and blotted dry
2 medium tomatoes, sliced and blotted dry
Salt and freshly ground black pepper to taste
1 tablespoon olive oil
1 small onion, sliced
2 garlic cloves, minced
1 teaspoon fennel seeds
2 tablespoons cumin seeds
1/4 teaspoon cayenne pepper
1 teaspoon cardamom
1 teaspoon turmeric
1/2 teaspoon coriander seeds
1/2 teaspoon ground cinnamon
4 (4-ounce) boneless, skinless fish fillets, sliced thin (use any firm-fleshed white fish such as snapper, roughy or sea trout)
1/4 cup chopped fresh parsley
1/4 cup chicken stock
1/4 cup white wine

Rinse and drain the salted eggplant; blot dry with paper towels. Arrange in a single layer on a baking sheet sprayed with nonstick cooking spray. Roast at 375 degrees until the eggplant is soft and beginning to brown. Remove from the oven and cool. Season the potatoes and tomato slices with salt and pepper. Arrange in a single layer on a baking sheet sprayed with nonstick cooking spray. Roast at 375 degrees until the vegetables are soft and beginning to brown. Remove from the oven and cool. Heat 1 teaspoon of the olive oil in a nonstick skillet over medium-high heat. Add the onion and sauté until soft. Add the garlic and sauté for 30 seconds longer. Grind the fennel seeds, cumin seeds, cayenne pepper, cardamom, turmeric, coriander seeds and cinnamon in a spice grinder; set aside. Spray a casserole dish with nonstick cooking spray. Add a layer of fish, sprinkle with some spice mix, chopped parsley, then drizzle some chicken stock and some white wine and some of the remaining olive oil over the fish. Add a layer of roasted vegetables, sprinkle with spice mix and chopped parsley. Drizzle some chicken stock and some white wine and some of the remaining olive oil over the vegetables. Bake at 375 degrees for 15 to 20 minutes or until the fish is cooked through. *Yield: 4 servings*

Nutrients Per Serving: Cal 263; Prot 20 g; Carbo 32 g; Fat 6 g; 19% Cal from Fat; Sod 101 mg

Lobster and Avocado Nori Rolls

Asian sushi has gained quite a following in this country over the last several years. Even if you're not quite ready for the raw fish experience, you can still enjoy nori rolls which, quite within tradition, are often filled with cooked seafood. Substitute shrimp or crabmeat for the lobster, or make them completely vegetarian, if you like. If you do not have sushi rice, you can substitute Arborio rice, a short grain Italian species with similar properties. In strict Asian custom, the pickled ginger would never be rolled inside the nori, but eaten between mouthfuls as a palate refresher. We like the contrast of flavor with the avocado, however, and so have bent the rules a little in our version.

2 cups uncooked sushi rice
3 1/2 cups water
1/4 teaspoon salt
2 tablespoons mirin or rice wine
1 tablespoon sugar
6 sheets nori seaweed
1 red bell pepper, roasted, peeled, seeded and sliced
1/2 avocado, peeled, seeded and sliced
1/2 carrot, julienned and blanched for 1 minute
12 slices pink pickled ginger
8 ounces cooked lobster meat, shredded

Combine the rice, water and salt in a saucepan over high heat. Bring to a boil and immediately reduce the heat to a simmer; cook, covered, for 15 minutes. Remove the saucepan from the heat and let the rice stand, covered, for 10 minutes. Combine the mirin and sugar in a small bowl; stir until the sugar dissolves. Fold the mirin mixture into the rice; set aside to cool. Place a sheet of nori, shiny side down, on a bamboo sushi mat or square of aluminum foil. Dampen your fingers with water, then spread a thin layer of rice on the nori; leave a 3/4-inch border at the top. Layer 1/6 of the bell pepper, avocado, carrot, ginger and lobster meat in a horizontal line over the rice, about 1 inch from the bottom. Using the mat as a guide, tightly roll the seaweed away from you. Dampen the exposed border of the nori with water and press to seal the roll. Repeat the process until you have 6 rolls. Chill the rolls in the refrigerator. Remove and slice into 1/2-inch-thick discs. Serve with wasabi paste (an Asian horseradish paste) and soy sauce. *Yield: 6 servings*

Nutrients Per Serving: Cal 375; Prot 14 g; Carbo 68 g; Fat 3 g; 7% Cal from Fat; Sod 348 mg

chefstip

Rice Is Nice ✳ Without question organic brown rice, as a whole grain, is the most nutritious variety of the genre; however, many rice-eating cultures have this outer husk removed for reasons of color, preference, or quickness in cooking. And while these white rices may lack the nuttiness and rustic appeal of their whole grain versions, many are more appropriate for the dishes in which they are used, and they still provide good food value. Since variety is the spice of life, and rice keeps very well, we keep 3 or 4 types around for specific applications. In addition to brown rice, we like Texmati (a Texas grown basmati derivative, available in white and brown), genuine basmati, and Arborio, a short grain, high starch rice wonderful in Italian risotto dishes and also quite suitable as sushi rice. Wild rice, which we also like, is actually not a true rice at all but a type of wild grass harvested in the Northern U.S. and Canada.

Coquille St. Jacques

For the better part of the twentieth century in the United States, fine dining simply meant French food. If you were going to a fancy restaurant for dinner, you were going to a French restaurant. Even our word for a person who is versed in the pleasures of the table — gourmet or gourmand — is French. And when Julia Child, arguably the most influential American cook of the twentieth century, burst upon the scene, what did she teach us? French cooking. The avant garde of this French revolution for Americans — dishes like crêpes, quiche, and Coquille St. Jacques — bore a common theme. Impeccably fresh, delicate ingredients were often swaddled (for better or worse) in heavy cream, egg yolks, and butter. And those foods that escaped such anointment were often as not doused with hollandaise, that definitively French dollop of emulsified butter and eggs festooning down in yellow ribbons onto the plate. This age of innocence — some would say indulgence — careened merrily along for some time until the medics (those nay-sayers) trip-wired the road with evidence linking consumption of saturated fats to arteriosclerosis, bringing the entire dinner party to a tumbling, clattering halt. Cholesterol and what to do about it dominated the media and consequently our imaginations. Many of us just stopped eating butter, cream, and eggs altogether; an understandable reaction and overreaction. The truth is, and always has been, that a wide variety of foods — sometimes even those previously outlawed — eaten in moderation is probably the best way for most of us to go. And the truth also is that many of those higher fat dishes we learned to love (before we learned to love wisely) adapt quite nicely to a lighter translation. Our Coquille St. Jacques is, we think, a case in point. So, vive and Vive La France!

1 cup clam juice
1/2 cup white wine
16 ounces sea scallops, sliced into bite-size pieces
1 tomato
1 tablespoon light butter
2 tablespoons minced shallots
2 teaspoons brandy
1/2 cup 2% milk
1 tablespoon flour
1 tablespoon 2% milk
1/8 teaspoon salt
1/8 teaspoon cayenne pepper
2 ounces reduced-fat Swiss cheese, shredded
4 teaspoons grated Parmesan cheese
Chopped fresh parsley or fresh tarragon leaves for garnish

Heat the clam juice and wine in a small nonreactive saucepan over medium heat. When hot, add the scallops and poach for 2 to 3 minutes. Remove the saucepan from the heat and cool the scallops in the liquid. Remove and reserve the scallops. Return the cooking liquid to medium-high heat and cook until reduced to 3/4 cup. Cut an X into the bottom of the tomato. Blanch it in boiling water in a saucepan for 30 seconds. Drain, peel, seed and chop the tomato. Heat the butter in a nonstick saucepan over medium-low heat. Add the tomato and shallots; cook gently until dry. Add the brandy, reserved scallop cooking liquid and 1/2 cup milk. Bring to a simmer. Combine the flour and 1 tablespoon milk; mix until a smooth paste forms. Whisk the flour mixture, salt and cayenne pepper into the simmering liquid. Cook, stirring constantly, until slightly thickened. Add the Swiss cheese and cook, stirring, until the cheese melts. Taste and correct the seasonings, if necessary. Divide the reserved scallops among 4 ramekins. Top each with 1/4 of the sauce. Sprinkle 1 teaspoon Parmesan cheese over the top of each ramekin and bake at 425 degrees until bubbly. *Yield: 4 servings*

Nutrients Per Serving: Cal 191; Prot 16 g; Carbo 7 g; Fat 8 g; 37% Cal from Fat; Sod 411 mg

Scallops Newburg

With the exception of steamed lobster, which isn't so much a recipe as it is a rite, the two most notable contributions from the Northeastern seaboard to our national cuisine are probably chowder (see Neo-Nantucket Clam Chowder, Page 59) and Newburg. A steaming tureen of buttery, rich Newburg, brimming with seafood — lobster, scallops, shrimp, or crab — graces many a table between New Brunswick and New Bedford on special occasions each year. Our Newburg, which uses many of the reduced-fat dairy products now available, is considerably lower in fat and calories, but still captures the rich and savory quality of the original. Serve it for Sunday supper and "sea" for yourself.

1 cup clam juice
1/4 cup white wine
16 ounces sea scallops
1 tablespoon light butter
1 tablespoon finely minced shallots
1 cup fat-free half-and-half or evaporated skim milk
2 teaspoons cornstarch
1 tablespoon brandy
1 tablespoon sherry
1/8 teaspoon cayenne pepper
1/4 cup egg substitute
1 ounce reduced-fat cream cheese
1 tablespoon minced fresh parsley

Heat the clam juice and wine in a saucepan over medium heat. Add the scallops and poach for 3 to 4 minutes. Strain, reserving the scallops and the cooking liquid. Heat the butter in a nonstick skillet over medium heat. Add the shallots and cook until soft. Add the reserved scallop liquid, increase the heat and cook until the mixture is reduced to 1/2 cup. Combine the cream and cornstarch in the top of a double boiler and mix well. Add the brandy, sherry, cayenne pepper and reserved scallop cooking liquid; mix well. Place over boiling water and cook, stirring occasionally, for 5 to 6 minutes or until slightly thickened. Pour the egg substitute into a bowl. Slowly drizzle about half the cream mixture into the bowl, stirring constantly. Return the double boiler over the pot of boiling water. Whisk in the egg and cream mixture. Cook, stirring constantly, until thickened. Add the cream cheese; cook, stirring constantly, until the cheese melts. Add the scallops and parsley; mix well. Serve with rice or pasta or, for a bit of elegance, over puff pastry. *Yield: 4 servings*

Nutrients Per Serving: Cal 182; Prot 15 g; Carbo 13 g; Fat 5 g; 26% Cal from Fat; Sod 344 mg

skin so soft

Refresh dry or irritated skin by combining 1/2 cup dried chamomile flowers and 1/2 cup dried sage leaves to one cup of oatmeal. Place in a cotton bath bag or a double layer of cheesecloth and tie up tightly. Steep the bag in bath water for a few minutes and then scrub the entire body to exfoliate and stimulate circulation. The chamomile and oatmeal will soften the skin and the sage acts as a natural antiseptic.

HOME SPA

New Orleans-Style Barbecue Shrimp

This recipe is our version of one of New Orleans' best and most beloved blue-collar dishes. Oh, you can peel the shrimp before cooking, but you'd be missing the point, and some of the flavor. Instead, roll up your sleeves, tuck that napkin into your collar, pop open a cold adult beverage, and get in and get after it!

2 teaspoons paprika
1 teaspoon onion powder
1 teaspoon garlic powder
1/4 teaspoon cayenne pepper
1/4 teaspoon ground white pepper
1/4 teaspoon dried thyme leaves
1/4 teaspoon dried leaf oregano
1/2 teaspoon salt
16 ounces medium to large shrimp, shells on
2 large garlic cloves, minced
1/4 cup minced onion
2 tablespoons flour
1/4 cup beer at room temperature
2 tablespoons Worcestershire sauce
1 cup seafood stock or clam juice
4 tablespoons light butter, cut into 4 pieces
1/4 cup chopped fresh parsley
French bread for dunking

Mix the paprika, onion powder, garlic powder, cayenne pepper, white pepper, thyme, oregano and salt in a bowl; set aside. Spray a nonstick skillet with nonstick cooking spray and place over medium-high heat. Add the shrimp and sauté just until the shrimp begin to turn pink. Add the spice mixture, garlic and onion. Cook, stirring constantly, for 30 seconds. Whisk the flour, beer, Worcestershire sauce and stock in a bowl. Pour into the skillet and cook, stirring constantly, for 1 minute. Reduce the heat and add the butter, 1 piece at a time. Shake the skillet gently just until the butter melts. Divide the shrimp and sauce among 4 wide-bottom soup bowls. Garnish with parsley and serve with bread for dunking. *Yield: 4 servings*

Nutrients Per Serving: Cal 153; Prot 16 g; Carbo 7 g; Fat 7 g; 39% Cal from Fat; Sod 731 mg

Shrimp and Black Bean Sopes with Guacamole and Chipotle Dressing

Masa is the mother of all things Mexican. From masa comes the tortilla, the tostado, the tamale, and amid these and a myriad of other such masa treats, the sope — a tasty semi-crisp receptacle for whatever you will. Beans are a good beginning. A Mayan-style guacamole, lightened with tomato and onion, and sharpened with chile and lime can play a leading role or support another protein such as shrimp, chicken, or cheese. Top everything with salsa and salad and you have some of the very best, most inventive eating imaginable. Offer one as an appetizer or two as an entrée in whatever combination of ingredients that serves both you and your guests well.

2 cups masa harina de maiz
1 1/2 cups water
2 tablespoons canola oil
1 medium avocado, peeled, seeded and cubed
1/2 cup diced tomato
3 tablespoons minced onion
1 large garlic clove, minced
1/2 serrano chile, seeded and minced
2 tablespoons chopped fresh cilantro leaves
2 teaspoons lime juice
1/4 teaspoon salt
1/4 cup fat-free mayonnaise
1/4 cup water
1 garlic clove, minced
1/2 teaspoon adobo paste from chipotle chiles
1/8 teaspoon salt
1 teaspoon annatto-infused olive oil*
2 teaspoons fresh lime juice
1 cup cooked black beans, whole or mashed, heated
16 medium shrimp, peeled, deveined and poached
Shredded lettuce
Sliced radishes
Diced tomato

Combine the masa harina and water in a bowl; mix well. Divide and shape the dough into eight 3-inch diameter disks. Heat a nonstick skillet over medium heat. Cook 1 side of each disk until it begins to brown. Remove from the skillet. With the cooked side up, pinch the sides up to make a cup with a half-inch rim. Add canola oil to the skillet and sauté the sopes until crisp, starting with the uncooked side down, then turning to brown and crisp the rims. Set aside. Mash the avocado in a bowl. Add the tomato, onion, garlic, chipotle chile, cilantro, lime juice and salt; mix well. Mix the mayonnaise, water, garlic, adobo paste, salt, olive oil and lime juice in a separate bowl. Arrange some black beans in each sope cup, top with a dollop of guacamole, 2 shrimp and some chipotle mayonnaise. Garnish with lettuce, radishes and tomato.

* Annatto is an indigenous seed used since pre-Columbian days to color and flavor food throughout the Americas. It is available in health food or ethnic food stores. To infuse, combine 1 tablespoon of seeds with 3 tablespoons olive oil in a saucepan over medium-low heat. Simmer for 3 to 4 minutes, but do not allow to burn. Strain and discard the seeds. Use the oil as needed and store the remainder in a tightly sealed container. *Yield: 4 servings*

Nutrients Per Serving: Cal 471; Prot 14 g; Carbo 66 g; Fat 19 g; 35% Cal from Fat; Sod 374 mg

Shrimp and Crab Tamales

We like to steam these tender and sweet seafood tamales in their traditional cornhusks because it's fun and it makes for a very nice presentation. For a little less work, but still a delicious meal, refer to the aluminum foil option in the Chicken Tamale Soup recipe (Page 107) for a quick wrap up.

1 cup chicken stock
8 ounces medium shrimp, shells on
1 1/2 cups masa harina de maiz
1 (15-ounce) can yellow hominy, drained, rinsed and puréed
1/2 teaspoon salt
1/4 cup light butter, softened
8 ounces Gulf crabmeat
12 cornhusks, soaked in hot water until very pliable
Extra cornhusks for strips for tying
1/2 cup Roasted Red Pepper Salsa (Page 20)

Heat the stock in a saucepan over medium heat. Add the shrimp and simmer for 2 minutes. Drain, reserving the stock and the shrimp. Peel the shrimp, discarding the shells. Coarsely chop the shrimp. Combine the masa harina, hominy, salt and reserved stock in a bowl and mix well. Whip the butter with a whisk in a bowl until light. Fold in the masa mixture. Fold in the shrimp and crabmeat. Divide the dough into twelve 1-inch diameter cylinders. Arrange 1 cylinder in the center of a cornhusk. Wrap the husk around the cylinder and tie the ends with strips of husk. Repeat until all tamales are completed. Arrange in a single layer in a steamer and steam for 1 1/2 hours. To serve, cut 1 end of each husk open, then spread to expose the tamale. Serve with Roasted Red Pepper Salsa. *Yield: 4 servings*

Nutrients Per Serving: Cal 397; Prot 23 g; Carbo 52 g; Fat 12 g; 27% Cal from Fat; Sod 1031 mg

chefstip

Tools of The Trade ✳ Most restaurant supply stores are happy to sell to the public. If you are more interested in utility, durability and function than cosmetic appearance, give them a try. You will find sturdily constructed wire whisks, rubber spatulas, basket strainers, storage containers, tongs, baking pans, cutting boards and other well-made and reasonably priced goods. The department store equivalents typically fall into the categories of "boutique sized and constructed" or "better made, but designer finished" and are priced accordingly.

Shrimp Crawfish Pie

"Me oh my, crawfish pie, filé gumbo. Son of a gun, we gonna have big fun on the bayou." Lyrics from a Fifties Hank Williams song. Not that they have a corner on it, but the folks in Louisiana do know how to eat. And, they do know how to have a good time. More often than not they roll the two together and when they do you can bet that the state's diminutive crustacean, the crawfish (a.k.a. the crawdad or mud bug) will be in evidence. Get your bugs hot, cold, boiled, or fried, in gumbo or casseroles or, even as the song suggests, in pies. Ours are wrapped in crispy phyllo, served with a slightly spicy red pepper sauce and a savory pea salad on the side. Me oh my, indeed, ma chérie.

2 teaspoons canola oil
1 cup minced onion
1/2 cup minced celery
1/2 cup minced carrot
1/2 cup minced chayote squash (or use zucchini)
4 garlic cloves, minced
1/4 teaspoon dried leaf oregano
1/8 teaspoon dried thyme
1/8 teaspoon garlic powder
1/8 teaspoon onion powder
1/8 teaspoon black pepper
1/4 teaspoon salt
12 ounces peeled shrimp, chopped
2 teaspoons Dijon mustard
2 tablespoons sherry
8 ounces crawfish meat
2 tablespoons chopped parsley
6 sheets frozen phyllo dough, thawed
Red Pepper Almond Sauce
Black-Eyed Pea Salad

Heat the canola oil in a large skillet over medium-high heat. Add the onion, celery and carrot; sauté until the vegetables are soft. Add the squash, garlic, oregano, thyme, garlic powder, onion powder, pepper, salt and shrimp. Sauté for 2 minutes. Add the Dijon mustard, sherry, crawfish and

as you like it

When was the last time you made a conscious decision to do as much or as little as you like? Life today tends to dictate to us what we have to get done and when it has to be completed. Rarely do we take time to sit quietly and read a book just because we want to. Recently, a guest at Lake Austin Spa Resort told a story that really hit home. As a mother of three young boys, she commented that the 10 minute portion of her facial in which she was under a masque and the technician left the room was the first time in five years that she could remember having a few minutes of solitude. Having "alone" time is essential to your long-term well being. Many of our guests arrive with their "Type A mentalities" working overtime. And because we offer so many classes and activities, many of them feel that they have to do and experience it all. We encourage you to let go and leave that mentality behind, if just for a short while. Make a conscious decision to do as much or as little as you like.

WELL BEING

parsley. Cook until fairly dry. Remove from the heat and cool completely. Arrange 1 sheet of phyllo dough on a clean flat surface with the long edge facing you. Spray the phyllo lightly with nonstick cooking spray. Fold the dough in half from left to right. Arrange about 1 cup of the filling along the bottom, leaving a 1-inch border on the bottom, left and right sides. Roll up once from the bottom. Fold in the sides. Spray the exposed phyllo surface with nonstick cooking spray. Continue rolling and spraying the dry surfaces with nonstick cooking spray until completely rolled. Repeat the process with the remaining sheets of dough. Arrange the pies, seam side down, on a baking sheet sprayed lightly with nonstick cooking spray. Bake at 375 degrees for about 20 minutes or until golden. Serve with Red Pepper Almond Sauce and Black-Eyed Pea Salad. *Yield: 6 servings*

The Red Pepper Almond Sauce

2 medium tomatoes, cut into halves
1 red bell pepper
6 garlic cloves, sprayed with nonstick cooking spray and wrapped in foil
6 whole almonds with skins
1/8 teaspoon cracked red pepper or red pepper flakes
2 tablespoons olive oil
1 tablespoon red wine vinegar
1/4 teaspoon salt

Arrange the tomatoes, bell pepper, wrapped garlic and almonds on a baking sheet. Roast at 400 degrees for 10 to 12 minutes. Remove and reserve the almonds. Roast the vegetables for 15 to 20 minutes longer. Remove from the oven. Peel and seed the bell pepper. Reserve 1/3 cup of the flesh for the sauce. Combine the cracked red pepper and olive oil in a small skillet over medium heat. Simmer for 30 seconds. Chop the reserved almonds. Combine the almonds, red pepper oil, roasted tomatoes, reserved bell pepper and garlic in a blender or food processor; process until smooth. *Yield: 6 servings*

The Black-Eyed Pea Salad

1/2 cup minced red onion
1/4 cup minced green bell pepper
1/4 cup minced celery
2 tablespoons chopped fresh parsley
1 garlic clove, minced
3 cups cooked black-eyed peas
1 tablespoon olive oil
1 tablespoon red wine vinegar
1/8 teaspoon sugar
1/8 teaspoon salt
1/8 teaspoon dry mustard
1/8 teaspoon black pepper

Combine the onion, bell pepper, celery, parsley, garlic, black-eyed peas, olive oil, vinegar, sugar, salt, dry mustard and pepper in a large bowl. Toss to mix well. Chill in the refrigerator until ready to serve. *Yield: 6 servings*

Nutrients Per Serving: Cal 375; Prot 24 g; Carbo 44 g; Fat 12 g; 28% Cal from Fat; Sod 526 mg

Tapas-Style Shrimp with Garlic and Almonds

Tapas are little meals served at wine and sherry bars throughout Spain. They're savory, appetizer-size portions of vegetables and/or meat and seafood intended to accompany the beverage of choice. Three or four can make an entire meal. This shrimp dish is our version of one of Spain's most famous tapas. We present it here in entrée-size portions, although we would urge you to consider it as part of a tapas party, too. As an entrée, serve it with steamed saffron rice and a green vegetable. Note that while this dish is moderately high in fat compared to some of our other entrées, approximately 75% of the fat comes from healthy monounsaturated olives, olive oil, and almonds — very typical of the Mediterranean diet.

1 tablespoon olive oil
4 large garlic cloves, minced
1/4 teaspoon cracked red pepper or red pepper flakes
16 ounces (21-25 count) shrimp, peeled (tails left on) and deveined
2 tablespoons chopped fresh parsley
1/8 teaspoon salt
1 small red bell pepper, roasted, peeled, seeded and sliced, or 1/2 cup pimentos, drained
1/4 cup toasted sliced almonds
8 pitted green olives
3 tablespoons medium-body sherry
Juice of 1 lemon
2 tablespoons light butter

Heat the olive oil in a heavy nonstick skillet over medium-high heat. Add the garlic and red pepper and sauté until the garlic turns golden. Add the shrimp and cook, spraying the shrimp with a little nonstick cooking spray if necessary until the shrimp are almost cooked; about 1 to 1 1/2 minutes. Add the parsley, salt, bell pepper, almonds, olives, sherry and lemon juice; mix well. Cook for 30 seconds. Add the butter and cook until the butter melts. *Yield: 4 servings as an entrée; 8 to 12 servings as tapas*

Nutrients Per Serving: Cal 233; Prot 20 g; Carbo 14 g; Fat 11 g; 43% Cal from Fat; Sod 488 mg

chefstip

Stick To It ✳ Grilled, skewered meats and vegetables can be a fast, fun and nutritious way to cook if you follow a few basic rules. Wooden skewers should be soaked in water for a couple of hours before using (so they will resist burning). If you have a rosemary bush, skewers made from the de-leafed branches make particularly aromatic skewers. You will want all of your skewered items to be about the same circumference for even cooking, not too large or small (about one inch is good). For vegetables, summer squashes, onions, and peppers are always good choices. Cherry tomatoes are nice with quick cooking items like shrimp but may overcook (and fall apart) with meats like lamb or beef. Always be sure you have a good hot fire but with a minimum of active flame so that the meats and vegetables will cook rapidly without becoming overly charred. Lightly mist the prepared skewers with a nonstick pan spray (away from the grill – the spray is flammable) to prevent sticking.

Pork and Shrimp Pot Stickers with Pineapple Ponzu Sauce

The story of pot stickers goes like this: an imperial chef was making steamed won tons as part of a royal banquet when he somehow became distracted and allowed all of the steaming liquid to evaporate from the pot, causing the won tons to stick to the bottom and turn crisp. Frantically, upon discovering his mistake — and no doubt sweating bullets because the emperor was a picky guy — the chef added more liquid to the pot. And, behold, the won tons released from the bottom. But, instead of having a velvety smooth texture, they retained a chewy, somewhat leathery resistance to the bite. Fearing the worst, but not knowing what else to do, the chef served the "pot stickers." (If you know anything about commercial kitchens, you know how entirely plausible this story is.) After consuming these new-style won tons the emperor promptly, (a) proclaimed the chef a blaspheming heretic and ordered his entrails to be fed to the royal koi, or (b) proclaimed the chef a culinary genius, a visionary without equal concerning all things edible, and showered him with rare gifts and precious jewels. Take your pick. For his part the chef would just as soon have had the day off.

8 ounces medium shrimp, peeled and deveined
8 ounces pork tenderloin, trimmed and finely chopped
1/4 cup diced green onions
2 tablespoons each: chopped cilantro leaves, chopped mint leaves and minced water chestnuts
1 tablespoon minced fresh gingerroot
2 garlic cloves, minced
1/2 teaspoon toasted sesame oil
2 tablespoons sherry
1/2 teaspoon salt
1 egg white
36 won ton wrappers
1/2 cup beaten egg whites or egg substitute
1 tablespoon cornstarch
1 1/2 tablespoons peanut oil or canola oil
1 cup chicken stock

Combine the shrimp, pork, onion, cilantro, mint, water chestnuts, gingerroot, garlic, sesame oil, sherry, salt and egg whites in a food processor; pulse until coarsely chopped. Follow the package directions to fill each won ton wrapper with the filling. Use egg whites or egg substitute to seal the won tons. Dust a baking sheet with cornstarch. Arrange the filled won tons on the sheet, covered with a cloth, until ready to cook. Heat the peanut oil in a large nonstick skillet over medium-high heat. Sauté 1/2 the won tons at a time for 2 minutes. Combine all the cooked won tons in the skillet; add the stock. Cover and cook for 2 minutes. Remove the lid and cook for 1 minute longer. Serve warm with Pineapple Ponzu Sauce. *Yield: 6 servings*

The Pineapple Ponzu Sauce

1 cup thawed frozen pineapple juice concentrate
1/2 cup water
1/4 cup cider vinegar
2 tablespoons sugar
1 tablespoon each: Asian chile paste and light soy sauce
2 teaspoons minced fresh gingerroot
1 tablespoon chopped fresh cilantro leaves or fresh mint leaves
1/4 cup minced fresh pineapple

Combine the pineapple juice concentrate, water, vinegar and sugar in a bowl. Stir until the sugar is dissolved. Add the chile paste, soy sauce, gingerroot, cilantro and fresh pineapple; mix well. *Yield: 6 servings*

Nutrients Per Serving: Cal 400; Prot 21 g; Carbo 63 g; Fat 7 g; 15% Cal from Fat; Sod 829 mg

meats

meats

meats

Rosemary Crusted Pork Loin Roast with Cherry Sauce, Pg.165

meats

Coffee-Crusted Sirloin with Jalapeño Red-Eye Gravy

Back in the 1800's, trail driving cowboys — some of the world's foremost experts at putting whatever was at hand to good use — made the first red-eye gravy by swirling some coffee, mixed with a little flour, in a skillet full of juices from pan-fried steaks. This concoction, along with pinto beans and Dutch oven biscuits, filled many a belly between Texas and the stockyards in Kansas City. Today, most of us are punching clocks instead of cattle, but a sizzling steak with red-eye gravy can still be mighty tasty. The dry rub for the steaks, made with ground coffee beans, doesn't taste anything like it sounds. Give it a try, lest folks take you for a complete greenhorn, podnah.

1/2 cup ground coffee beans
1/4 teaspoon garlic powder
1/2 teaspoon black pepper
1/2 teaspoon salt
4 (4-ounce) all-natural sirloin steaks, trimmed
1 teaspoon canola oil
1 cup brewed coffee
1 cup beef stock
1/4 cup jalapeño jelly
1 tablespoon brown sugar
1 tablespoon lemon juice
2 teaspoons cornstarch, dissolved in a little additional coffee

Combine 1/2 cup ground coffee, garlic powder, pepper and salt in a flat-bottom soup bowl or pie plate. Dredge the steaks in the mixture, coating both sides. Heat the canola oil in a cast-iron skillet with an ovenproof handle over high heat. Spray the steaks with nonstick cooking spray. Sear the steaks in the skillet, turning to sear both sides. Transfer the skillet to a 450-degree oven to finish cooking the steaks to the desired doneness. Remove the skillet from the oven; transfer the steaks to a plate, cover and keep warm. Combine 1 cup brewed coffee and the stock in the hot skillet, stirring with a wooden spoon to incorporate all the brown bits. Cook over medium-high heat until the liquid is reduced to 1 cup. Add the jelly, brown sugar, lemon juice, cornstarch mixture and any accumulated juices from the steaks; mix well. Serve the gravy over the steaks. *Yield: 4 servings*

Nutrients Per Serving: Cal 236; Prot 27 g; Carbo 22 g; Fat 6 g; 23% Cal from Fat; Sod 518 mg

Orange-Flavored Beef

We love Chinese food for its bright colors, assertive flavors, distinctive textures, and quick-cooking techniques. Substitute extra-firm tofu for the beef to make this a delicious and completely vegan dish. Omit the Asian chile paste for a milder version.

12 ounces all-natural sirloin, trimmed and cut into strips
1 tablespoon cornstarch for dusting
1 tablespoon canola oil
2 cups broccoli florets
2 cups vertically sliced onions
1 cup cubed red bell pepper
Grated zest and juice of 1 orange
3 tablespoons orange marmalade
1 tablespoon soy sauce
1 teaspoon Asian chile paste
1/4 cup ketchup
2 tablespoons Ginger Sauce (Page 126)

Dredge the beef strips in cornstarch; shake off any excess. Heat 1 1/2 teaspoons of the canola oil in a heavy nonstick skillet or wok, then rapidly stir-fry the beef. Remove the beef; set aside. Add the remaining canola oil, broccoli, onions and bell pepper and stir-fry for 1 minute. Mix the orange zest, orange juice, marmalade, soy sauce, chile paste, ketchup and Ginger Sauce in a bowl. Return the beef to the pan, add the orange mixture and cook, stirring constantly, for 1 minute. Serve hot with steamed rice, if desired. *Yield: 4 servings*

Nutrients Per Serving: Cal 266; Prot 23 g; Carbo 34 g; Fat 8 g; 27% Cal from Fat; Sod 639 mg

betty crocker vs. superwoman

Did you know that the average three-car garage is the same size as a house built in the 1950's? In those days, only 25% of married women were in the paid workforce, versus almost 80% today. There is no question that the life of a typical family has changed dramatically in the past 50 years. But have the "advances" made during that time allowed us to live fuller, happier and more contented lives? An alarming pair of statistics tells us that per capita spending has increased almost 45% in the past 20 years, yet the quality of life index has decreased 51% over that same time period. Perhaps "having it all" isn't the point after all. Life continues to move faster, daily demands become greater and something important may be getting lost. Take time to remember that the business of life is not so much about business as it is about life.

Beef Stroganoff

Beef with egg noodles may be the classic presentation of Vienna, but on this side of the pond we like our meat and gravy with potatoes — crispy shoestrings, piled high on top. Broccoli and the Blue Danube waltz would make excellent accompaniments.

16 ounces organic beef tenderloin
2 medium potatoes, peeled and cut into 1/8-inch wide matchsticks
2 tablespoons flour
1 teaspoon dry mustard
1 1/2 cups beef stock, reduced to 1 cup
1/4 cup fat-free sour cream
1 tablespoon light butter
1 tablespoon canola oil
1 cup thinly sliced onion
12 medium mushrooms, quartered
2 garlic cloves, minced
Salt and freshly ground black pepper to taste
2 tablespoons chopped fresh parsley

Cut the beef into strips 2 inches long by 3/4-inch wide by 1/8-inch-thick; set aside. Blot the potatoes dry with paper towels. Spray a baking sheet with nonstick cooking spray. Arrange the potatoes in a single layer without touching one another on the baking sheet. Bake at 400 degrees for 20 minutes or until crisp. Set aside. Heat a heavy skillet over medium-high heat. Add the flour and cook, stirring constantly with a wooden spoon, for 5 minutes. Add the dry mustard and cook, stirring constantly, for 1 minute. Whisk in the stock and cook, stirring constantly, for 2 to 3 minutes. Remove the skillet from the heat and whisk in the sour cream and butter. Heat the canola oil in a separate skillet over medium-high heat. Add the onion and mushrooms and sauté until the onions are golden. Increase the heat to high and add the beef. Sear the beef just until done. Reduce the heat to medium-low. Season the beef with salt and pepper; add the sauce. Heat just until hot; do not boil. Divide the beef mixture equally among 4 plates, top each with a mound of potatoes hot from the oven and sprinkle parsley over the top. *Yield: 4 servings*

Nutrients Per Serving: Cal 330; Prot 31 g; Carbo 32 g; Fat 11 g; 30% Cal from Fat; Sod 330 mg

chefstip

Mas Masa ✳ Corn tortillas, tamales and the like are all fashioned from a corn flour, "masa harina de maiz," which can be found in the flour section of many major grocery stores. It's different than cornmeal, but just as easy to work with, and if you are a person who would make corn bread from scratch, then you should consider making your Mexican food from scratch as well. "Maseka," the most popular brand of masa in Mexico is our favorite, but Quaker also makes a very good masa. Once you have discovered the goodness of a homemade corn tortilla or sope and the ease with which they can be made, you will be hard-pressed to buy those commercially produced. And, even if you do not use it every day (although you will be tempted to), your unused masa will keep indefinitely in your freezer as you work your way through the many recipes in this book that call for it.

Beef and Veal Bolognese

The region around Bologna, Italy, has been well-known for centuries for its fine beef and dairy products. A number of famous dishes have emanated from there, but perhaps the best known is the Bolognese meat sauce with pasta. Rather than being the tomato-based version you may be more familiar with, traditional Beef Bolognese relies upon cream for its foundation. We've lightened things up by using less oil, very lean meats, milk, and reduced-fat cream cheese for our delicious adaptation.

2 teaspoons olive oil
1/2 cup diced onion
3 tablespoons diced carrot
3 tablespoons diced celery
2 garlic cloves, minced
6 ounces ultra lean, all-natural ground beef
6 ounces ultra lean, all-natural ground veal
1 ounce brandy
Salt and freshly ground black pepper to taste
4 medium tomatoes, peeled, seeded and diced
1 teaspoon chopped fresh thyme leaves, or 1/2 teaspoon dried thyme
3/4 cup white wine
1 1/2 cups 2% milk
2 teaspoons minced fresh chives
2 ounces reduced-fat cream cheese
6 cups cooked capellini noodles
2 tablespoons grated Parmesan cheese
1 tablespoon chopped fresh parsley

Heat the olive oil in a heavy nonstick skillet over medium heat. Add the onion, carrot and celery and sauté gently until they begin to soften. Add the garlic, ground beef and ground veal. Cook until the beef and veal turn gray, but not brown. Add the brandy, salt, pepper, tomatoes and thyme. Cook slowly, stirring occasionally, until the mixture is fairly dry. Add the wine, milk, chives and cream cheese. Cook, stirring frequently, until the mixture is reduced and creamy. Serve over the capellini garnished with Parmesan and parsley. *Yield: 4 servings*

Nutrients Per Serving: Cal 564; Prot 33 g; Carbo 74 g; Fat 12 g; 19% Cal from Fat; Sod 202 mg

Chili Cheeseburgers and Fries

Go ahead and snicker if you like, but in the Southwest, chili and cheese are considered foundation foods, and putting them on a burger is a potential epiphany in eating experiences. For carnivores, it just doesn't get much better than meat on meat with fried potatoes on the side. We promise that many Texans, if asked to ponder the choice of a final meal, would have this one on the short list. So, rather than wasting our efforts in feeble and futile protestation — and fully embracing our philosophy of "no forbidden foods" — we offer you this enlightened recipe. Perhaps with a few judicious ingredient choices and alternative cooking techniques we can put a little blessing on this blasphemy. At Lake Austin Spa Resort we use locally ranched, certified, organic beef that is more than 95% lean and serve it on a 100% whole wheat bun with our tasty — and almost fat-free — chili. By the way, you can take this recipe and with just a little tinkering and a few corn tortillas make yourself some of the best Tex-Mex enchiladas (another pillar of the chili-cheese foundation) that you've ever eaten.

16 ounces ultra lean, all-natural ground beef
1/2 cup minced onion
1 small garlic clove, minced
1 tablespoon chili powder
1 teaspoon ground cumin
2 tablespoons flour
1 tablespoon tomato purée
1 cup beef stock
1/2 cup (2 ounces) shredded reduced-fat Cheddar cheese
4 whole wheat buns, split

Make four 3-ounce beef patties, reserving the remaining ground beef. Arrange the patties on a plate and chill, covered, in the refrigerator. Spray a nonstick skillet with nonstick cooking spray and place over medium heat. Add the remaining ground beef and sauté until the beef turns gray. Add 2 tablespoons of the onion; cook, stirring frequently, for 30 seconds. Add the garlic, then sprinkle the chili powder, cumin and flour over the ground beef. Cook, stirring frequently, for 30 seconds. Whisk in the tomato purée and stock. Cook, stirring occasionally, until the mixture thickens slightly. Remove from the heat and keep warm. Grill the beef patties over hot coals until done to your liking. Arrange 1 patty on the bottom slice of each bun. Top with chili, some of the remaining minced onion, cheese and the top of the bun. *Yield: 4 servings*

The Fries

2 medium potatoes, peeled and cut into thick slices
Salt and freshly ground black pepper to taste
1/8 teaspoon paprika

Blanch the potatoes in boiling water in a saucepan for 1 minute; drain, cool and pat dry. Spray a large baking sheet with nonstick cooking spray. Arrange the potatoes on the baking sheet in a single layer without touching one another. Bake at 400 degrees for 20 to 25 minutes or until crisp and slightly brown. Remove from the oven and sprinkle with salt, pepper and paprika. *Yield: 4 servings*

Nutrients Per Serving: Cal 305; Prot 34 g; Carbo 39 g; Fat 7 g; 21% Cal from Fat; Sod 366 mg

Moussaka

This homey Greek-style casserole, with its slightly exotic but subtle spicing, is one of our favorite Mediterranean comfort foods. We usually serve it with a tomato, cucumber, parsley, and chick-pea salad tossed in a simple vinaigrette as a contrasting side dish.

2 teaspoons olive oil
1 1/2 cups diced onions
12 ounces ultra lean, all-natural ground beef, crumbled
3 garlic cloves, minced
2 cups canned diced tomatoes with juice
1/2 cup tomato purée
1/4 cup red wine
1/2 teaspoon ground cinnamon
1/8 teaspoon each: ground cloves and ground allspice
1 small bay leaf
1/4 teaspoon salt and freshly ground black pepper to taste
2 medium eggplants sliced lengthwise into 1/4-inch-thick slices, lightly salted
1 cup 2% milk
2 tablespoons flour
1/8 teaspoon ground nutmeg
1 ounce reduced-fat cream cheese
Salt and freshly ground black pepper to taste
1/2 cup grated Parmesan cheese

Sauté the onions slowly with the oil, covered, until soft. Add the ground beef and garlic and cook, stirring occasionally, until the ground beef is lightly browned. Add the next nine ingredients. Reduce the heat and simmer until the mixture thickens (30 min). Rinse the eggplant and pat dry with paper towels. Arrange the eggplant on a sprayed baking sheet. Bake at 400 degrees for 10 to 15 minutes or until soft and lightly browned. Simmer the milk, flour and nutmeg in a saucepan over medium heat, stirring frequently, until slightly thickened. Melt in the cream cheese. Taste and correct the seasonings. Spray a baking dish with nonstick cooking spray. Layer 1/2 the eggplant in the bottom of the dish, top with the ground beef mixture and add the remaining eggplant. Pour the cream sauce over the eggplant. Sprinkle the Parmesan cheese over the top. Bake, uncovered, at 350 degrees for 45 minutes or until golden and bubbly. *Yield: 6 servings*

Nutrients Per Serving: Cal 227; Prot 21 g; Carbo 26 g; Fat 7 g; 28% Cal from Fat; Sod 483 mg

iron it out

Many women and children have difficulty obtaining adequate iron from their diet alone. However, eating a small amount of meat, fish or poultry with beans or tofu increases your body's ability to absorb and utilize iron. Iron is absorbed best when in an acid environment, so drink your orange and grapefruit juice. You can triple iron absorption by taking in at least 30 mg of vitamin C with a veggie or other non-meat source of iron. The best-absorbed form of iron, glycolytic iron, is found in iron-fortified infant cereal. Add it to muffins, bread, meatloaf or cooked cereal. Try cooking in Grandma's cast-iron cookware. Scrambling an egg in a cast-iron skillet triples the amount of iron in the egg. And be aware that the tannins in tea decrease the absorption of iron, so drink your tea between meals.

Kressnopita

From the earliest annals of recorded history, the lamb has played a pivotal role in the development of Western civilization. This small, hardy animal, prized both for its meat and wool, adapted perfectly to sustain the nomadic lifestyles of early peoples. And, for centuries, lamb has been a symbol of both sacrifice and celebration. Our favorite cut by far is London broil. While not inexpensive, it is extremely lean, yields almost 100% when cooked, and is conveniently sized (1 to 1 1/2 pounds) for most uses. Prepare several simple celebratory roasts, then freeze the leftovers until you have enough for this Greek lamb pie.

2	**teaspoons olive oil**
3/4	**cup diced onion**
1/2	**cup each: diced carrot and diced zucchini**
3	**garlic cloves, minced**
2	**tomatoes, peeled, seeded and diced**
1/4	**cup raisins**
12	**pitted kalamata olives, cut into halves**
1	**teaspoon dried leaf oregano**
1/2	**teaspoon ground cinnamon**
1/2	**cup white wine**
	Salt and freshly ground black pepper to taste
16	**ounces cooked lean lamb, cubed**
1	**tablespoon each: chopped fresh parsley and chopped fresh mint leaves**
3	**ounces feta cheese, cut into small cubes**
6	**sheets frozen phyllo dough, thawed**
1/2	**cup Tzatziki Sauce (Page 88)**

Heat the olive oil in a nonstick skillet over medium heat. Add the onion and carrot and sauté until the vegetables are soft. Add the zucchini and garlic; cook for 30 seconds. Stir in the tomatoes, raisins, olives, oregano, cinnamon, wine, salt and pepper. Simmer until most of the liquid has evaporated. Remove from the heat; set aside and cool to room temperature. When cool, add the lamb, parsley, mint and cheese; stir and set aside. Place a sheet of phyllo dough on a clean, flat, dry surface with the long edge facing you. Cut into halves. Spray both pieces lightly with nonstick cooking spray. Arrange 1 piece on top of the other. Arrange 1/6 of the lamb mixture on the bottom of the dough, leaving a 3/4-inch border on the bottom and each side. Roll away from you 1 full roll to encase the lamb. Fold the sides in toward the middle. Spray the exposed dough lightly with nonstick cooking spray. Continue to roll, spraying exposed dry surfaces with cooking spray as you go. Repeat the process with the remaining lamb and phyllo dough until you have 6 rolls. Arrange the rolls in a single layer without touching one another on a baking sheet. Bake at 350 degrees for 25 minutes or until golden. Serve with a dollop of Tzatziki Sauce on the side. *Yield: 6 servings*

Nutrients Per Serving: Cal 323; Prot 25 g; Carbo 24 g; Fat 12 g; 33% Cal from Fat; Sod 500 mg

The Berry Best ✳ They say what separates the professional chef from the amateur cook is the sauce work. Well here's a "saucy" secret to put you in front of the pack. Take a bag of unsweetened frozen fruit (berries are best). Thaw. Purée. Strain. Add confectioners' sugar and lemon juice to taste. Voila! You have produced a professional-quality fruit sauce in mere minutes. And fruit sauces are not just for dessert - try them with smoked and grilled foods. Our smoked pork tenderloin with a blackberry sauce is a perennial favorite with guests.

Chilaquiles de Estudiante

The direct translation of chilaquiles is "broken up old sombrero," a reference to the use of stale tortilla strips. A more useful, if less colorful, definition might be "casserole with stale tortilla strips," and there are a limitless number of Mexican recipes that would fit that definition. This one, a student's casserole, would traditionally be made with a less expensive, higher fat cut of pork — students can't afford tenderloin. But using the tenderloin here goes a long way toward leaning up the final results and, in the amount used, should be quite affordable. In spite of its relatively low fat content, this is a very substantial dish. Serve with a green salad and black or pinto beans to complete the meal.

12 **corn tortillas**
16 **ounces pork tenderloin, trimmed or boneless skinless chicken or turkey breast**
4 **cups water**
1 **cup chopped onion**
1 **garlic clove, minced**
1/2 **teaspoon salt**
3 **medium tomatoes, peeled and chopped**
1 1/2 **cups chopped onions**
2 **garlic cloves, minced**
1/4 **cup raisins**
18 **small pimento-stuffed green olives, cut into halves**
1 **tablespoon cider vinegar**
1 **teaspoon sugar**
Salt and freshly ground black pepper to taste
4 to 5 medium ancho chiles
1 1/2 **cups chopped onions**
2 **garlic cloves, minced**
1/8 **teaspoon each: ground cinnamon and ground cloves**
2 **teaspoons canola oil**
2 **tomatoes, peeled and chopped**
2 **tablespoons shredded reduced-fat Cheddar cheese**
1/4 **cup chopped fresh cilantro leaves**
2 **tablespoons crumbled queso fresco or feta cheese**

Cut the tortillas into 1/2-inch wide strips. Arrange on a baking sheet and bake at 300 degrees for 10 to 15 minutes or until stiff but not browned. Remove from the oven and set aside. Cut the pork into 2-inch lengths. Combine the pork, water, 1 cup onion, 1 garlic clove and salt in a saucepan over medium heat. Simmer for 20 to 25 minutes or until the pork is tender. Drain, reserving the liquid. Chop or shred the pork; set aside. Combine 3 tomatoes, 1 1/2 cups onions and 2 garlic cloves in a blender or food processor; process until smooth. Remove the mixture to a saucepan over medium heat. Add the reserved pork, raisins, olives, vinegar, sugar, salt, pepper and 1 cup of the reserved cooking liquid. Simmer until the mixture begins to thicken. Add the tortilla strips. Remove from the heat and set aside. Toast the chiles in a heavy, dry skillet over medium-high heat for 2 to 3 minutes, turning the chiles frequently. Remove the skillet from the heat; stem and seed the chiles. Soak the chiles in hot water in a bowl for 20 minutes or until soft. Combine the chiles, 1/2 cup onions, 2 garlic cloves, cinnamon, cloves and a little of the chile soaking liquid, if necessary, in a blender or food processor; purée. Heat the canola oil in a heavy saucepan over medium heat. Add the chile purée and cook for 3 to 4 minutes. Purée 2 tomatoes in a blender or food processor and add to the chile pepper mixture. Cook for 2 minutes; add 2 cups of reserved pork cooking liquid. Simmer until the mixture reduces and thickens slightly. Arrange the pork mixture in a casserole dish. Pour the chile sauce over the pork; top with Cheddar cheese. Bake at 350 degrees for 30 minutes. Serve garnished with cilantro and queso fresco. *Yield: 6 servings*

Nutrients Per Serving: Cal 393; Prot 24 g; Carbo 52 g; Fat 9 g; 21% Cal from Fat; Sod 522 mg

Chiles Rellenos en Nogadas

This is the stuffed chile of Mexico; the one by which all others are measured. The pungent, dark green peppers are filled with pork, nuts, fruit, and vegetables, then topped with a chilled walnut cream sauce and a sweet-jeweled sprinkling of pomegranate seeds. The complementary and contrasting flavors, colors, and texture mariachi through your mouth with every bite. Citron (candied pineapple) is another common and delicious addition to the filling. Bear in mind, and be comforted by the fact, that a substantial amount of the fat in this dish comes from healthy monounsaturated walnuts.

1 medium onion, diced
12 ounces pork tenderloin trimmed and cut into 2-inch lengths
3 garlic cloves, minced
1/8 teaspoon salt
6 black peppercorns
1 teaspoon olive oil
2 tablespoons each: minced red bell pepper and minced carrot
1/2 cup minced apple
2 tomatoes, roasted, peeled and chopped
2 tablespoons raisins
3 tablespoons chopped walnuts
1/2 teaspoon sugar
1/4 teaspoon ground cinnamon
6 poblano chiles, roasted, peeled and seeded
2 tablespoons pomegranate seeds

Set aside 1/4 cup of the minced onion. Combine the remaining onion, pork, half of the garlic, all of the salt and peppercorns in a saucepan over medium heat. Add enough water to cover. Simmer for 30 minutes. Remove from the heat and cool. Remove and shred the pork; set aside. Heat the olive oil in a nonstick skillet over medium-low heat. Add the reserved 1/4 cup onion, remaining garlic, bell pepper, carrot and apple; cook, covered, until the vegetables are soft. Remove the lid and add the shredded pork, tomatoes, raisins, walnuts, sugar and cinnamon. Simmer until fairly dry. Remove from the heat and cool. Cut the tops off of the chiles. Stuff some of the pork mixture into each of the chiles. Arrange the stuffed chiles on a baking sheet. Bake at 350 degrees until heated through. Remove from the oven. Arrange 1 chile on each of 6 plates, cover with Walnut Cream Sauce and garnish with pomegranate seeds. *Yield: 6 servings*

The Walnut Cream Sauce

1/2 cup walnut pieces
2 cups boiling water
4 ounces reduced-fat cream cheese
1/4 cup fat-free sour cream
1/4 cup skim milk
2 tablespoons sherry
3 garlic cloves, minced
1/8 teaspoon ground cumin
1 teaspoon sugar

Drop the walnuts into the boiling water in a saucepan. Remove from the heat, cover and set aside for 5 minutes. Drain, discarding the soaking liquid, and rub or pick off as much of the brown exterior walnut skin as possible. Combine the walnuts, cream cheese, sour cream, milk, sherry, cumin and sugar in a blender or food processor; process until smooth. Chill in the refrigerator until ready to use. *Yield: 6 servings*

Nutrients Per Serving: Cal 315; Prot 19 g; Carbo 23 g; Fat 15 g; 43% Cal from Fat; Sod 153 mg

Honey Mustard Pork with Shiner Bock

Just about all the meats in the United States have become considerably leaner in the last ten years, primarily because consumers have said that's what they want. Charging from the rear to the lead of this pack is pork — now even boldly billing itself as "the other white meat," alluding to its new similarity to chicken breast in terms of fat content. If we choose the leanest cuts — the loin or tenderloin — trim them of visible fat, and consume them in moderate portions, we can indeed enjoy pork as part of a healthy diet without "pigging out." This recipe, a fall favorite at the resort, pan sears the tenderloin and finishes it with a quick pan reduction sauce provincially featuring (some might say providentially) a locally brewed dark beer of some renown.

16 ounces pork tenderloin, trimmed
Salt and freshly ground black pepper to taste
1 teaspoon canola oil
1/2 cup minced onion
2 garlic cloves, minced
1 (12-ounce) bottle Shiner Bock beer or other bock beer
1/2 cup beef stock
1/4 cup Dijon mustard
2 tablespoons honey
1 teaspoon minced fresh rosemary, or 1/2 teaspoon dried rosemary
1 tablespoon cider vinegar
2 teaspoons green peppercorns in brine, drained
1/4 cup fat-free sour cream

Cut the pork into 8 medallions. Season each with salt and pepper. Heat the canola oil in a heavy cast-iron skillet over medium-high heat. Sear the pork for 2 minutes per side. Remove the pork to a plate; cover and set aside. Add the onion to the skillet; cook, stirring, until it begins to brown. Stir in the garlic. Add the beer, stock, Dijon mustard, honey, rosemary, vinegar and peppercorns. Cook, stirring with a wooden spoon to incorporate all the brown bits, until reduced to 3/4 cup. Whisk in the sour cream and add any pork juices accumulated from the plate. Arrange 2 pork medallions on each of 4 plates. Top with sauce and serve immediately. *Yield: 4 servings*

Nutrients Per Serving: Cal 299; Prot 26 g; Carbo 18 g; Fat 5 g; 15% Cal from Fat; Sod 572 mg

Stop what you are doing, set this cookbook down, close your eyes and take a few really good, deep cleansing breaths. Feel your shoulders relax and settle. Notice the intoxication as these deep inhalations breathe new life into you. Consciously move from a state of stress to a relaxed repose. Now promise yourself to treat yourself to this wonderful feeling several times a day. Taking time to breathe will help you to calm your mind and stop the constant chatter. Breathe deeply and clear your mind of the ongoing chatter of things to do, information to remember, people to call and places to be. Each day, our clear thinking becomes cluttered by thousands of background thoughts. Let go of these repetitive thoughts and relax. Focus on one task at a time, one breath at a time.

WELL BEING

Molasses-Glazed Pork with Papaya and Avocado Salsa and Crispy Hoppin' John Cakes

Many of our favorite dishes — those that brim over with bright, bold flavors, create a sensation we describe as "a circus for the mouth." This island-inspired entrée invokes, if not a circus, then surely a carnival — every bite a cascade of fire and ice, sugar and spice. Sweet and cool tropical fruits are spiked with chile and lime. A splash of vinegar sasses up a warm pool of rum and molasses for the smoky pork. And the pea and rice fritter with a famous namesake brings a welcome chew and crunch, in addition to substantial nutrition. It's all designed to put you on "island time" — the next best thing to "spa time."

1 cup diced, seeded and peeled papaya
1/2 cup diced, seeded and peeled avocado
2 green onions, minced
2 tablespoons diced red bell pepper
1 garlic clove, minced
1/2 serrano chile, minced
2 tablespoons chopped fresh cilantro leaves
1/2 teaspoon sugar
1/8 teaspoon salt
1 tablespoon each: lime juice and canola oil
8 (2-ounce) pork tenderloin medallions seasoned with salt and freshly ground pepper
1/4 cup minced onion
1 tablespoon rum
1/2 cup beef stock
1/4 cup molasses
2 tablespoons cider vinegar

Toss the first ten ingredients in a bowl. Chill. Sear the pork on both sides over medium-high heat with canola oil; remove from the skillet. Cover and set aside. Add the onion to the skillet and cook, stirring occasionally, until it begins to brown. Add the rum, stock, molasses and vinegar. Cook, stirring occasionally, until the liquid is reduced to a sauce consistency. Stir in any juices accumulated around the pork. Pool some sauce in the middle of each of 4 plates. Top with 2 pork medallions and some fruit salsa. Arrange a Hoppin' John Cake on the side. *Yield: 4 servings*

The Hoppin' John Cakes

1/2 cup dried black-eyed peas, soaked for 8 hours or overnight
2 tablespoons chopped onion
1 garlic clove, minced
1 tablespoon each: chopped red bell pepper, chopped celery, chopped fresh cilantro leaves
1/4 teaspoon salt
1/8 teaspoon each: black pepper and cayenne pepper
1/4 cup cooked rice
1/3 cup cornmeal
2 tablespoons flour
4 teaspoons canola oil

Drain the peas; blanch in boiling water in a saucepan for 5 minutes and drain again. Combine the peas with the onion, garlic, bell pepper, celery, cilantro, salt, black pepper and cayenne pepper in a blender or food processor; pulse until of coarse meal consistency. Remove to a bowl and add the rice, cornmeal and flour. Work with your hands, using a little water if needed, until the dough comes together when you press it. Shape the mixture into 8 patties. Heat the canola oil in a heavy nonstick skillet over medium-high heat. Sauté the patties until crispy on both sides. *Yield: 4 servings*

Nutrients Per Serving: Cal 501; Prot 31 g; Carbo 48 g; Fat 16 g; 29% Cal from Fat; Sod 366 mg

Phat Thai

This dish, often called Pad Thai, is, in a sense, a national Thai treasure. It is as common and as celebrated as our hamburger, and like the hamburger, Phat Thai represents a basic recipe with countless variations on the central theme. Also, like our burger, you will find this spicy noodle dish sold on almost every street corner and in nearly every restaurant. Look for rice stick noodles and fish sauce in an Oriental grocery store, or in the Oriental section of your supermarket. You can make a vegetarian version of this dish by substituting additional tofu for the shrimp and pork, and soy sauce for the fish sauce, but it is the variety of flavors and textures that makes this dish so special.

8 ounces rice stick noodles
1 tablespoon peanut oil
1 1/2 tablespoons minced garlic
4 ounces medium shrimp, peeled and deveined
4 ounces pork tenderloin, sliced thin or chicken breast
3 tablespoons Thai fish sauce (nam pla)
1/3 cup white vinegar
1/3 cup sugar
2 tablespoons ketchup
1/4 cup diced firm tofu
1/2 cup egg substitute
2 serrano chiles, thinly sliced
4 green onions, cut into 1-inch lengths
1 cup bean sprouts
1/4 cup finely chopped dry-roasted peanuts
1/4 cup chopped fresh cilantro leaves

Soak the rice noodles in hot water to cover in a bowl for about 15 minutes or until soft. Heat the peanut oil in a heavy nonstick skillet over medium-high heat. Add the garlic and stir-fry until it begins to color. Add the shrimp and pork; stir-fry for 1 minute. Mix the fish sauce, vinegar, sugar and ketchup in a bowl. Add to the stir-fry; stir and bring mixture to a boil. Drain the noodles and add them to the sauce. Add the tofu and mix well. Add the egg substitute and cook, without stirring, until the egg begins to set. Add the chiles and green onions; stir-fry until the egg is completely cooked. Mix in the bean sprouts, peanuts and cilantro. Serve immediately. *Yield: 4 servings*

Nutrients Per Serving: Cal 569; Prot 23 g; Carbo 90 g; Fat 10 g; 16% Cal from Fat; Sod 1266 mg

chefstip

"A Peeling" Fruit ✳ Peeling mangoes, pineapples, papayas, and melons is easy once you know the trick. With each of these fruits, you begin the same way. Using a sharp French or chef's knife, cut a strip from both the top and bottom of the fruit large enough to allow it to stand firmly upright (with the pineapple you will be cutting off the entire crown at the top). Now pare away the skin with the knife, starting at the top and carving downward strips until you have gone all around the fruit. At this point each fruit presents its own individual challenge. The mango contains a large elliptical seed that mimics the shape of the fruit. Feel for it with the knife and carve closely around it. The pineapple has a cylindrical core. Simply quarter the fruit vertically and then carve out the core. The papaya and melon have hollow centers with seeds. Cut the fruit in half and scrape out the seeds.

Pueblo Pork and Red Bean Chili

Many macho Texas "chili heads" insist that the real thing must be made with beef — lots of it — and no beans. Just sear up a couple of pounds of steer, throw in some onions, a bunch of chili powder, water and tomatoes, and let 'er rip. In New Mexico, however, pork is at least as likely to be the meat of choice, and beans are welcome. Using leaner cuts, like the loin, can produce a steaming bowl of red that sticks to the ribs and satisfies, while keeping the fat and meat intake at reasonable levels. A little bit of crisped, natural bacon provides a lot of flavor and not as much fat as you might think (1 1/4 grams per serving). The coffee rounds everything out with a slightly bitter, toasty undercurrent that plays against the sweetness of the tomatoes and pork. Score one for the neighbors.

4 slices all-natural, nitrate-free bacon
4 teaspoons olive oil
24 ounces pork loin, trimmed and cut into 3/4-inch cubes
Salt and freshly ground black pepper to taste
3 cups diced onions
2 to 3 serrano chiles, seeded and minced
6 garlic cloves, minced
1/3 cup chili powder
1 tablespoon ground cumin
2 teaspoons dried leaf oregano
1/4 teaspoon cayenne pepper
2 cups beef stock
1 cup brewed coffee
1 cup water
1 (28-ounce) can crushed tomatoes with purée
6 cups cooked red beans
6 tablespoons chopped red onion
1/4 cup chopped fresh cilantro leaves
1/4 cup diced avocado
8 lime wedges

Cook the bacon in a heavy skillet over medium-high heat until crisp. Drain, blot dry and crumble; set aside. Discard the bacon grease from the skillet. Add half the olive oil and return the skillet to medium-high heat. Season the pork with salt and pepper. Add to the skillet and brown on all sides. Remove the pork to a plate, cover and keep warm. Add the remaining olive oil and onion to the skillet; sauté until the onions turn golden. Add the chiles and garlic; cook, stirring constantly, for 30 seconds. Add the chili powder, cumin, oregano and cayenne pepper; cook, stirring, for 30 seconds. Add the stock, coffee, water, tomatoes and reserved pork. Simmer until the pork is tender. Add the beans; cook until heated through. Taste and adjust the seasonings, if necessary. Serve garnished with red onion, cilantro, avocado and a lime wedge. *Yield: 8 (2-cup) servings*

Nutrients Per Serving: Cal 453; Prot 36 g; Carbo 50 g; Fat 9 g; 18% Cal from Fat; Sod 451 mg

Rosemary-Crusted Pork Loin Roast with Cherry Sauce

Slow-roasted, herb-crusted meat or poultry, finished with a fruit-accented pan sauce, is a classic theme with a dozen or more delicious variations. One of our fall and winter holiday favorites is a mild, lean pork roast, slathered first with a spicy rosemary rub, then served sliced with a ribbon of dark, sweet cherry sauce fortified by deglazed pan juices.

1	**(32-ounce) boneless pork loin roast**
2	**tablespoons minced fresh rosemary leaves**
3	**garlic cloves, minced**
1	**tablespoon each: coarsely ground black pepper and brown sugar**
1/8	**teaspoon cayenne pepper**
1/4	**teaspoon garlic powder**
1	**tablespoon soy sauce**
1	**teaspoon canola oil**
3	**cups beef stock, reduced to 1 1/2 cups**
1 1/2	**cups fresh or thawed frozen pitted cherries**
2	**tablespoons orange liqueur**
1/2	**teaspoon grated orange zest**
1/8	**teaspoon salt**
1/4	**cup sugar**
3	**tablespoons raspberry vinegar**
2	**tablespoons cornstarch, dissolved in a little beef stock**

Trim the roast of all but 1/8 inch of top fat. Arrange the roast in a baking pan. Combine the rosemary, garlic, black pepper, brown sugar, cayenne pepper, garlic powder, soy sauce and canola oil in a bowl; mix until a paste forms. Rub the paste all over the roast. Refrigerate the roast for 1 to 2 hours. Preheat the oven to 450 degrees. Arrange the roast on a rack, fat side up, in a roasting pan and place in the oven. Immediately reduce the temperature to 325 degrees and roast for 1 1/2 hours or until a meat thermometer inserted into the center registers 150 degrees. Remove the roast to a platter for 20 minutes. Set the roasting pan over medium heat and add 1/2 cup of reduced beef stock. Cook, stirring with a wooden spoon to incorporate all the brown bits, for 1 to 2 minutes. Remove the mixture to a saucepan over medium-high heat. Add the remaining reduced beef stock, cherries, liqueur, zest, salt, sugar, vinegar and cornstarch mixture. Cook, stirring frequently, until the mixture thickens. Serve the roast sliced with sauce drizzled over the top. *Yield: 6 servings*

Nutrients Per Serving: Cal 351; Prot 36 g; Carbo 26 g; Fat 7 g; 18% Cal from Fat; Sod 641 mg

give your immunity a boost

To increase hydration and boost your immune system, add a two-ounce blend of Echinacea, ginger, vitamin C, zinc or other immune-building herbs to your daily intake of water. You can also add the mixture to your favorite juice or other caffeine-free beverage. The anti-oxidant and healing properties of green tea are also well known and there are many ways to dress up the flavor with fresh herbs from your garden. Catnip and chamomile can be added to tea for a calming effect. Lemon balm, lemon verbena and lemon basil are also tasty and healthy additions.

HOME SPA

Shrimp and Pork Satay on Thai Cucumber and Eggplant Salad

Chinese food has been popular in this country for quite some time. But, in recent years, other Asian foods, notably those from Thailand and Japan, have increasingly tantalized our taste buds. These cuisines, with their big, bright flavors, emphasis on vegetables, and quick-cooking techniques, are made to order for twenty-first century American tastes. This dish, with small amounts of lean meat and seafood grilled quickly over charcoal, then served with our slimmed-down version of a traditional spicy peanut sauce on a crisp cool salad, is a perfect example.

1/4 cup reduced-fat smooth all-natural peanut butter
1/3 cup hot water
Grated zest and juice of 1 lime
2 tablespoons brown sugar
2 tablespoons light soy sauce
1 tablespoon minced fresh gingerroot
1 teaspoon minced garlic
2 teaspoons Asian chile paste
2 teaspoons pure coconut extract
2 tablespoons chopped fresh cilantro leaves
1 serrano chile, minced
2 garlic cloves, minced
1 tablespoon brown sugar
2 teaspoons Thai fish sauce (nam pla)
1/8 teaspoon ground white pepper
1/4 cup fresh lemon juice
1 large cucumber, peeled, split, seeded and thinly sliced
2 medium tomatoes, cut into thin wedges
1/2 cup thinly sliced red onion
1/3 cup chopped fresh mint leaves
8 ounces Japanese eggplant, sliced vertically or regular eggplant
8 ounces pork tenderloin, trimmed and cut into 3/4-inch cubes
8 ounces medium shrimp, peeled and deveined
8 wooden skewers, soaked in hot water for 30 minutes

Combine the peanut butter, hot water, lime zest, lime juice, brown sugar, soy sauce, ginger, garlic, chile paste and coconut extract in a bowl; mix well and set aside. Combine the cilantro, chile, garlic, brown sugar, fish sauce, white pepper and lemon juice in a separate bowl and mix well. Add the cucumber, tomatoes, red onion and mint; stir to combine. Grill the eggplant over hot coals until soft and golden. Add to the cucumber mixture. Thread pork and shrimp onto wooden skewers. Grill over hot coals until done. Serve over eggplant-cucumber salad with peanut sauce on the side. *Yield: 4 servings*

Nutrients Per Serving: Cal 320; Prot 28 g; Carbo 29 g; Fat 9 g; 25% Cal from Fat; Sod 751 mg

Spaghetti with Red Swiss Chard and Bacon

True story. A vegetarian friend of ours, traveling across the South a couple of years ago, found himself in a small town diner for lunch. Noting the meat-heavy bent of the menu, he asked the waitress if he might simply have a plate of vegetables. Eager to please (Southern Hospitality ever present), the waitress cheerfully complied and before he knew it, he had before him a steaming platter of collard greens — with visible bits of ham intertwined — mashed potatoes with chicken-based cream gravy, and fried okra. Any bets on the fat they used to fry the okra? In the South, you see, it really isn't a vegetable dish unless it has meat in it. Well, truth be told, unless you're a vegetarian, there is a real affinity between pork and greens. So, the trick for many of us is not whether to use pork, it's making sure to use the right pork. We use a lean, chemical-free bacon in modest amounts. We pour off the saturated fat and replace it with monounsaturated olive oil. We use organic greens grown in our own gardens, some garlic, pasta, and naturally low-fat Parmesan cheese. It all adds up to a low-fat, hearty supper that would please any vegetarian who plays by Southern rules.

4 Roma tomatoes, cut lengthwise into halves
1 bunch red Swiss chard
4 strips all-natural, nitrate-free bacon
1 tablespoon olive oil
1 cup sliced onion
2 garlic cloves, minced
Salt and freshly ground black pepper to taste
6 cups cooked spaghetti
1/2 cup grated Parmesan cheese

Spray a baking sheet with nonstick cooking spray. Arrange the tomatoes on the baking sheet and bake at 300 degrees for 2 hours. Trim the stems from the chard. Chop the stems and leaves separately. Blanch the stems in boiling water in a saucepan for 2 minutes. Add the leaves and blanch for an additional 2 minutes; drain and set aside. Sauté the bacon in a heavy skillet over medium-high heat until crisp. Remove the bacon to paper towels to drain. Discard the bacon fat in the skillet, then add the olive oil and onion. Reduce the heat to medium and cook, stirring occasionally, until the onion is caramelized. Add the garlic and cook, stirring constantly, for a few seconds. Add the chard; mix well. Season with salt and pepper. Cut the roasted tomatoes into quarters and add them to the chard mixture. Crumble the bacon into the mixture. Heat thoroughly and toss with the hot spaghetti. Sprinkle the cheese over the top. *Yield: 4 servings*

Nutrients Per Serving: Cal 460; Prot 18 g; Carbo 68 g; Fat 9 g; 18% Cal from Fat; Sod 407 mg

chefstip

Land Of The "Free" ✱ In recent years, manufacturers have begun to offer us many of our favorite products in reduced-fat and even fat-free versions. Leading the pack has been the dairy industry, and today there is scarcely a product which cannot be purchased with these options. Regular, reduced-fat, low-fat, fat-free, take your pick. But how low can you go, and still get what you want? Being fat-free is not a sufficient enough virtue to stand alone – the product has to produce. We experiment with a lot of them, embracing the good ones, rejecting those that do not work, trying to strike a positive nutritional balance, but remembering that taste, texture and eating satisfaction are our bottom line. We hope that you can take a look at some of the things we use and apply them to your own recipes to produce healthier and better tasting food. Because the land of the free is really about freedom of choice.

desserts

desserts

desserts

Polenta Pound Cake with Oranges, Pg.182

desserts

Golden Carrot Almond Cake

The idea of including one or two ounces of nuts or seeds in your daily diet as part of a healthy regimen has gained widespread credibility in recent years. These little packets of encapsulated energy are bursting with vital nutritional elements and are an excellent source of monounsaturates. One of our favorite ways of practicing such a healthy regimen is this deliciously light carrot cake, which derives virtually all of its fat from almonds.

1/4 cup (or more) fine dry bread crumbs
1 cup whole almonds with skins, chopped
1 cup egg substitute
3/4 cup sugar
1/2 pound finely shredded carrots
1 1/2 tablespoons dark or amber rum
1 teaspoon pure almond extract
2 teaspoons baking powder
1 teaspoon grated lemon zest
1/2 teaspoon salt
2 tablespoons confectioners' sugar
1 teaspoon grated nutmeg
1 1/2 cups fat-free whipped topping

Combine the bread crumbs and almonds in a food processor. Process until finely ground, but not paste. Remove and set aside. Combine the egg substitute and sugar in a mixing bowl and beat on high for 2 minutes. Add the ground nut mixture, carrots, rum, almond extract, baking powder, lemon zest and salt. Beat until all the ingredients are incorporated. Spray a 9-inch springform pan with nonstick cooking spray, then dust with bread crumbs. Pour the batter into the pan. Bake at 350 degrees for 40 to 45 minutes. Remove from the oven and cool. Remove the side from the springform pan; dust the top of the cake with confectioners' sugar and nutmeg. Serve with a dollop of whipped topping. *Yield: 16 servings*

Nutrients Per Serving: Cal 132; Prot 4 g; Carbo 17 g; Fat 5 g; 35% Cal from Fat; Sod 185 mg

why weight?

Strength training is a vital component of any balanced exercise program. This includes any weight bearing exercise, such as machines, free weights, resistance tubing or bands, Yoga, Pilates, or any activity where you are lifting against gravity. Weight bearing exercises have been shown to strengthen muscles, increase metabolism and bone density and improve posture and balance. Since we tend to lose bone density as we age, weight bearing exercise is an effective tool in the prevention of osteoporosis. Best of all, increased strength will enable you to perform everyday tasks with greater ease and less stress to the body, allowing you to participate in life more fully.

FITNESS

Buttermilk Fig Cake

A higher-fat version of this recipe first came to our attention in an old Carolina Inns Cookbook. The trick was to see if we could ratchet down the fat grams without giving up on all that homespun goodness. We have to say we are right pleased with the results. As dense and moist as you could hope for, this cake has been a Lake Austin Spa Resort favorite for years.

2 eggs
2 egg whites
1 1/2 cups sugar
1 tablespoon canola oil
3 (2 1/2-ounce) jars of baby food prunes
2 cups flour
1 teaspoon ground nutmeg
1 teaspoon ground allspice
1 teaspoon ground cinnamon
1 teaspoon salt
2 teaspoons baking soda
1 teaspoon baking powder
2/3 cup buttermilk
1 teaspoon pure vanilla extract
1 1/2 cups chopped preserved figs or canned figs, drained
1/3 cup chopped pecans (optional)

The Glaze

1/4 cup buttermilk
1/2 cup sugar
1/4 teaspoon baking soda
1 1/2 teaspoons cornstarch
1 tablespoon light butter
1 1/2 teaspoons pure vanilla extract

Combine the eggs and egg whites in a mixing bowl. Beat on high until frothy. Beat in the 1 1/2 cups sugar, oil and prunes. Sift the flour, nutmeg, allspice, cinnamon, salt, 2 teaspoons baking soda and baking powder together. Add the sifted dry ingredients and buttermilk alternately to the egg mixture, mixing well after each addition. Mix in the vanilla. Fold in the figs and pecans. Spray a 9-inch springform pan lightly with nonstick cooking spray. Pour the batter into prepared pan. Bake at 350 degrees for approximately 55 minutes or until the cake tests done. Remove from the oven and cool in the pan for 10 minutes. Combine the buttermilk, 1/2 cup sugar, 1/4 teaspoon baking soda, cornstarch and butter in a saucepan over medium-high heat. Bring to a boil. Cook for 2 minutes, stirring frequently. Remove from the heat and cool completely. Stir in the vanilla. Remove the side from the springform pan. Drizzle the glaze over the cake. *Yield: 16 servings*

Nutrients Per Serving: Cal 287; Prot 5 g; Carbo 65 g; Fat 3 g; 8% Cal from Fat; Sod 392 mg

Chocolate Cappuccino Pudding Cake

Listed as the first definition under "Comfort Desserts" in the Lake Austin Spa Resort's Book of Things We'd Rather Not Do Without, a warm cup of this double-Chocolate Cappuccino Pudding Cake, served with a dollop of frozen vanilla yogurt is a combination that cannot be improved upon. Part of the molten magic is that the cake portion starts on the bottom, but rises during the baking to replace the pudding ingredients, which originally start on the top.

1 1/2 teaspoons baking powder
1 cup flour
1/2 cup sugar
2 tablespoons baking cocoa
1/4 teaspoon salt
1/2 cup evaporated skim milk
1 teaspoon canola oil
1 teaspoon pure vanilla extract
1 egg white
1/4 cup semisweet chocolate morsels, melted
1 cup packed brown sugar
1/4 cup baking cocoa
1 3/4 cups hot water
1/4 cup instant cappuccino mix (2 envelopes)

Combine the baking powder, flour, sugar, 2 tablespoons baking cocoa and salt in a large bowl. Mix the evaporated milk, canola oil, vanilla and egg white in a separate bowl. Whisk the liquid ingredients into the dry ingredients. Stir in the chocolate. Spray a 4 x 6-inch baking pan with nonstick cooking spray, then dust with flour. Spread the chocolate batter in the pan. Mix the brown sugar and 1/4 cup baking cocoa in a bowl. Sprinkle over the cake batter. Combine the hot water and cappuccino mix in a bowl. Gently pour over the top of the cake batter. Do not stir. Bake at 350 degrees for 1 hour or until the top springs back when touched. Serve warm in soup cups with a dollop of fat-free or low-fat frozen vanilla yogurt. *Yield: 9 servings*

Nutrients Per Serving: Cal 286; Prot 4 g; Carbo 60 g; Fat 4 g; 13% Cal from Fat; Sod 244 mg

chefstip

Setting A Good Eggsample ✳ Twenty years ago or so, when the words "cholesterol and saturated fat" began making headlines, we all looked around for something we could give up to lower our intake of these products. The poor egg took a beating. We just stopped eating them (at least compared to previous years). Egg white omelets began showing up on restaurant menus and egg substitutes lined grocery store shelves. Now, a large egg does contain five grams of fat, mostly saturated, and some cholesterol (all in the yolk). However, a more reasoned examination by the medicos seems to indicate that maybe we went too far in our condemnation. The egg is an excellent source of protein and other nutrients, and, for most of us, two or three per week do not seem to have any deleterious effects. At the resort, where we offer both eggs and their substitutes, we have taken an additional step towards the good by using local, organically produced eggs (lower in saturated fat and higher in healthy omega3 fatty acids). For our omelets, scrambles and desserts, we often combine these with additional whites for a healthy, tasty compromise.

Chocolate-Glazed Poppy Seed Cake with Rum Custard and Tropical Fruit

By our standards, this is a "big" dessert — a bit of a production with four separate components (cake, filling, frosting and fruit) and fairly high in sugar and calories. The good news? By most dessert makers' standards, it's a low-fat no-brainer. Whatever your perspective, it's delicious. Serve it as a special ending to a light summer supper or plantation Sunday brunch.

1/4 cup light butter, softened, plus 1 cup sugar and 1/4 cup applesauce
2 cups sifted cake flour
2 teaspoons baking powder
1/3 teaspoon salt
3/4 cup skim milk
1 teaspoon pure vanilla extract
2 tablespoons poppy seeds

Cream the butter, sugar and applesauce in a mixing bowl at high speed for 3 minutes. Beat the dry ingredients into the creamed mixture gradually, alternating with the milk. Add the vanilla and poppy seeds. Spray a 9-inch springform pan with nonstick cooking spray. Pour the batter into the prepared pan. Bake at 375 degrees for 45 to 50 minutes or until the cake tests done. Cool completely.

The Filling

1/4 cup sugar, plus 2 tablespoons cornstarch, 1/8 teaspoon salt and 1 cup 2% milk
1/2 cup egg substitute
2 tablespoons rum
1/4 teaspoon pure vanilla extract

Combine the first four ingredients in a saucepan over medium heat. Cook until slightly thickened, stirring constantly. Pour the egg substitute into a small bowl; whisk in about 1/4 cup of the hot sugar mixture. Pour the egg and sugar mixture quickly back into the saucepan, whisking constantly. Add the rum. Cook until thickened, stirring constantly. Stir in the vanilla. Chill, with a sheet of plastic wrap pressed against the surface of the filling.

The Glaze

1 cup confectioners' sugar, sifted
3 tablespoons baking cocoa
2 tablespoons 2% milk
1 teaspoon melted light butter
1/2 teaspoon light corn syrup

Combine all ingredients in a bowl until smooth. To assemble, split the cake horizontally into 2 layers. Carefully remove the top layer and cover the bottom layer with filling. Replace the top layer and frost with the chocolate glaze.

The Tropical Fruit Garnish

2 cups water, plus 1 cup sugar
6 cups cubed papaya, or mango, pineapple, or a combination
Zest and juice of one lime
1 (2-inch) cinnamon stick

Combine the water and sugar in a 3-quart saucepan over medium-high heat. Bring to a boil and cook until a light syrup forms. Add the fruit, lime juice, lime zest and cinnamon. Simmer for 8 minutes. Strain the syrup into a clean saucepan; place the fruit in a bowl and discard the cinnamon. Cook the syrup over high heat until reduced to 1 cup. Pour over the fruit and chill. *Yield: 16 servings*

Nutrients Per Serving: Cal 254; Prot 4 g; Carbo 54 g; Fat 3 g; 10% Cal from Fat; Sod 178 mg

Collapsed Chocolate Soufflé Cake

Appreciated as much for its ethereal, billowy texture as for its flavor, the difficulty of executing a classic French dessert soufflé is not so much in the making as it is in the timing of the presentation. The soufflé must be rushed directly from the oven to the table to display its grandiose height, for as soon as it begins to cool, it begins to shrink. Converging this tiny time window with the completion of a dinner's entrée is, at best, an uncertain proposition. The dedicated dessert chef must, like the tightrope walker, the high-rise window washer, or the buxom middle-aged movie star, contend with the constant fear of falling. This bane can be made beneficent, however, and its vice turned into virtue, if we allow the soufflé to collapse on purpose. Gravity condenses it to a rich, velvety texture and tastes completely unlike, but equally as appealing, as its progenitor. Best of all, you may now serve it at your leisure.

2/3 cup baking cocoa
1/4 cup flour
1/3 cup sugar
1/8 teaspoon salt
2/3 cup each: brewed hazelnut decaffeinated coffee and 1% milk
2 tablespoons light butter
2 ounces semisweet chocolate, chopped
2 egg yolks
6 egg whites
1/4 cup (or more) sugar

Sift the baking cocoa, flour, 1/3 cup sugar and salt into a 2-quart saucepan. Whisk in the coffee and milk. Cook over medium heat until the mixture thickens, stirring constantly. Remove the mixture to a large bowl and whisk in the butter, chocolate and egg yolks. Beat the egg whites in a mixing bowl until soft peaks form. Add the sugar, beating until the whites are thick and glossy. Fold the egg whites into the chocolate mixture. Spray a 9-inch springform pan with nonstick cooking spray, then dust with sugar. Pour in the batter. Bake at 375 degrees for 35 to 40 minutes or until the cake is puffy and set. Remove from the oven to cool and fall before cutting. If desired, serve with fat-free commercial caramel sauce, low-fat frozen vanilla yogurt or a teaspoon of chopped toasted pecans. *Yield: 12 servings*

Nutrients Per Serving: Cal 116; Prot 4 g; Carbo 18 g; Fat 4 g; 31% Cal from Fat; Sod 72 mg

candle sense

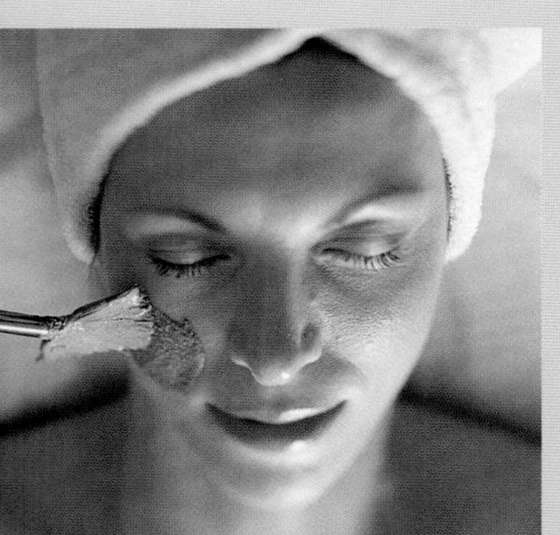

When shopping for scented candles, smell the bottom of the candle, where the fragrance tends to be stronger. When burning candles containing essential oils take care to keep the flame short. High flames give off more smoke, causing soot damage on walls and ceilings. If the flame starts to get higher, blow out the candle at least once an hour and trim the wick as low as possible, then relight. This will also help your candles last longer. And let your candles do double duty by storing them in your linen closet - they'll give your sheets and towels a lovely, fresh scent.

HOME SPA

Mocha-Glazed Chocolate Cake

Here is a dark, dense, and moist chocolate cake made without any oil or butter. Early on in the crusade to produce lower-fat desserts that still tasted good, some wise (or perhaps desperate) soul discovered that certain fruit purées work admirably well as fat replacements, supplying much of the moisture and rich mouth-feel previously provided by fat. Prune purée, conveniently available in the form of baby food, is especially useful in this regard for chocolate or spice cakes. This recipe, one of our oldest, still gets good reviews.

2 cups flour
1 cup baking cocoa
2 cups sugar
2 teaspoons baking soda
1 teaspoon baking powder
1/4 teaspoon salt
1/2 teaspoon ground cinnamon
4 (2 1/2-ounce) jars of baby food prunes
2 teaspoons pure vanilla extract
2 eggs, beaten
1 cup skim milk
1 cup strong brewed coffee

Sift the flour, baking cocoa, sugar, baking soda, baking powder, salt and cinnamon into a large bowl. Whisk the prunes, vanilla, eggs, milk and coffee in a separate bowl. Pour the prune mixture into the dry ingredients; stir just until blended. Spray a 9-inch springform pan with nonstick cooking spray. Pour in the batter. Bake at 350 degrees for 45 to 50 minutes or until the cake tests done. Cool in the pan for 10 minutes. Remove to a wire rack to cool completely. *Yield: 16 servings*

The Glaze

1/3 cup brewed coffee
1/3 cup packed brown sugar
1/3 cup baking cocoa
3 tablespoons cornstarch

Combine the coffee, brown sugar, baking cocoa and cornstarch in a saucepan over medium heat. Cook, stirring, until the mixture thickens. Spoon over the top of the cooled cake. *Yield: 16 servings*

Nutrients Per Serving: Cal 241; Prot 4 g; Carbo 55 g; Fat 1 g; 5% Cal from Fat; Sod 246 mg

Chocolate Mocha Dacquoise

Dacquoise (dak-quaz) is a classically elegant French meringue cake, typically filled with a flavored ganache (read heavy cream and chocolate), and frosted with a rich buttercream frosting (read 2 sticks of butter). It's dizzily delicious, but definitely in the special indulgence category with its hefty saturated fat gram count (read about a gazillion). Our version, still borderline ethereal, derives almost all of its fat from healthy monounsaturated toasted nuts. Even the coffee-flavored frosting, which encases the chocolate and the slightly crunchy, chewy meringue, is fat-free. Although this recipe contains several steps, and needs to be made the day before serving, the actual construction is really quite quick and simple, if you own a food processor and an electric mixer. Your reward is a dinner party level dessert, guaranteed not to go to waist.

1/2 cup blanched and toasted hazelnuts
1/2 cup blanched and toasted almonds
1/2 cup confectioners' sugar
2 tablespoons cornstarch
5 egg whites, at room temperature
3/4 cup sugar
2 teaspoons pure vanilla extract
8 ounces fat-free cream cheese, softened
3/4 cup confectioners' sugar
3/4 cup baking cocoa
1 ounce semisweet chocolate, melted
1/2 cup skim milk
1 tablespoon rum
2 tablespoons coffee-flavored liqueur
2 tablespoons instant coffee granules
12 ounces fat-free cream cheese, softened
3/4 cup confectioners' sugar
1 tablespoon sliced almonds

Combine the hazelnuts, 1/2 cup toasted almonds, confectioners' sugar and cornstarch in a food processor; process until finely ground. Beat the egg whites at low speed in a mixing bowl, then increase the speed to high and beat until soft peaks form. Add the granulated sugar 3 tablespoons at a time, beating after each addition, until the mixture is very thick and glossy. Gently fold in the nut mixture and vanilla using a rubber spatula or wooden spoon. Line an 11 x 17-inch baking pan with parchment paper. Trace two 8-inch circles onto the paper. (The bottom of an 8-inch springform pan works perfectly.) Remove the meringue mixture to a plain-tipped pastry bag and pipe into the circles, starting in the center and spiraling outward. Or simply spread the meringue carefully into the circles using a rubber spatula. Bake the meringues at 300 degrees for 30 minutes; reduce the heat to 275 degrees and bake for 1 1/2 hours longer. Remove from the oven and cool on the parchment to room temperature. Beat 8 ounces cream cheese, 3/4 cup confectioners' sugar, baking cocoa, chocolate, milk and rum in a mixing bowl until smooth. Cover with plastic wrap pressed onto the mixture's surface; set aside. Combine the coffee liqueur and instant coffee in a small saucepan over low heat. Cook just until the coffee granules dissolve. Remove to a mixing bowl and beat in 12 ounces cream cheese and 3/4 cup confectioners' sugar until smooth; set aside. To assemble the dacquoise, peel the parchment paper away from the meringues. Trim with a sharp knife, if necessary, to make them as uniform as possible. Place 1 meringue on a serving plate. Spread the chocolate filling evenly over the top. Top with the second meringue. Frost the top with the coffee mixture. Scatter the almond slices over the frosting. Chill in the refrigerator for 12 hours. *Yield: 16 servings*

Nutrients Per Serving: Cal 226; Prot 9 g; Carbo 33 g; Fat 7 g; 25% Cal from Fat; Sod 215 mg

Coconut Tres Leches Cake with Caramelized Bananas

This is arguably Mexico's most famous special occasion cake. Tres leches means three milks — typically heavy cream, sweetened condensed milk, and whole milk. Our version opts for a lighter more tropical soaking — reduced-fat coconut milk, fat-free sweetened condensed milk, and skim milk. You would think that all of this fluid infusion would turn the cake to sodden disintegration. But, in fact, it absorbs the liquids beautifully, much as does the equatorial earth absorb a sudden downpour. Accompanied by rum-caramelized bananas and topped with toasted coconut, this cake has become our most popular dessert.

2 cups sifted cake flour
2 teaspoons baking powder
1/3 teaspoon salt
1 cup sugar
1/4 cup light butter, softened
1/2 cup puréed bananas (approximately 1/2 banana)
3/4 cup skim milk
1 teaspoon pure vanilla extract
1 teaspoon pure coconut extract
1/2 cup egg whites, stiffly beaten
1/2 (14-ounce) can fat-free sweetened condensed milk
3/4 cup evaporated skim milk
2/3 cup light coconut milk
1/4 cup packed brown sugar
2 tablespoons dark rum
4 bananas, sliced
12/3 cups fat-free whipped topping
2 tablespoons toasted shredded coconut

Sift the cake flour, baking powder and salt into a bowl. Cream the sugar, butter and banana purée in a mixing bowl until light and fluffy. Add 1/3 flour mixture and 1/3 skim milk alternately; mixing well after each addition. Mix in the vanilla and coconut extracts. Fold in the egg whites. Spray a 6 x 8-inch cake pan with nonstick cooking spray. Flour the pan. Pour the batter into the prepared pan. Bake at 375 degrees for 50 minutes or until the cake tests done. Remove from the oven and cool in the pan for 10 minutes. Remove to a wire rack to cool completely. Combine the condensed milk, 3/4 cup skim milk and coconut milk in a bowl; mix well. Arrange the cake on a serving platter. Poke holes all over the cake with a wooden pick or skewer. Spoon the milk mixture over the cake. Cover the cake and chill in the refrigerator for 4 hours. Combine the brown sugar and rum in a saucepan over medium heat. Cook until the mixture reduces to a syrupy consistency. Add the bananas and stir gently to coat the fruit. Remove from the heat and cool to room temperature. Top each serving of cake with whipped topping and a scattering of toasted coconut. Serve the bananas on the side. *Yield: 16 servings*

Nutrients Per Serving: Cal 233; Prot 5 g; Carbo 46 g; Fat 3 g; 11% Cal from Fat; Sod 182 mg

chefstip

Temper, Temper ✳ You will find a lot of recipes in the dessert section of this book, particularly those that involve a custard, with a curious instruction about heating liquid over a double boiler and drizzling it slowly into a bowl of egg product (rather than heating everything together), then continuing to cook. The importance of these two steps, the double boiler and the drizzling, has to do with "tempering" the eggs – changing their temperature gradually so that they do not scramble (generally not a desirable condition unless you are making "scrambled-egg pie").

Double-Ginger Gingerbread with Lemon Sauce

In spite of its unlikely culinary application as construction material, and its penchant for running away as fast as it can, gingerbread remains our best-loved spice cake. This recipe doubles your pleasure with two forms of ginger — candied or crystallized ginger (found in health food and upscale grocery stores) and the ground or powdered form.

1 1/2 cups flour
1 teaspoon each: baking soda and baking powder
1/2 teaspoon black pepper
2 teaspoons ground ginger
1 teaspoon ground cinnamon
1/2 teaspoon salt
3 tablespoons light butter
1/2 cup packed brown sugar
1 egg plus 2 egg whites
2 (2 1/2-ounce) jars of baby food prunes
1/4 cup molasses
2/3 cup buttermilk
1/4 cup chopped candied ginger

Combine the flour, baking soda, baking powder, pepper, ground ginger, cinnamon and salt in a large bowl. Cream the butter in a mixing bowl until fluffy. Beat in the brown sugar, egg and egg whites. Add the prunes and molasses and beat until smooth. Stir in half the dry ingredients, then the buttermilk, followed by the remaining dry ingredients, mixing well after each addition. Fold in the candied ginger. Spray an 8 x 11-inch baking pan with nonstick cooking spray; dust with flour. Pour in the batter. Bake at 325 degrees for 45 minutes or until the cake tests done. Cut the cake into 16 squares; top with Lemon Sauce and, if desired, a dollop of fat-free whipped topping and a sprinkling of grated nutmeg. *Yield: 16 servings*

The Lemon Sauce

1 1/2 cups water
2 tablespoons cornstarch
Juice of 3 lemons
Grated zest of 1 lemon
1 tablespoon light butter
3 tablespoons honey

Combine the water, cornstarch and lemon juice in a small saucepan. Bring to a boil and whisk until the mixture thickens and becomes clear. Whisk in the lemon zest, butter and honey. Remove from the heat and cool to room temperature. *Yield: 16 servings*

Nutrients Per Serving: Cal 138; Prot 3 g; Carbo 28 g; Fat 2 g; 13% Cal from Fat; Sod 228 mg

orange you healthy

Oranges contain more than 170 different phytochemicals, including more than 60 flavonoids which provide anti-inflammatory and anti-tumor agents, inhibit blood clots, and act as antioxidants. They also contain limonoids, which stimulate a detoxifying enzyme system and inhibit tumor formation, and 20 different types of carotinoids, strong anti-oxidants which decrease the risk of age-related blindness (macular degeneration).

NUTRITION

Torta Limoncello

With the possible exception of the scenery, Italy's ruggedly beautiful Amalfi coast is best known for its fragrant, flourishing lemon orchards. Some of these luscious lemons are distilled into a liqueur known as Limoncello, the ubiquitous after-dinner offering found in the local cafés. It's perfect as a sunset- and seacoast-gazing apéritif, and makes a pretty good cake, too.

6 tablespoons light butter, softened
1 1/2 cups confectioners' sugar, sifted
2 eggs, separated
1/2 cup each: fat-free plain yogurt and frozen lemonade concentrate
2 tablespoons lemon liqueur or lemon juice plus 1 tablespoon grated lemon zest
2 teaspoons pure vanilla extract
2 cups cake flour plus 2 teaspoons baking powder and 1/2 teaspoon salt
1/2 cup egg substitute

Cream the butter and sugar in a mixing bowl for 3 minutes. Add the next six ingredients; beat until smooth. Add the flour mixture to the creamed mixture; mix well. Beat the egg whites and egg substitute in a mixing bowl until soft peaks form. Fold into the batter. Spray a 5 x 9-inch loaf pan with nonstick cooking spray; dust with flour. Pour in the batter. Bake at 350 degrees for 1 hour. Cool. To serve, slice into 16 pieces, arrange each slice on a plate topped with a dollop of Lemon Cream Topping and a few Candied Lemon Peels. *Yield: 16 servings*

The Lemon Cream Topping

2 tablespoons cornstarch
1/4 cup sugar
1/2 cup fresh lemon juice
1/3 cup water
1/4 cup egg substitute
8 ounces fat-free cream cheese, softened
4 ounces reduced-fat cream cheese, softened
1/2 cup confectioners' sugar
1 cup fat-free whipped topping
2 tablespoons lemon liqueur or lemon juice

Combine the cornstarch, sugar, lemon juice and water in a nonreactive saucepan over medium heat. Simmer until the mixture thickens, stirring constantly. Remove 1/4 cup of the lemon mixture to a bowl containing the egg substitute; mix thoroughly. Pour the egg mixture back into the saucepan and cook for 2 minutes, stirring constantly. Combine the cream cheese and confectioners' sugar in a mixing bowl; beat until smooth. Add the lemon mixture; beat until smooth. Add the whipped topping and liqueur; beat well. Chill in the refrigerator until ready to use. *Yield: 16 servings*

The Candied Lemon Peel

4 lemons
3/4 cup sugar
1/3 cup water
3/4 cup sugar, finely ground in a blender or food processor

Peel the lemons vertically. Slice the peel into 1/8-inch strips. Boil the peel in water to cover in a saucepan for 1 minute. Drain and repeat 3 times. Combine the sugar and water in a saucepan over medium-high heat. Bring to a boil and add the lemon peel. Reduce the heat and simmer for 8 minutes, stirring frequently. Spray a piece of parchment paper with nonstick cooking spray. Drain the lemon peel and arrange on the parchment paper. Set aside at room temperature for 3 hours. Toss the peel with finely ground sugar, then store in a tightly sealed container until ready to use.

Nutrients Per Serving: Cal 315; Prot 7 g; Carbo 62 g; Fat 5 g; 14% Cal from Fat; Sod 296 mg

Lemon Roll with Blackberry Sauce

These elegant pinwheel swirls of fat-free genoise cake and tart lemon custard floating on a shimmering pool of blackberry sauce are picture — and palate — perfect.

8 egg whites
1/8 teaspoon salt
3/4 cup sugar
3/4 cup sifted cake flour
1/4 cup confectioners' sugar
2 teaspoons fresh lemon juice
1/2 teaspoon pure vanilla extract

Line a 10 x 15-inch cake pan with parchment paper. Spray thoroughly with nonstick cooking spray; set aside. Beat the egg whites and salt in a mixing bowl at high speed until soft peaks form. Add the sugar and beat until the mixture is thick and glossy. Sift half the flour over the egg whites, then fold it in while pulsing the mixer on and off very briefly. Do not overfold, or the whites will collapse. Sift the remaining flour over the egg whites and repeat the process. Fold in the lemon juice and vanilla. Spread the batter in the prepared pan. Bake at 300 degrees for 25 minutes or until the cake is dry to the touch. Remove the cake from the oven. Sift half the confectioners' sugar over the top, arrange a piece of parchment paper over the cake, then invert the cake onto the clean parchment. Remove the pan and gently peel away the original parchment. Sift the remaining confectioners' sugar over the cake. Roll the warm cake as for a jelly roll from the short side and place on a wire rack to cool. Unroll the cooled cake carefully and remove the parchment. Spread the lemon filling to within 1 inch of the edge and reroll. Wrap in parchment paper and chill in the refrigerator for at least 2 hours. To serve, unwrap and slice into 3/4-inch-thick roulades. Pool some blackberry sauce in the middle of each plate and arrange a slice of cake in the center. *Yield: 13 servings*

The Lemon Filling

1/3 cup cornstarch
2/3 cup sugar
1 teaspoon grated lemon zest
1 cup fresh lemon juice
1 cup water
1/3 cup egg substitute
1 tablespoon light butter

Combine the cornstarch and sugar in a saucepan over medium heat. Whisk in the lemon zest, lemon juice and water. Cook until the mixture thickens, stirring constantly. Remove about 1/2 cup of the hot lemon mixture and slowly pour it into a bowl containing the egg substitute, whisking constantly. Return the mixture to the saucepan. Cook, stirring over low heat for 2 minutes. Whisk in butter. Remove from the heat and cool to room temperature.

The Blackberry Sauce

2 cups fresh or thawed frozen blackberries
1/4 cup sugar
1 teaspoon fresh lemon juice

Combine the berries, sugar and lemon juice in a blender or food processor; process until smooth. Strain mixture into a clean container, such as a squeeze bottle, and refrigerate until ready to use. *Yield: 13 servings*

Nutrients Per Serving: Cal 177; Prot 4 g; Carbo 40 g; Fat 1 g; 4% Cal from Fat; Sod 74 mg

Pineapple Pound Cake with Spiced Pineapple Syrup

Most reduced-fat butters sport disclaimers regarding their use in baking. But, in our recipe, it helps to produce a dense, fine-crumbed cake, not too sweet, and with all the taste and texture of its higher-fat antecedent. If you are unable to find pure pineapple extract, simply substitute lemon or coconut. The candied ginger, a nice touch, is available in upscale grocery stores or health food stores, but can be omitted.

1/2 cup (1 stick) light butter, softened
1 1/2 cups confectioners' sugar
2 eggs, separated
4 ounces low-fat pineapple yogurt
1/3 cup thawed frozen pineapple juice concentrate
1 teaspoon pure vanilla extract
1 tablespoon each: pure pineapple extract and fresh lemon juice
1 teaspoon grated lemon zest
2 cups cake flour
2 teaspoons baking powder
1/2 teaspoon salt
1/2 cup egg substitute
1/2 cup minced candied ginger

Cream the butter and confectioners' sugar in a mixing bowl for 2 to 3 minutes. Add the egg yolks, yogurt, pineapple juice concentrate, vanilla, pineapple extract, lemon juice and lemon zest; beat at medium speed to blend well. Sift the flour, baking powder and salt in a separate bowl. Add to the creamed mixture, beating at low speed until smooth. Beat the egg whites and egg substitute in a mixing bowl at medium-high speed until soft peaks form. Fold into the batter, then fold the ginger into the batter. Line the bottom of a 5 x 9-inch loaf pan with parchment paper. Spray the paper and inside of the pan with nonstick cooking spray, then dust with flour. Pour in the batter. Bake at 350 degrees for 1 hour or until the cake tests done. Cool in the pan for 10 minutes. Remove to a wire rack to cool completely. Slice the cake into 1/2-inch slices and serve with Spiced Pineapple Syrup spooned over the top. *Yield: 16 servings*

The Spiced Pineapple Syrup

1 cup each: thawed frozen pineapple juice concentrate and water
1 (3-inch) cinnamon stick
3 cloves
2 star anise (optional)
1 cup diced pineapple

Combine the pineapple juice concentrate, water, cinnamon, cloves and star anise in a nonreactive saucepan over medium heat. Simmer for 10 minutes. Remove from the heat, strain into a clean bowl and stir in the pineapple. Cool to room temperature. *Yield: 16 servings*

Nutrients Per Serving: Cal 217; Prot 4 g; Carbo 42 g; Fat 4 g; 17% Cal from Fat; Sod 197 mg

chefstip

Be "Zest" Full ✳ In cookbook parlance, "zest" refers to the grated peel of a citrus fruit which imparts the very quality the name implies. The trick is to not grate too deeply, as the white pith beneath the exterior peel can impart bitterness. Although dependable old-style box graters still do an adequate job of zesting, there are some new "micro-plane" graters, generally shaped like files, that are truly superior, giving higher yields with less pith - and less chance of injury.

Polenta Pound Cake with Oranges

The polenta part of this recipe, in addition to having a nice alliterative ring, refers to the use of cornmeal — the integral ingredient in a savory Italian side dish of the same name. And, just as it does in this savory dish, the use of cornmeal in this cake adds a pleasant granular texture and rustic appeal to this straightforward, good-natured dessert.

2 large oranges
1 1/2 cups confectioners' sugar
1 1/4 cups flour
1/2 cup yellow cornmeal
1 teaspoon baking powder
1/2 teaspoon salt
1/2 cup fat-free plain yogurt
3 tablespoons canola oil
1 teaspoon pure vanilla extract
2 eggs, lightly beaten

Grate enough orange zest to equal 1 tablespoon. Remove and discard the remaining peel. Section the oranges into wedges; set aside. Sift the confectioners' sugar, flour, cornmeal, baking powder and salt into a large mixing bowl. Combine the orange zest, yogurt, canola oil, vanilla and eggs in a separate bowl. Add the yogurt mixture to the dry ingredients, beating with an electric mixer until the batter is smooth. Spray a 5 x 9-inch loaf pan with nonstick cooking spray. Pour in the batter. Bake at 325 degrees for 50 minutes or until the cake tests done. Remove to a wire rack to cool. To serve, cut the cake into 1/2-inch slices and spoon Orange Sauce over each slice. *Yield: 16 servings*

The Orange Sauce

2 cups orange juice
1 cup sugar
3 cloves
Reserved orange segments (above)

Combine the juice, sugar and cloves in a saucepan over medium heat. Cook until reduced to 1 1/2 cups, stirring occasionally. Remove from the heat and strain into a clean bowl. Add orange wedges. *Yield: 16 servings*

Nutrients Per Serving: Cal 205; Prot 3 g; Carbo 41 g; Fat 4 g; 15% Cal from Fat; Sod 117 mg

create your sacred space

Do you have your own special place? Perhaps it's a private room in your house or someplace special from your childhood memories. Or maybe it's the bathtub each night after the kids are settled in. Creating a sacred space is essential to your well being. At Lake Austin Spa Resort, we have designed the property and the guest rooms with this philosophy in mind. Our guests enjoy sacred spaces for quiet contemplation and small group gatherings. And whether we use these spaces to pause and reflect or laugh hysterically with a group of lifelong friends, they immediately take us to a place of comfort. Take time to find a sacred space in your life, a place where you can sit quietly, read or make a phone call to your best friend. Fill your space with special items - photos, children's drawings, your favorite music, candles, and the most comfortable furniture you can find. Then use it as often as possible.

WELL BEING

Strawberry Charlotte

Truly one of the world's greatest and richest desserts, a classical charlotte consists of delicate ladyfingers compressed around a creamy, ground almond and butter filling. Fruit and/or flavorings are added, then the whole thing is weighted for 24 hours before being unmolded and sliced. It's as delicious and decadent a dessert as you will ever encounter. A little piece of heaven, but with equally stratospheric calorie and fat-gram counts to match. Our charlatan of a charlotte, however, gets tricked down to more terrestrial numbers with low-fat vanilla yogurt, low-fat ricotta cheese and fat-free whipped topping. It may taste like a deal made with the devil, but we promise you will emerge from this eating experience with whatever portion of your virtue you still possess intact. This is not the simplest dessert to prepare — it requires patience and advance planning — but the spectacular results of the créme — without the cream — are well worth it.

32 ounces low-fat vanilla yogurt
6 egg whites
1 cup sugar
1/4 teaspoon salt
3 eggs
1/4 cup egg substitute
1 1/4 cups flour, sifted
1 tablespoon confectioners' sugar
1/4 cup orange-flavored liqueur
1 envelope unflavored gelatin
7 1/2 ounces low-fat ricotta cheese, squeezed dry
2/3 cup ground blanched almonds
2 1/2 cups fat-free whipped topping
1 teaspoon pure almond extract
1 tablespoon confectioners' sugar
2 cups sliced fresh strawberries or thawed frozen strawberries

Drain the yogurt in a cheesecloth-lined mesh strainer over a bowl in the refrigerator for 8 hours or overnight. Beat the egg whites in a large mixing bowl until soft peaks form. Add the sugar and salt and beat until the mixture is thick and glossy. Combine the eggs and egg substitute in a separate mixing bowl; beat until thick and fluffy. Beat in the flour at slow speed just until combined. Fold into the egg white mixture. Line an 11 x 17-inch baking pan with parchment paper. Spray with nonstick cooking spray. Spread the batter evenly into the baking pan. Bake at 325 degrees for 30 to 35 minutes. Remove from the oven and cool in the pan for 10 minutes. Place a piece of parchment paper on a clean work surface; dust the surface with 1 tablespoon confectioners' sugar. Invert the cake onto the parchment. While the cake is baking, pour the liqueur into a microwave-safe dish. Sprinkle the gelatin over the surface of the liqueur; let stand for 10 minutes. Microwave on High for 20 seconds or just long enough to dissolve the gelatin. Beat the ricotta cheese in a mixing bowl until smooth. Add the gelatin mixture; mix well. Add the yogurt, almonds, whipped topping and almond extract; mix well. Chill until the mixture starts to thicken, stirring occasionally. Cut two 8-inch circles from the cake using the bottom of an 8-inch springform pan as a template. You should have a 4 x 17-inch strip of cake left over. Cut the strip into two 4 x 8 1/2-inch strips. Cut each strip lengthwise into 2 pieces to create a total of 4 strips of cake; two 2 3/4 x 8 1/2 inches, and two 1 1/4 x 8 1/2 inches. Spray an 8-inch springform pan with nonstick cooking spray; dust with 1 tablespoon confectioners' sugar. Arrange 1 circle of cake in the bottom. Line the sides with two 2 3/4 x 8 1/2-inch pieces, plus a third piece formed by combining the two thinner pieces. Arrange the strawberries over the circle of cake. Top with the cream filling, followed by the remaining circle of cake. Cover with plastic wrap. Top with an 8-inch circle of cardboard and a heavy object such as a brick, or equivalent. Refrigerate the charlotte for 8 hours or overnight. Remove the weight, cardboard, plastic wrap and side of the springform pan before serving. *Yield: 16 servings*

Nutrients Per Serving: Cal 233; Prot 10 g; Carbo 37 g; Fat 5 g; 19% Cal from Fat; Sod 138 mg

Zucchini, Cranberry and Walnut Cake

When, where, or why some presumably desperate soul first decided to put shredded zucchini into a cake we do not know. It's not that we're unfamiliar with the concept of using certain vegetables in desserts (See Sweet Potato Pie, Page 195.) Even carrots have found a place on the dessert cart — and in FRESH (See Golden Carrot Almond Cake, Page 170.) But, zucchini? Well, guess what folks? It works. And every time we serve this cranberry and walnut beauty — a fall favorite with our guests — we tip our hat to the singular leap of faith taken by that unknown culinary pioneer. (Wonder who it was who ate the first snail?) When cranberries are not in season, substitute golden raisins for a Lemon Iced Italian Spice Cake.

1 cup whole wheat flour
2 cups unbleached white flour
1 1/4 cups sugar
1 teaspoon baking powder
1 teaspoon baking soda
2 teaspoons ground cinnamon
1 teaspoon salt
2 eggs
1/2 cup egg substitute
2 (2 1/2-ounce) jars of baby food prunes
2 tablespoons canola oil
2/3 cup buttermilk
3 tablespoons thawed frozen orange juice concentrate
2 teaspoons pure vanilla extract
3 cups shredded zucchini, blotted dry
1 1/2 cups fresh cranberries
1/2 cup chopped walnut pieces
1 tablespoon grated orange zest
1 tablespoon grated lemon zest

Mix the whole wheat flour, unbleached white flour, sugar, baking powder, baking soda, cinnamon and salt in a large bowl. Whisk the eggs, egg substitute, prunes, canola oil, buttermilk, orange juice concentrate and vanilla in a separate bowl. Add the dry ingredients and whisk until smooth. Fold in the zucchini, cranberries, walnuts, orange zest and lemon zest. Spray two 5 x 9-inch loaf pans with nonstick cooking spray. Divide the batter between the pans. Bake at 350 degrees for 1 hour and 20 minutes. Cool in the pans for 10 minutes. Remove to a wire rack to cool completely. Glaze with Lemon Icing. *Yield: 16 servings*

The Lemon Icing

1 1/2 cups confectioners' sugar
1 teaspoon grated lemon zest
1/4 cup fresh lemon juice

Combine the confectioners' sugar, lemon zest and juice in a bowl; whisk until smooth and sugar is completely dissolved. Spoon over the top of the cake. *Yield: 16 servings*

Nutrients Per Serving: Cal 134; Prot 3 g; Carbo 25 g; Fat 3 g; 18% Cal from Fat; Sod 145 mg

Chocolate Espresso Cheesecake

This is a cheesecake for chocolate lovers. The recipe originally started out as a mocha latte cheesecake, then one of our chefs accidentally tripled the amount of cocoa powder. Our guests couldn't order it fast enough. They raved; we smiled, said thanks, and quickly changed the recipe.

20 reduced-fat chocolate wafers, crumbled
4 teaspoons light butter, melted
3 tablespoons instant espresso powder
3 tablespoons coffee-flavored liqueur
2 cups fat-free ricotta cheese
1 1/2 cups fat-free sour cream
6 ounces fat-free cream cheese, softened
6 ounces reduced-fat cream cheese, softened
1 1/4 cups sugar
6 tablespoons flour
4 egg whites
1 cup baking cocoa
1/4 teaspoon salt
1/8 teaspoon ground cinnamon

Combine the cookie crumbs and butter in a bowl and mix well. Spray a 9-inch springform pan with nonstick cooking spray. Press the crumb mixture evenly into the bottom of the pan. Bake at 325 degrees for 10 minutes. Remove and cool to room temperature. Combine the espresso powder and liqueur in a small bowl; stir until the powder dissolves. Place the ricotta cheese in cheesecloth or a clean dish towel and squeeze out as much moisture as possible. Remove to a mixing bowl and beat at high speed until puréed. Add the sour cream, cream cheese, sugar, flour, egg whites, baking cocoa, salt and cinnamon; beat well. Pour the mixture over the cooled crust. Bake at 325 degrees for approximately 1 hour. Turn off the oven, but leave the cake in the oven for 30 to 40 minutes longer. Remove and cool to room temperature. Chill in the refrigerator for at least 4 hours. *Yield: 16 servings*

Nutrients Per Serving: Cal 196; Prot 9 g; Carbo 32 g; Fat 3 g; 15% Cal from Fat; Sod 207 mg

chefstip

A Matter Of Concentration * Frozen fruit juice concentrate is a wonderful example of great convenience food. The concentration saves space, generally requires no preservatives, is usually made with all-natural ingredients, and is ready to go in minutes. And not just as juice! We use fruit juice concentrates in desserts, in salad dressings, and to bolster savory sauces. Instead of reaching for the butter, try just a teaspoon of orange, lemonade, or raspberry concentrate on steamed carrots, whipped sweet potatoes, or green beans, and savor the possibilities.

Cranberry Cheesecake

If you are sympathetic to the idea that one of the heaviest burdens in life is unlimited potential, then pity the poor cranberry. This bright red denizen of the bogs, introduced almost 300 years ago to the Pilgrims by their indigenous neighbors, is still trying to get legs. In spite of its high nutritive value (cranberries contain more vitamin C than orange juice, more iron than prunes), gorgeous crimson color, and clean, spirited flavor, the cranberry still suffers the abuse of underuse. As juice, it is often mixed with more popular flavors like apple or raspberry to give it more marketability. As a berry, it has been relegated almost exclusively to the role of the obligatory afterthought at the traditional Thanksgiving dinner — pushed to the perimeter of the plate, a tiny beacon soon buried under an avalanche of potatoes, turkey, and dressing. This is a shame, because cranberries make wonderful baked goods, (give us cranberry nut bread anytime and keep your more popular banana), scintillating sauces, a remarkable sherbet and, we think, the very best cheesecake.

10 reduced-fat cinnamon graham crackers, crumbled
1 egg white
1 tablespoon light butter, melted
12 ounces cranberries (3 cups)
1 cup water
3/4 cup sugar
1 teaspoon grated orange zest
12 ounces fat-free cream cheese, softened
8 ounces reduced-fat cream cheese, softened
2 teaspoons pure vanilla extract
1/3 cup lemon juice
1/3 cup flour
1/4 teaspoon salt
4 egg whites
1/4 cup sugar
1 (14-ounce) can fat-free sweetened condensed milk

Spray a 9-inch springform pan with nonstick cooking spray. Combine the graham cracker crumbs, egg white and butter in a bowl and mix well. Press the mixture into the bottom of the prepared pan. Bake at 325 degrees for 10 minutes. Remove and cool. Combine the cranberries, water, sugar and orange zest in a nonreactive saucepan over high heat. Bring to a boil; immediately reduce the heat to a simmer and cook for 10 minutes. Remove from the heat and cool. Beat the cream cheese in a mixing bowl until fluffy. Add the vanilla, lemon juice, flour, salt, egg whites, sugar and condensed milk; beat until smooth. Fold in 1/3 cup of the cranberry mixture by hand. Pour the mixture over the cooled crust. Bake at 325 degrees for 50 minutes. Turn off the oven, but leave the cake in the oven for 30 minutes longer. Remove and cool completely. Top with remaining cranberry mixture. *Yield: 16 servings*

Nutrients Per Serving: Cal 206; Prot 9 g; Carbo 35 g; Fat 4 g; 15% Cal from Fat; Sod 260 mg

Lemon Cherry Cheesecake

Old-fashioned goodness from new-fangled ingredients — even though it's made with reduced-fat and fat-free ingredients, this traditional cheesecake has all the richness, density, and mouth-feel of its New York deli relatives. You may, of course, substitute a variety of other fruit toppings.

1 1/2 cups reduced-fat graham cracker crumbs
2 tablespoons light butter, melted
16 ounces fat-free cream cheese, softened
8 ounces reduced-fat cream cheese, softened
1 1/2 (14-ounce) cans fat-free sweetened condensed milk
6 egg whites
3 eggs
2 tablespoons grated lemon zest
3/4 cup fresh lemon juice
2 teaspoons vanilla extract
2/3 cup flour
1 (16-ounce) package frozen tart red cherries
1/2 cup sugar
2 tablespoons cornstarch

Mix the crumbs and butter in a bowl. Spray a 9-inch springform pan with nonstick cooking spray. Press the crumb mixture into the bottom of the pan. Bake at 300 degrees for 10 minutes. Remove and cool. Beat the cream cheese in a mixing bowl until fluffy. Add the milk; beat until smooth. Add the egg whites, eggs, lemon zest, lemon juice and vanilla; beat well. Sift the flour over the creamed mixture; beat well. Pour the mixture into the prepared pan. Bake at 325 degrees for 55 to 60 minutes. Turn off the oven, but leave the cake in the oven for 30 minutes longer. Remove and cool completely. Combine the cherries, sugar and cornstarch in a saucepan over medium heat. Bring to a simmer. Cook until the sugar is dissolved and the mixture is slightly thickened, stirring frequently. Remove from the heat and cool. Spread the cherry mixture over the top of the cheesecake. Chill for 4 to 6 hours. *Yield: 16 servings*

Nutrients Per Serving: Cal 301; Prot 13 g; Carbo 47 g; Fat 4 g; 12% Cal from Fat; Sod 317 mg

a garden of memories

If you have ever wanted to share the beauty of your gardens with friends and family, or simply create a memento of each year's passing bounty, try these simple techniques. Take flowers that are fresh, beautiful and very dry and place them in an old phone book, 20 to 30 pages apart. Then carefully close the book and put something heavy on it - books, hand weights or rocks. Be sure to keep the flowers from touching each other and make sure there is no dew or moisture on them. Leave the flowers in the book for 7-10 days. When dry, they're ready to use for cards, bookmarks, candles, and other crafts. Glue the pressed flowers to cardstock and then use decoupage to cover them or have them laminated. Sunlight will fade the flowers, so keep your finished artwork out of direct sunlight. Some of the best flowers for pressing are pansies, violas, snapdragons, bluebonnets, larkspur, Indian paintbrush and verbenas. Herb flowers and foliage are wonderful too.

Collapsed Lemon Chèvre Cheesecake with Raspberry Sauce

Here's an adult dinner party cheesecake with rich, sophisticated, and not-too-sweet flavors for the slightly adventurous. Chèvre is a soft, mild goat cheese available in most supermarkets. It's the perfect partner — and a fabulous finish — for a meal featuring beef or, better yet, lamb.

1/2 cup flour
3/4 cup sugar
1/8 teaspoon salt
1 1/2 cups 2% milk
Grated zest of 2 lemons
2 tablespoons light butter
3 ounces reduced-fat chèvre, softened
2 egg yolks
Juice of 1 lemon
6 egg whites
1/4 cup sugar

Combine the flour, sugar, salt and milk in a saucepan over medium heat. Cook until the mixture thickens, stirring frequently. Add the lemon zest, butter, cheese, egg yolks and lemon juice; beat with a whisk. Remove the mixture to a large bowl. Beat the egg whites in a mixing bowl until stiff, but not dry. Fold the egg whites into the cheese mixture. Spray a 9-inch springform pan with non-stick cooking spray. Pour the batter into the pan. Bake at 375 degrees for 40 to 45 minutes. Remove from the oven. Cool completely in the pan. Pool raspberry sauce in the middle of each plate; top with a slice of cheesecake. *Yield: 16 servings*

The Raspberry Sauce

1/4 teaspoon black peppercorns
2 (2-inch) cinnamon sticks
Peeled zest and juice of 1 orange
Juice of 1 lemon
2 cups red wine
1 cup sugar
1 1/2 cups thawed frozen raspberries

Combine the peppercorns, cinnamon, orange zest, orange juice, lemon juice, wine and sugar in a saucepan over medium-high heat. Cook until the mixture is reduced to 1 cup. Strain the mixture into a blender or food processor; discard the solids. Add the raspberries and purée. Strain the mixture into a clean container; a squeeze bottle works well. *Yield: 16 servings*

Nutrients Per Serving: Cal 200; Prot 4 g; Carbo 37 g; Fat 2 g; 11% Cal from Fat; Sod 86 mg

Spring For A Springform ✳ The recipes for all of our pies and cheesecakes, and a good number of our cakes, are designed to be made in springform pans. These versatile receptacles are made with round bases and round, removable (spring loaded) sidewalls. This feature gives the pan two major advantages: it provides a very protective housing (which can be covered with plastic wrap) for desserts you may wish to transport, and makes it easy to cut and portion desserts, especially those with a bottom crumb crust. The most commonly available sizes for springforms are 8", 9", and 10". Most of our recipes are written for the 9" size.

Banana Coconut Cream Pie

The old joke we learned as children goes — the visiting math professor says, "pi r squared." "No," replies the Southerner. "Pie are round. Corn bread are square!" Slanderous linguistics aside, Southerners do know a thing or two about this subject, particularly "pie." If you find yourself the fortunate guest in a Southerner's home for Sunday supper, the table absolutely groaning under the weight of platters of fried chicken, pork ribs, sweet potatoes, mashed potatoes, green beans, collard greens, okra, summer squash — and, oh yes — corn bread, you will likely find yourself the subject of your hostess' cheerful admonition to "save room for pie!" Thick, double-crusted fruit pie, oozing sweet berries. Or, lemon meringue pie with a cumulus of beaten egg whites floating over a lemon curd so tart and sweet that your tongue suffers from a sort of benevolent schizophrenia. Or, perhaps, an icebox cream pie with thick slabs of chilled custard mortaring slices of banana or shredded coconut underneath a shingle slathered with billowy whipped cream. Too many of these Sunday suppers, however, and you might just as likely find yourself in the cardiopulmonary ward at Atlanta General pondering a Jell-O cup. So, for some occasions at least, we offer this delicious, lighter alternative, which respects the traditions from which it comes, yet still minds its manners regarding fat and calories. An awful lot of fat in many of these Southern favorites is in the butter or shortening cut into the flour for that crisp, flaky crust. We've tried every low-fat version of this traditional approach we've ever heard of, and have even tried a few experiments of our own. They all come up woefully short. So, instead of cardboard, we've opted for crumb crusts, which we think do a much better — and tastier — job. So, enjoy, and ya'll come back soon, you hear?

14 pieces melba toast
2 tablespoons sugar
4 teaspoons light butter, melted
1 envelope unflavored gelatin
3 tablespoons cornstarch
1/2 (14-ounce) can fat-free sweetened condensed milk
1 1/4 cups evaporated skim milk
1/2 cup sugar
1 egg
3/4 cup egg substitute
1 teaspoon vanilla
1/4 cup pure coconut extract
1/4 cup shredded sweetened coconut
4 bananas, sliced
3 cups fat-free whipped topping
1 tablespoon toasted shredded coconut

Grind the melba toast to fine crumbs in a food processor. Remove to a bowl and add the sugar and butter; mix well. Spray a 9-inch springform pan with nonstick cooking spray. Press the crumb mixture into the bottom of the prepared pan. Bake at 350 degrees for 10 minutes. Remove from the oven and cool. Combine the gelatin, cornstarch, condensed milk, skim milk and sugar in the top of a double boiler over boiling water. Cook for 6 to 8 minutes or until the mixture thickens, stirring constantly. Whisk the egg and egg substitute in a separate bowl. Slowly add about 1/2 cup of the hot milk mixture, whisking constantly. Pour the egg and milk into the hot milk mixture. Continue to cook over boiling water for 2 to 3 minutes or until the mixture thickens, stirring constantly. Remove from the heat and stir in the vanilla, coconut extract and shredded coconut. Arrange the banana slices over the cooked crust. Spread the custard mixture over the bananas. Chill in the refrigerator for 3 to 4 hours. Spread the whipped topping over the top and sprinkle with a small amount of toasted coconut, if desired. Return to the refrigerator to chill completely. *Yield: 12 servings*

Nutrients Per Serving: Cal 252; Prot 8 g; Carbo 46 g; Fat 3 g; 10% Cal from Fat; Sod 156 mg

Chocolate Bourbon Swirl Cream Pie

Healthy cooking classes are an optional part of our program at the resort. This particular recipe was part of a class whimsically titled "Whiskey, Red Meat, Gravy and Pie — and other Spa Specialties." This provocative prologue had a two-pronged purpose: to take advantage of the old teacher's adage that "If you're going to teach them anything, first you have to get their attention," and to remind the participants that our philosophy is that there are no forbidden foods. Healthy eating is about balance and variety. Almost any food, taking into account quantity (generally, we eat too much), and frequency (generally, we eat too often), can and should be part of a healthy diet. The meat and gravy you will find discussed in other parts of this book, but we've got your whiskey and pie right here!

20 reduced-fat chocolate wafers
4 teaspoons light butter, melted
2 1/2 cups 2% milk
1/2 (14-ounce) can fat-free sweetened condensed milk
1/4 cup bourbon
3 tablespoons cornstarch
1 envelope unflavored gelatin
1/2 cup sugar
2 eggs
1/2 cup egg substitute
1 teaspoon pure vanilla extract
2 tablespoons baking cocoa
1 tablespoon hot water
1 ounce semisweet chocolate, melted
3 cups fat-free whipped topping
1 teaspoon grated nutmeg
1 tablespoon grated semisweet chocolate

Grind the wafers to fine crumbs in a food processor. Remove to a bowl and add the butter; mix well. Spray a 9-inch springform pan with nonstick cooking spray. Press the crumb mixture into the bottom of the prepared pan. Bake at 350 degrees for 10 minutes. Remove from the oven and cool. Combine the 2% milk, condensed milk, bourbon, cornstarch, gelatin and sugar in the top of a double boiler over boiling water. Cook for 5 to 7 minutes or until the mixture thickens, stirring constantly. Whisk the egg and egg substitute in a separate bowl. Slowly add about 1 cup of the hot milk mixture, whisking constantly. Pour the egg mixture into the hot milk mixture. Continue to cook over boiling water for 2 to 3 minutes or until the mixture thickens, stirring constantly. Stir in the vanilla. Remove two-thirds of the custard to a separate bowl; cool, stirring occasionally. Dissolve the baking cocoa in the hot water; add to the mixture remaining in the top of the double boiler. Add the melted chocolate and mix well. Remove from the heat and cool, stirring occasionally. When the custards just begin to set, pour the chocolate custard into the vanilla custard and swirl gently with a knife. Pour the combined custards into the cooled crust. Chill in the refrigerator for 4 hours. Spread the whipped topping over the top, then sprinkle with grated nutmeg and grated chocolate. *Yield: 12 servings*

Nutrients Per Serving: Cal 222; Prot 7 g; Carbo 36 g; Fat 5 g; 18% Cal from Fat; Sod 116 mg

Chocolate Cream Pie

The Night Hawk Frisco Shop is a small restaurant in Austin, Texas, that specializes in chopped steaks and burgers. It is the sole surviving member of a small chain of beef emporiums that flourished locally under the Night Hawk marquee for almost half a century. Although the beef and burgers are still good, it's the pies that are worth shouting about. Big, luscious cream pies like your mama wished she could make. Coconut. Banana. And the best chocolate cream pie you have ever eaten. Our recipe is not as good. No recipe is as good. But if you can't get by the Frisco, or if you don't want to squander a whole week's worth of fat grams on a single serving, you'll find this version quite serviceable — tasty even. So, enjoy.

5 reduced-fat graham crackers
4 teaspoons light butter, melted
1/3 cup baking cocoa
1/3 cup warm water
1 envelope unflavored gelatin
1 (14-ounce) can fat-free sweetened condensed milk
1 ounce semisweet chocolate, melted
12 ounces fat-free cream cheese, softened
4 ounces reduced-fat cream cheese, softened
1/2 teaspoon vanilla extract
3 cups fat-free whipped topping

Grind the crackers to fine crumbs in a food processor. Remove to a bowl and add the butter; mix well. Spray a 9-inch springform pan with nonstick cooking spray. Press the crumb mixture into the bottom of the prepared pan. Bake at 350 degrees for 10 minutes. Remove from the oven and cool. Combine the baking cocoa and water in a microwave-safe dish. Sprinkle the gelatin over the top; set aside for 10 minutes. Microwave on High for 20 seconds. Combine the baking cocoa mixture, milk, chocolate, cream cheese and vanilla in a mixing bowl; beat until smooth. Pour into the cooled crust. Chill in the refrigerator for 3 hours. Spread the whipped topping on top. Refrigerate until ready to serve. *Yield: 12 servings*

Nutrients Per Serving: Cal 209; Prot 9 g; Carbo 33 g; Fat 4 g; 18% Cal from Fat; Sod 248 mg

do your breathwork

Breathwork can be used to engage the mind and body by awakening the nervous system and sharpening the senses. Various breathing techniques can calm, balance, heat, cool, energize, and detoxify. A complete breath will make full use of your lung capacity by engaging the muscles of the rib cage and abdominal area, resulting in the expansion of your chest, back, and abdomen. Breathing through the nose allows you to warm, filter, and moisten incoming air before it enters the lungs. Inhalations allow the spine to lengthen and the back to be subtly strengthened; exhalations are opportunities to strengthen the pelvic floor and abdominal muscles.

Orange Chocolate Mousse Pie

A rare intersection of elegant and easy, this sophisticated, rich, chocolate-crusted chocolate pie definitely qualifies as a dinner party dessert. But, happily, it's one that requires no other cooking than a brief stint in the oven for the crust.

20 **reduced-fat chocolate wafers**
4 **teaspoons light butter, melted**
Grated zest and juice of 1 orange
2 **tablespoons orange-flavored liqueur**
1 **envelope unflavored gelatin**
8 **ounces fat-free cream cheese, softened**
8 **ounces reduced-fat cream cheese, softened**
1 **(14-ounce) can fat-free sweetened condensed milk**
3/4 **cup baking cocoa**
2 **ounces semisweet chocolate, melted**
3 **cups fat-free whipped topping**

Grind the wafers to fine crumbs in a food processor. Remove to a bowl and add the butter; mix well. Spray a 9-inch springform pan with nonstick cooking spray. Press the crumb mixture into the bottom of the prepared pan. Bake at 350 degrees for 10 minutes. Remove and cool. Combine the orange zest, orange juice and liqueur in a microwave-safe dish. Sprinkle the gelatin over the top; set aside for 10 minutes. Microwave on High for 20 seconds. Combine the orange mixture, cream cheese, milk, baking cocoa and chocolate in a mixing bowl; beat until smooth. Add the whipped topping and beat just until the color is uniform. Pour the mixture into cooled crust. Chill for 3 to 4 hours. *Yield: 12 servings*

Nutrients Per Serving: Cal 262; Prot 10 g; Carbo 41 g; Fat 7 g; 24% Cal from Fat; Sod 238 mg

chefstip

A Case For Chocolate ✳ Those whose credo is "life is too short to give up chocolate" will be heartened to know that at least one major medical study has shown that people who eat chocolate live longer than those who abstain! No surprise here. Chocolate makes people happy, and we have at least one chocolate dessert on our menu every night. Using a little ingenuity and some of the products now available, we've created several desserts with reduced-fat counts that still taste like "the real deal." For example, we're often able to substitute lower fat products for some of the higher fat non-chocolate ingredients: reduced-fat cream cheese or whipped topping instead of heavy cream; a light butter or fruit purée instead of whole butter. To achieve "the proper state of chocolate" we combine a good quality cocoa powder with a measure of good quality real chocolate. The result is almost as rich as the "no holds barred" version but with a considerable savings in fat. We encourage you to try some of these conversions with your own favorite recipes.

Coconut Custard Tart

We've all been cautioned, and rightfully so, about limiting our intake of the saturated fats in so-called tropical fats — primarily coconut and palm oils. Good quality extracts, which are fat-free, are a great way to enjoy the flavors without suffering the adverse side effects. Unfortunately, many of the extracts sold in supermarkets are imitation flavors. In the case of imitation coconut extract, the flavor of the finished dish is disquietingly reminiscent of suntan lotion. It's definitely worth the time and trouble to hunt up the genuine article made with pure coconut. Your reward will be a densely creamy and decidedly delightful taste of the tropics.

1/2 cup sliced and blanched almonds
6 pieces melba toast
2 tablespoons sugar
1 tablespoon light butter, melted
2 eggs
1/2 cup egg substitute
4 ounces fat-free cream cheese, softened
4 ounces reduced-fat cream cheese, softened
1/2 cup sugar
2 tablespoons cornstarch
1/2 (14-ounce) can fat-free sweetened condensed milk
2 cups evaporated skim milk
2 teaspoons pure vanilla extract
2 tablespoons pure coconut extract
1/2 teaspoon pure almond extract
1/2 teaspoon ground cinnamon
2 tablespoons toasted shredded coconut
Strawberry Sauce

Arrange the almonds on a baking sheet. Toast at 350 degrees for about 10 minutes. Remove from the oven and cool. Combine toasted almonds, melba toast and sugar in a food processor. Grind to fine crumbs. Remove to a bowl and add the butter; mix well. Spray a 9-inch springform pan with nonstick cooking spray. Press the crumb mixture into the bottom of the pan. Bake at 350 degrees for 10 minutes. Remove and cool. Press heavy-duty foil tightly over the outside bottom and side of the springform pan to prevent leakage; set aside. Combine the eggs, egg substitute, cream cheese, sugar, cornstarch and condensed milk in a mixing bowl; beat until smooth. Strain the mixture into a clean bowl. Whisk in the skim milk, vanilla, coconut and almond extracts and cinnamon. Pour over the prepared crust. Sprinkle toasted coconut over the top. Set the springform pan into a larger shallow pan. Add hot water to the larger pan to the depth of 1 inch. Bake at 350 degrees for 1 1/2 hours. Remove from the oven. Remove the springform pan to a wire rack to cool to room temperature. Chill for 3 to 4 hours. To serve, pool some Strawberry Sauce in the middle of a plate. Top with a piece of pie and garnish with a mint sprig, if desired. *Yield: 12 servings*

The Strawberry Sauce

2 cups strawberries, fresh or thawed frozen
2 tablespoons confectioners' sugar
1 tablespoon fresh lemon juice

Combine the strawberries, sugar and lemon juice in a food processor. Process until smooth. Chill until ready to use.

Nutrients Per Serving: Cal 176; Prot 9 g; Carbo 32 g; Fat 1 g; 1% Cal from Fat; Sod 207 mg

Key Lime Pie

Key lime pie is a marvelous example of how inspiration born out of necessity can sometimes produce unexpected and triumphant results. As the name implies, this pie was created down in the Florida Keys early in the twentieth century using a small and uniquely tart local lime. It was a time and place where fresh milk was generally not available, so canned sweetened condensed milk provided the alternative. And what an alternative it was! Even today — generations and countless key lime pie variations later — when fresh milk is available on every street corner, we still rely upon the canned version to give this pie its special character. Today, however, we can get this essential ingredient, with its unctuous sweetness, in a fat-free version. This fact, coupled with a few other tricks of the trade, has allowed us to produce a low-fat, but remarkably luscious, pie — simple to make, true to tradition, and by all accounts, one of the most popular desserts we offer.

1 cup reduced-fat graham cracker crumbs
4 teaspoons light butter, melted
3/4 cup fresh lime juice
1 teaspoon grated lime zest
1 envelope unflavored gelatin
8 ounces fat-free cream cheese, softened
8 ounces reduced-fat cream cheese, softened
1 (14-ounce) can fat-free sweetened condensed milk
1 cup fat-free sour cream
1 cup fat-free whipped topping
1/2 cup confectioners' sugar

Combine the graham cracker crumbs and butter in a bowl; mix well. Spray a 9-inch springform pan with nonstick cooking spray. Press the crumb mixture into the bottom of the pan. Bake at 350 degrees for 10 minutes. Remove from the oven and cool. Combine the lime juice and lime zest in a microwave-safe dish. Sprinkle the gelatin over the surface; set aside for 10 minutes. Combine the cream cheese in a mixing bowl; beat until smooth. Microwave the gelatin mixture on High for 20 seconds. Add the gelatin mixture and condensed milk to the cheese mixture; beat until smooth. Pour into the prepared springform pan. Refrigerate for 30 minutes. Gently whisk the sour cream, whipped topping and confectioners' sugar in a bowl. Spread over the top of the pie. Chill for 3 hours. *Yield: 12 servings*

Nutrients Per Serving: Cal 244; Prot 10 g; Carbo 40 g; Fat 5 g; 18% Cal from Fat; Sod 249 mg

take your time

There's an old expression, "time is a gift." Time is a precious commodity. So it is vital in this day of instant everything – coffee, meals, messages, etc., that we take time to consider what truly matters in life. If we evaluate the really important aspects of our life, we will see that it is not so much about owning or collecting things as it is about spending time with special people in our lives. Did you know that the average American spends one year of his or her life watching commercials? But we spend an average of only 40 minutes per week playing with our children. In families where both partners work outside the home, it is estimated that couples talk with one another just 12 minutes a day. At Lake Austin Spa Resort, we encourage our guests to balance work with pleasure, alone time with family time and valuable commitments with unstructured down time. Remember: time you enjoy wasting is not wasted time. So take a moment today to measure what matters in your life. Then spend your gift of time wisely.

WELL BEING

Sweet Potato Pie

Vegetables for dessert? Now, that's a concept. We actually prefer this low-fat gingersnap crust to the more traditional one because of the way the flavors harmonize. Substitute an equal amount of canned pumpkin for the Thanksgiving standard — although we can hardly tell the difference.

20 gingersnap cookies
1 tablespoon light butter, melted
3 cups cooked and mashed sweet potatoes
2 eggs
1 1/2 cups evaporated skim milk
3/4 cup packed brown sugar
1 tablespoon cornstarch
1 teaspoon each: ground cinnamon, ground ginger and ground nutmeg
1/4 teaspoon salt
1 teaspoon pure vanilla extract

Grind the gingersnaps to fine crumbs in a food processor. Remove to a bowl and add the butter; mix well. Spray a 9-inch springform pan with nonstick cooking spray. Press the crumb mixture into the bottom of the pan. Bake at 350 degrees for 10 minutes. Remove from the oven and cool. Increase the oven temperature to 450 degrees. Combine the sweet potatoes, eggs, milk, sugar, cornstarch, cinnamon, ginger, nutmeg, salt and vanilla in a mixing bowl; beat until smooth. Pour the batter over the prepared crust. Bake at 450 degrees for 10 minutes. Reduce the temperature to 350 degrees and cook for 50 to 60 minutes longer or until set. Remove from the oven and cool completely. Serve with a dollop of fat-free whipped topping, if desired. *Yield: 12 servings*

Nutrients Per Serving: Cal 230; Prot 6 g; Carbo 47 g; Fat 3 g; 11% Cal from Fat; Sod 194 mg

Café Créme Brûlée

Even people who don't like coffee often enjoy coffee-flavored deserts. This silky café latte custard with a sweet, crunchy crust doubles as a memorable finish to a sophisticated dinner and as a perfect cup of java to start the following day.

2 cups 2% milk
1 1/2 cups evaporated skim milk
2 tablespoons each: instant coffee granules and coffee-flavored liqueur
1 teaspoon cornstarch
3 eggs
4 egg whites
2 teaspoons pure vanilla extract
1/2 (14-ounce) can fat-free sweetened condensed milk
2 tablespoons sugar
5 ounces fat-free cream cheese, softened
3 ounces reduced-fat cream cheese, softened
1 1/2 cups sifted confectioners' sugar

Combine the 2% milk, skim milk, coffee granules and liqueur in a saucepan over medium heat. Cook, stirring, until the coffee granules dissolve. Combine the cornstarch, eggs, egg whites, vanilla, condensed milk, sugar and cream cheese in a mixing bowl. Add the coffee mixture and beat until smooth. Pour into 12 individual custard cups. Place the custard cups in a shallow pan of hot water. Bake in the water bath at 325 degrees for 1 1/2 hours, or until set. Remove from the water bath to cool. Chill for 4 hours. Before serving, sift the confectioners' sugar over the tops of the custards, covering them completely. Caramelize the sugar quickly under a broiler or with a propane torch. *Yield: 12 servings*

Nutrients Per Serving: Cal 211; Prot 10 g; Carbo 33 g; Fat 4 g; 15% Cal from Fat; Sod 194 mg

Double-Chocolate Créme Icebox Dessert

Not so long ago an icebox dessert was synonymous with a summer celebration. Birthdays, baptisms, bar mitzvahs, and a ledger of lesser occasions most commonly concluded with some version of this cool custard confectionery. Even today, when the concept of refrigerated desserts is as common as dot coms, this homey dessert is beloved by children and adults alike. It travels well (doubles well, too), and is equally at home served at a post-season soccer party or a holiday office function. And the fact that it's made all in one pot won't make you any enemies in the kitchen, either!

1 envelope unflavored gelatin
1/4 cup cornstarch
1/2 (14-ounce) can fat-free sweetened condensed milk
2 1/4 cups evaporated skim milk
3/4 cup sugar
3 tablespoons baking cocoa
1 egg
3/4 cup egg substitute
2 ounces fat-free cream cheese, softened
2 ounces reduced-fat cream cheese, softened
1 cup fat-free whipped topping
10 reduced-fat graham crackers
1 cup fat-free chocolate sundae topping

Combine the gelatin, cornstarch, condensed milk, skim milk, sugar, baking cocoa, egg and egg substitute in the top of a double boiler over boiling water. Cook for 6 to 8 minutes or until the mixture thickens, stirring constantly. Add the cream cheese; cook until the cheese melts, stirring constantly. Remove from the heat and cool the custard until partially set, stirring occasionally. Fold in the whipped topping. Line the bottom of an 8-inch baking pan with 5 graham crackers. Top with half the custard filling. Arrange the remaining graham crackers over the filling. Top with the remaining filling. Chill for 1 hour. Warm the chocolate topping slightly in a microwave-safe cup or over hot water. Spread over the top of the dessert. Chill for an additional 4 hours. To serve, scoop out individual portions with a large spoon. *Yield: 10 servings*

Nutrients Per Serving: Cal 340; Prot 13 g; Carbo 66 g; Fat 3 g; 8% Cal from Fat; Sod 273 mg

chefstip

An Eye On Caramelizing * One of the delights of flan or a pot au crème (the French version of flan) is the contrast between the cool creamy custard and the dark intensity of its thin, caramelized sugar sauce. When making the sauce, there are several things to note. First, don't stir. This causes the sugar to crystallize. Instead, swirl gently in the pan. The sugar will go from granulated solid to clear syrup and will begin to color. At this point, stay right with it, swirling it gently to a darker, amber color, but not allowing it to burn. Second, remember that this sauce is extremely hot, so take care when pouring. And finally, it does cool rapidly, so pour it promptly into the desired container(s).

Flan

All the world, it seems, loves custard. The English have their trifle, the French have crème brûlée, and the Hispanics have the quintessential flan. All the world, however, does not love a heart attack, and unfortunately, all of these cool, creamy concoctions — at least in their original iterations — rely upon a disquieting number of whole eggs, further enriched with additional egg yolks and a double measure of heavy cream to achieve their silken texture and goodness. Total fat grams for a single serving can achieve a number to rival your zip code — a reality check that definitely puts all of these desserts in the special occasion category for most of us. After trying for some time to navigate around this obstacle, and yet arrive at the same destination, the advent of some nifty low-fat and fat-free dairy products and a chance encounter with a Mexican cheese-based flan recipe finally provided the solution. The result is one of the very best desserts in this book. Make a sauce by puréeing the flesh of a ripe mango with some water and the juice of one lime for an extra special treat.

1 1/2	**cups sugar**
2	**tablespoons water**
3	**eggs**
4	**egg whites**
2	**teaspoons pure vanilla extract**
2	**cups 1% milk**
3/4	**cup evaporated skim milk**
2	**teaspoons cornstarch**
1/2	**(14-ounce) can fat-free sweetened condensed milk**
2	**tablespoons sugar**
4	**ounces fat-free cream cheese, softened**
4	**ounces reduced-fat cream cheese, softened**

Combine the sugar and water in a saucepan over medium-high heat. Cook until the mixture turns to a dark golden syrup; do not stir. Remove from the heat and immediately pour into 16 individual ovenproof dessert cups, or into one 8 x 8-inch baking pan. Combine the eggs, egg whites, vanilla, 1% milk, skim milk, cornstarch, condensed milk, sugar and cream cheese in a mixing bowl. Beat at high speed until smooth and creamy. Pour batter into the prepared dessert cups or baking pan. Set the cups or pan into a larger shallow pan. Add hot water to a depth of 1 inch. Bake at 325 degrees until the custard is set — individual cups will take about 1 hour, a single pan will take about 1 1/2 hours. Remove the custard from the water bath; cool. Chill for 4 hours. Run a sharp knife blade around the inside edge of each cup or pan and invert the flans onto serving plates or a platter. *Yield: 16 servings*

Nutrients Per Serving: Cal 178; Prot 7 g; Carbo 32 g; Fat 3 g; 13% Cal from Fat; Sod 128 mg

Pineapple Flan

In much of the tropics, people have more pineapples than chickens and more chickens than cows. We offer you then, especially for the lactose-challenged, an entirely traditional, dairy-free flan that makes the most of what you have the most of.

2 cups sugar combined with 3 tablespoons water
1 (12-ounce) can frozen pineapple juice concentrate
3 cups water
2 tablespoons cornstarch
9 egg yolks
2 cups egg substitute
2 teaspoons pure coconut extract
1 teaspoon pure vanilla extract

Cook the sugar and water mixture in a saucepan over medium-high heat until the mixture turns a light caramel color; do not stir. Remove from the heat and immediately pour into 12 individual custard cups or one 4 x 6-inch baking pan. Chill the cups or pan until the sugar sets. Combine the remaining sugar, pineapple juice concentrate, 3 cups water and cornstarch in a saucepan over medium heat. Cook just until the sugar dissolves, stirring constantly. Beat the egg yolks, egg substitute, coconut extract and vanilla in a mixing bowl. Add the pineapple mixture and beat well. Pour the mixture into the prepared custard cups or pan. Set the cups or pan in a large shallow pan. Add enough hot water to reach 1 inch up the side of the cups or baking pan. Bake at 325 degrees until the custard sets — individual cups will take about 1 hour; a single pan will take about 1 1/2 hours. Remove the custard from the water bath; cool. Chill for 4 hours. Run a sharp knife blade around the inside edge of each cup, or pan, and invert the flans onto serving plates or a platter. *Yield: 12 servings*

Nutrients Per Serving: Cal 267; Prot 7 g; Carbo 48 g; Fat 5 g; 18% Cal from Fat; Sod 81 mg

Natillas

Spanish in origin, natillas (nah-tee-yas) is a delicate custard with the texture of just-melted ice cream. It made its way across the ocean long ago — a gift from the Old World to the New. Today it is also very popular in Mexico. Laced with a drop of orange liqueur, as befits its heritage, and dusted with a bit of cinnamon, natillas provides a cooling, comforting finish to the robust food common to both cultures — somewhat like its more famous cousin, flan. Unlike flan, however, which requires considerable time to make, this custard can be ready in less than one hour. Make it before dinner, and it will be ready in time for dessert.

2 eggs, separated
1/2 cup sugar
1/4 cup cornstarch
3 cups 2% milk
1/4 cup orange-flavored liqueur
1 teaspoon salt
1/4 cup sugar
1/8 teaspoon ground cinnamon (try canela, a soft Mexican cinnamon, if you can find it)

Combine the egg yolks, 1/2 cup sugar, cornstarch and milk in a saucepan over medium heat. Cook until the mixture thickens, stirring constantly. Remove from the heat and stir in the liqueur and salt. Strain into a clean bowl; set aside to cool to room temperature, stirring occasionally to prevent a skin from forming on the surface. Beat the egg whites in a mixing bowl until soft peaks form. Add 1/4 cup sugar, 1 tablespoon at a time, beating well after each addition. Fold egg whites into the custard mixture. Place a piece of plastic wrap onto the surface of the mixture; chill thoroughly. Divide natillas among 6 stemmed wine glasses. Sprinkle with a pinch of ground cinnamon. *Yield: 6 servings*

Nutrients Per Serving: Cal 217; Prot 6 g; Carbo 40 g; Fat 4 g; 16% Cal from Fat; Sod 471 mg

Poppy Seed Pound Cake

There's something about the straightforward simplicity and honest-to-goodness goodness of a pound cake that appeals to almost all of us. It's not too sweet, for one thing, lending versatility uncommon in most desserts. It's the perfect companion for an afternoon cup of coffee or tea, or a substantive component of breakfast with fruit and yogurt. This virtue of understatement also provides a flexible neutral palette that welcomes direction or adornment. Finish it with fresh strawberries and a dollop of whipped topping, add pineapple and ginger to the batter, or sprinkle in a few poppy seeds and crown it with a sweet-tart lemon glaze. However and whenever you decide to serve pound cake, this humble loaf is still the cake that takes the cake.

1/2 cup (1 stick) light butter, softened
1 cup sugar
1 egg
1/4 cup egg substitute
1 tablespoon lemon zest
1 teaspoon pure vanilla extract
2 cups cake flour
2 tablespoons poppy seeds
1 teaspoon baking powder
1/4 teaspoon baking soda
1/8 teaspoon salt
3/4 cup buttermilk
1 cup confectioners' sugar
2 tablespoons fresh lemon juice

Cream the butter and sugar in a mixing bowl until light and fluffy. Beat in the egg and the egg substitute, mixing well after each addition. Beat in the lemon zest and vanilla. Combine the flour, poppy seeds, baking powder, baking soda and salt in a separate bowl. Add to the creamed mixture alternately with the buttermilk, mixing well after each addition. Spray a 5 x 9-inch loaf pan with nonstick cooking spray; dust with flour. Pour in the batter. Bake at 350 degrees for 1 hour or until the cake tests done. Cool in the pan for 10 minutes. Remove to a wire rack to cool completely. Combine the confectioners' sugar and lemon juice in a bowl; stir until the sugar is completely dissolved. Drizzle over the cooled cake. *Yield: 16 servings*

Nutrients Per Serving: Cal 183; Prot 3 g; Carbo 34 g; Fat 4 g; 20% Cal from Fat; Sod 127 mg

motion sickness potion

If you suffer from motion sickness while traveling, put a little peppermint essential oil on a tissue and inhale deeply - the oil will also perk you up. For a really queasy stomach onboard ship, mix a drop or two of chamomile or ginger essential oil into a tablespoon of unscented lotion and rub on pulse points and over the abdomen. This can also help with traveler's "digestive trauma" when you are exposed to different foods or water.

HOME SPA

Butternut Squash Bread Pudding with Bourbon Cream

Another winner from the vegetables-for-dessert category. Don't miss the Sweet Potato Pie or Zucchini Cranberry Cake recipes for other ribbon holders. A heartier heart healthy hearth warmer (repeat this phrase three times rapidly without twisting your tongue and you can have a second helping) would be hard to find.

6 cups cubed butternut squash (1/2-inch cubes)
1 baking apple, cored and diced
3/4 cup raisins
1 baguette, cut into 3/4-inch cubes (about 6 cups)
4 cups skim milk
1 (14-ounce) can fat-free sweetened condensed milk
1/2 cup sugar
4 eggs, lightly beaten
1 1/2 cups egg substitute
1/2 teaspoon ground cinnamon
1/4 teaspoon ground allspice
1/4 teaspoon ground nutmeg
1 teaspoon pure vanilla extract

Spray a baking pan with nonstick cooking spray and arrange the squash in a single layer. Roast at 400 degrees for 15 minutes. Combine the apple and raisins in a bowl. Spray a 4 x 8-inch baking pan with nonstick cooking spray. Arrange the bread in the bottom. Scatter the apple-raisin mixture over the bread. Whisk the skim milk, condensed milk, sugar, eggs, egg substitute, cinnamon, allspice, nutmeg and vanilla in a bowl. Pour over the fruit. Place the baking pan in a larger shallow pan and add hot water to a depth of 3/4-inch. Bake at 350 degrees for 1 1/2 hours or until set. Remove from the water bath and cool slightly. Serve warm with Bourbon Cream. *Yield: 16 servings*

The Bourbon Cream

3 cups evaporated skim milk
1/2 cup fat-free sweetened condensed milk
1/2 cup sugar
6 tablespoons bourbon
2/3 cup egg substitute
2 teaspoons pure vanilla extract

Combine the skim milk, condensed milk, sugar, bourbon and egg substitute in the top of a double boiler over boiling water. Cook until the mixture thickens, stirring constantly. Remove from the heat. Cool until tepid, stirring constantly. Stir in the vanilla. Cover and refrigerate until thoroughly chilled. Serve spooned over warm pudding. *Yield: 16 servings*

Nutrients Per Serving: Cal 321; Prot 15 g; Carbo 57 g; Fat 3 g; 8% Cal from Fat; Sod 215 mg

Lemon Pistachio Crisp

Perhaps because of their understandable association with sunshine and warm climates, lemons — or more specifically lemon desserts — are primarily considered to be cool summertime treats. You will find a number of recipes in this book that bear out that penchant. In this recipe, however, we're giving the lemon a slightly different twist, combining the zest and juice with sugar and eggs to create a warm custard under a slightly crisp, slightly nutty homespun crust. Temper this insouciantly tart filling with a cool, creamy dollop of frozen yogurt and you will have a dessert for all seasons; as welcome in December as it is in May.

5 lemons
2 cups sugar
1/4 teaspoon salt
2 eggs
1/2 cup egg substitute
2 tablespoons light butter, melted
1 cup flour
1/2 cup Grape Nuts cereal
1/3 cup chopped pistachio nuts
1/3 cup sugar
1 teaspoon baking powder
1/2 teaspoon baking soda
1/2 teaspoon salt
3 tablespoons light butter, cut into bits
2/3 cup buttermilk

Slice the peel from the lemons; cut into strips. Blanch in boiling water in a saucepan for 1 minute; drain. Repeat the process 2 additional times, using fresh water each time. Pare the white pith away from the peel with a sharp knife and discard. Chop the remaining zest. Slice the lemons into very thin slices; discard the seeds. Combine the zest, lemon slices and 2 cups sugar in a stainless steel bowl; set aside, covered, for 24 hours. Add the eggs, egg substitute, butter and 1/4 cup of the flour; mix well. Mix the remaining flour, Grape Nuts, pistachios, 1/3 cup sugar, baking powder, baking soda and salt in a separate bowl. Work the butter bits into the dry mixture with your hands, squeezing the butter and flour together between your thumb and fingers until incorporated. Add the buttermilk and stir just until combined. Spray an 8-inch baking dish with nonstick cooking spray. Pour the lemon mixture into the dish. Scatter the nut topping over the top. Bake at 350 degrees for 1 hour or until the top is browned. Remove from the oven and cool slightly. Serve warm with vanilla frozen yogurt, if desired. *Yield: 12 servings*

Nutrients Per Serving: Cal 281; Prot 6 g; Carbo 55 g; Fat 6 g; 17% Cal from Fat; Sod 343 mg

chefstip

Meringue Methodology * Creamy, or sometimes crunchy, cloud-like meringues are a delicious (and fat-free) component to many desserts. To ensure that yours are successful, remember that the whites must not contain any foreign matter (including yolk), and should be at room temperature. The mixing bowl should be dry, and completely clean. Add the sugar gradually and beat until very thick. Some recipes in other cookbooks call for a pinch of cream of tartar to stabilize the meringue structure, so you might try that if you're having problems with its volume and thickness.

Blueberry Cobbler

Whether you're on the production or consumption side, cobblers are one of the friendliest desserts going. They couldn't be easier to make and almost no one can resist warm fruit under a wholesome, crunchy crust with a scoop of frozen vanilla yogurt served on the side.

8 cups fresh blueberries or thawed frozen blueberries
2/3 cup sugar
3 tablespoons cornstarch
Grated zest and juice of 1 lemon
1 cup flour
1/2 cup rolled oats
1/3 cup sugar
1 teaspoon baking powder
1/2 teaspoon baking soda
1/2 teaspoon salt
1/2 teaspoon ground cinnamon
4 tablespoons light butter, cut into small cubes and chilled
3/4 cup buttermilk

Combine the blueberries, 2/3 cup sugar, cornstarch, lemon zest and lemon juice in a large bowl. Let stand for 15 to 20 minutes, stirring occasionally. Combine the flour, rolled oats, 1/3 cup sugar, baking powder, baking soda, salt and cinnamon in a separate bowl. Refrigerate until thoroughly chilled. Work in the butter with your hands, pinching the bits between your thumb and fingers until the butter is mostly incorporated. Add the buttermilk and stir just until combined. Spray a 4 x 8-inch baking pan with nonstick cooking spray. Arrange the blueberry mixture in the bottom; top with the dough mixture. Bake at 375 degrees for 45 minutes or until the top is crisp and browned. Remove from the oven and serve hot with a scoop of low-fat frozen vanilla yogurt.

A variety of other fruit, fresh or frozen, can be successfully substituted for the blueberries. We particularly like apples, peaches and cherries. For a citrus version see the Lemon Pistachio Crisp recipe, Page 201. *Yield: 10 servings*

Nutrients Per Serving: Cal 246; Prot 4 g; Carbo 53 g; Fat 4 g; 12% Cal from Fat; Sod 283 mg

putting first things first

Our financial advisors tell us to pay ourselves first. Flight attendants tell us to secure our own mask first, then help those around us. Instinctively, we understand that in order to help and take care of others, we must take care of ourselves. Yet, overwhelmingly, research tells us that women rarely put themselves first. Recent studies indicate that the average woman with children spends six to seven hours each day taking care of others – children, spouses, parents, friends, etc. And although statistics indicate that more than half of these women know that making time for themselves is important, the vast majority do not make it a priority. So please, put yourself on your own list of loved ones. Set aside time each day to do something nice for yourself. By taking special care of yourself, you ensure that you will continue to have the energy and focus necessary to take care of others.

WELL BEING

Nutritional Guidelines

The editors have attempted to present recipes in a form that allows approximate nutritional values to be computed. Persons with dietary or health problems or whose diets require close monitoring should not rely solely on the nutritional information provided. They should consult their physicians or a registered dietitian for specific information.

Abbreviations for Nutritional Profile

Cal – Calories
Sod – Sodium
g – grams
Prot – Protein
Fat – Total Fat
Carbo – Carbohydrates
mg – milligrams

Nutritional information for these recipes is computed from information derived from many sources, including materials supplied by the United States Department of Agriculture, computer databanks and journals in which the information is assumed to be in the public domain. However, many specialty items, new products and processed foods may not be available from these sources or may vary from the average values used in these profiles. More information on new and/or specific products may be obtained by reading the nutrient labels. Unless otherwise specified, the nutritional profile of these recipes is based on all measurements being level.

* Artificial sweeteners vary in use and strength so should be used "to taste" using the recipe ingredients as a guideline. Sweeteners using aspartame (Nutrasweet and Equal) should not be used as a sweetener in recipes involving prolonged heating which reduces the sweet taste. For further information on the use of these sweeteners, refer to package information.
* Alcoholic ingredients have been analyzed for basic ingredients, although cooking causes the evaporation of alcohol, thus decreasing caloric content.
* Buttermilk, sour cream and yogurt are the types available commercially.
* Chicken, cooked for boning and chopping, has been roasted; this method yields the lowest caloric values.
* Cottage cheese is cream-style with 4.2% creaming mixture. Dry curd cottage cheese has no creaming mixture.
* Eggs are all large. To avoid raw eggs that may carry salmonella as in eggnog or 6-week muffin batter, use an equivalent amount of commercial egg substitute.
* Flour is unsifted all-purpose flour.
* Garnishes, serving suggestions and other optional additions and variations are not included in the profile.
* Butter is reduced-fat or light and in stick form.
* Lowfat milk is 1% butterfat. Evaporated milk is skim milk with 60% of the water removed.
* Oil is olive or canola oil.
* Salt and other ingredients to taste as noted in the ingredients have not been included in the nutritional profile.
* If a choice of ingredients has been given, the nutritional profile reflects the first option. If a choice of amounts has been given, the nutritional profile reflects the greater amount.

index

ORDER FORM

CHECKS PAYABLE TO
Lake Austin Spa Resort
Natural Expressions
Boutique
1705 S. Quinlan Park Rd.
Austin, TX 78732

PHONE
512-372-7300

FAX
512-266-1572

WEBSITE
www.lakeaustin.com

EMAIL
info@lakeaustin.com

For more information on Lake Austin Spa Resort or to purchase additional copies of **FRESH** or our previously published and very popular cookbook, **Lean Star Cuisine**, mail in this postcard or call us at 1-800-847-5637. You may also find more information on our website at **www.lakeaustin.com**. Volume discounts and merchandising opportunities are available—call us for more information.

SOLD TO (please print):

Name

Address

City State Zip

Telephone

Email

FORM OF PAYMENT:

[ ] American Express [ ] Diners Club
[ ] Discover [ ] MasterCard
[ ] Visa [ ] Check or Money Order

Account Number

Expiration Date

Name as it appears on credit card

Signature

SHIP TO (please print):

Name

Address

City State Zip

Telephone

Email

TITLE	PRICE	QTY	TOTAL
FRESH: HEALTHY COOKING AND LIVING FROM LAKE AUSTIN SPA RESORT	$30.00		$
Lean Star Cuisine	$19.95		$
Subtotal			$
Sales Tax (where applicable)			$
Shipping/Handling*			$
TOTAL			$

*Determined by location, call for information.